Teachers
in the
Middle

Joseph L. DeVitis & Linda Irwin-DeVitis
GENERAL EDITORS

Vol. 38

PETER LANG
New York • Washington, D.C./Baltimore • Bern
Frankfurt am Main • Berlin • Brussels • Vienna • Oxford

ADVANCE PRAISE FOR

Teachers in the Middle

"*Teachers in the Middle* is an enormously important book, one of a relative few that takes us beyond the often trivialized treatment of young adolescents and their schools. In its place we see the possibility of democratic middle schooling complete with student voice, collaborative relationships, intellectually challenging and meaningful curriculum, and much more. Set in Australia, *Teachers in the Middle* speaks to policies, politics, and practice in middle schooling everywhere."

James Beane, National College of Education,
National-Louis University, Illinois

"With his usual scholarly insight, John Smyth illustrates along with his collaborator Peter McInerney, the intellectual failure of neo-conservative assumptions about youth and their schooling while concurrently providing readers with compelling alternatives to such bankrupt pedagogical practices. An intellectually savvy and practical must read for those concerned with middle school education."

Joe L. Kincheloe, Canada Research Chair
in the Faculty of Education, McGill University

"Reminiscent of progressive writings of the 1930s and 1940s when efforts to bring about more humane schools held sway, this serious work is scholarly and readable. It offers a needed, fresh, and counter perspective on the problem of educating adolescents in today's world. The inclusion of many poignant and pithy comments and scenarios made by students and teachers give this thought-provoking work an engaging richness and relevance."

John Lounsbury, Emeritus Professor,
Georgia College and State University

John Smyth & Peter McInerney

Teachers
in the
Middle

Reclaiming the Wasteland
of the Adolescent Years of Schooling

PETER LANG
New York • Washington, D.C./Baltimore • Bern
Frankfurt am Main • Berlin • Brussels • Vienna • Oxford

Library of Congress Cataloging-in-Publication Data

Smyth, John.
Teachers in the middle: reclaiming the wasteland of the adolescent years
of schooling / John Smyth, Peter McInerney.
p. cm. — (Adolescent cultures, school and society; 38)
Includes bibliographical references and index.
1. Middle school education—Australia.
2. Middle school students—Australia.
3. Middle school teachers—Australia.
I. McInerney, Peter. II. Title.
LB1623.53.A8S69   373.2360994—dc22   2006024141
ISBN-13: 978-0-8204-7459-5
ISBN-10: 0-8204-7459-2
ISSN 1091-1464

Bibliographic information published by **Die Deutsche Bibliothek**.
Die Deutsche Bibliothek lists this publication in the "Deutsche
Nationalbibliografie"; detailed bibliographic data is available
on the Internet at http://dnb.ddb.de/.

Cover design by Lisa Barfield

The paper in this book meets the guidelines for permanence and durability
of the Committee on Production Guidelines for Book Longevity
of the Council of Library Resources.

Printed in the United States of America

Table of Contents

Introduction

"This place hurts my spirit"

(HIGH SCHOOL STUDENT, POPLIN & WEERES, 1992, P. 11)

At the time of writing this book, there is a profound and deepening crisis in secondary education—but at its essence, it is a crisis of a very different kind from the one portrayed by the media, the business community, politicians and policy-makers. While barely a day goes by without some reference in the mainstream media to a crisis in schooling, just what constitutes the crisis is somewhat problematic. What is being constructed for us through a concerted 'conservative assault' and a 'new authoritarianism' (Giroux, 2005) is one of failure by young people, their schools and teachers. But as with any moral panic, there are undisclosed interests and agenda operating, and they are not those of the people most directly affected, in this case young people. If we are to believe the ideologues of the right, schools— especially middle schools—are failing young people because they lack clear guidelines in terms of curriculum content and standards, overemphasize the social dimensions of learning at the expense of rigorous academic studies, fail to concentrate on the basics of literacy and numeracy, and place too much stress on student-centered learning. The solution to this crisis, as advocated by critics like Yecke (2005) and Donnelly (2004), is to name and shame failing schools, define what and how students must learn through a prescriptive subject-based syllabus, enforce strict accountability standards through standardized testing regimes, maintain strong discipline approaches and place more emphasis on formal, whole-class learning. In short, the answer to 'falling standards' is greater uniformity and compliance.

By most accounts, somewhere between 30 and 40 percent of young people in Western countries are not completing their secondary education and are actively rejecting the version of schooling being served up to them. Furthermore, it has been estimated (Cothran & Ennis, 2000) that as much as two-thirds of the US high school population may be disengaged from schooling and actively contemplating leaving school or else remaining tuned out. Official responses to this alarming situation have been jackbooted, to say the least—bearing down with harsher accountability and testing regimes, and requiring teachers to teach in increasingly meaningless and scripted ways. Failure to comply brings its own swift forms of retribution. 'Quick fixes' of this kind are precisely the wrong kind of remedies for alienation, disaffection and disconnectedness, which lie at the heart of students 'not-learning' (Kohl, 1994). What is going on here is a major disconnection between the curriculum on offer in contemporary high schools, and the lives and experiences of young people (see Brown & Saltman, 2005). Put simply, schools are boring places for many young people and being made even more so by ill-conceived and damaging policies and reforms. The causes of this 'crisis' have much more to do with the failure of schools, governments and societies to challenge inequitable educational policies and practices that contribute to social exclusion and the escalating school 'dropout' rates and palpable disaffection being felt by minority groups (Gibson, 2005).

As our opening quote from a high school student indicates, the crisis lies deep in the construction of school systems that are wounding and damaging large numbers of young people. The real crisis is one of paradigmatic paralysis fed by an impoverishment of political will and imagination capable of listening to and embracing the lives, experiences and aspirations of young people, and the teachers and schools who work with them.

We have decided to tackle the issues raised above by framing our research and writing in this book around Charles Silberman's (1970) provocative image of 30 years ago of high schools, at least in the United States, as being mindless "wasteland[s]" (p. 324). We invoke Silberman as a way of acknowledging what is being *done* *to* large numbers of young people by current policy directions through testing, benchmarking, standards, competitive league tables, and similar measures that are making high schools more like prisons and boot camps than vibrant and lively places of learning. Framed in this way, the 'crisis' is a crisis of equity arising from savage economic inequalities (Kozol, 1992; 2005), an under-funded and constantly vilified public education system, and a 'manufactured crisis' in education (Berliner &

Biddle, 1995) used to justify the imposition of discriminatory high stakes testing regimes. As Lounsbury and Vars (2003) argue:

> Gains in test scores, when and if achieved, will have no immediate impact on the serious problems that beset our society. The greater need is to guide the overall development of young adolescents in ways that will equip them with the behavioral attributes, attitudes, and values they need to make wise choices in all aspects of their lives. Success in doing so will in no way handicap the school's clear responsibility for the intellectual development of students but will, in fact, fulfill that responsibility more effectively. (p. 8)

Part of the solution to this "crisis" has to lie in rejecting the "yellow-school-bus model of education" (Eisner, 2002, p. 576), and instead embracing diversity in all its forms and creating "conditions that enable students to pursue what is distinctive about themselves" (Eisner, 2002, p. 581) rather than having to endure an alien, imposed and rigid curriculum.

Unashamedly, we identify ourselves with the view that schools should be guided by higher purposes other than the reproduction of the *status quo*; that education should not merely serve the economy by turning out compliant workers but should encourage the acquisition of critical literacies and democratic practices; that all children should be able to participate in a challenging curriculum that will assist them to make sense of their lives and their identities. If there is a 'crisis' in education, it is a crisis that has been manufactured by those who seek to undermine the democratic and egalitarian purposes of public schooling. The starting point in any kind of reconstrual has to be with 'a pedagogy of respect' (MacKenzie, 1998), and that is what we try to portray in this book.

Acknowledgments

This book draws extensively on projects funded by the Australian Research Council (ARC): a Small ARC Project (2000), *Middle Schooling and Improved Educational Provision for Young Adolescents*, and an ARC Discovery Grant Project (2002–2004), *On Becoming a Middle School Teacher: Reclaiming the Wasteland of the Middle Years of Schooling*. Both these projects focused on the educational arrangements for young people in the adolescent years of schooling, generally taken to be students between the ages of 10 and 15 years in the so-called 'middle years.'

The research builds directly on a Collaborative ARC Project (1997–2000), *Students' Voices on Retention in Post-compulsory Schooling*, which documented the experiences of students who fail to complete formal high school requirements (Smyth, Hattam, Cannon, Edwards, Wilson & Wurst 2000). Taking account of the issues of youth alienation and disengagement described in this study, the main intent of the present research was to explore the ways in which teachers and schools are reinventing themselves for young adolescents. The research was conducted by Professor John Smyth, Chief Investigator, and Dr. Peter McInerney, Research Associate. We wish to acknowledge the role of Associate Professor Rob Hattam in assisting with the development of the research proposal (2000–2002) that led to the ARC grant, and to his intellectual ideas that informed us in the early fieldwork stages and that were never far away as we wrote this book.

We want to acknowledge the financial support from the ARC and the cooperation of the Department of Education and Children's Services (DECS) in facilitating access to the six project schools in the study. We especially want to record our appreciation to the 104 participants from the project schools—the teachers, principals, students, education administrators and community personnel—who gave so generously of their time and knowledge in sharing their views of what is needed to make schools more humane and educationally enriching places for young people.

John Smyth, who held the position of Roy F. and Joann Cole Mitte, Endowed Chair in School Improvement, College of Education, Texas State University-San Marcos (2004–2005) at the time of writing, explicitly expresses his grateful appreciation to the Mitte Foundation for its generous support. He also held other institutional positions in respect of which he expresses his gratitude for supporting this research, including: Professorial Fellow, University of Ballarat; Visiting Professor, Wilf Malcolm Institute for Educational Research, The University of Waikato; Adjunct Professor, Charles Darwin University; and Emeritus Professor, Flinders University. The research undertaken and reported in this book is, therefore, directly attributable to these multiple institutional affiliations. The referencing, formatting and bringing this book together in a coherent manner was made possible through the resourceful and cheerful skills of Solveiga, who was there all the way through. Many thanks to Jan McInerney for her ongoing support and encouragement. Appreciation is expressed to Chris Myers, Joe DeVitis and the wonderful editing and production staff of Peter Lang Publishing.

John Smyth and Peter McInerney
October 26, 2005

Glossary

AET   Aboriginal Education Teacher: a teacher with specific responsibilities for indigenous education programs

AEW   Aboriginal Education Worker: a non-teaching indigenous staff member who provides educational support for Aboriginal students

DSP   Disadvantaged Schools Program

ESL   English as a Second Language

LOTE   Languages Other Than English

NEP   Negotiated Education Program: a mandated program for students with disabilities and special needs, formerly known as Negotiated Curriculum Plan (NCP)

NSN   National Schools Network

OECD   Organization for Economic Cooperation and Development

R   Reception year of schooling, equivalent to K in the United States

SRC   Student Representative Council

SSO   School Service Officer: non-teaching personnel who provides ancillary support in schools

STAR   STudents At Risk

TAFE   Technical and Further Education

VET   Vocational Education and Training

PART ONE

An Orientation to the Study

CHAPTER ONE

Setting the scene

The research issue

Against the backdrop of a 'conservative restoration' (Apple, 1996) and neo-liberal reforms that have corroded the democratic and egalitarian purposes of public schooling, this book explores the ways in which teachers and schools are working with and against policy discourses to build 'geographies of trust' (Scott, 1999) and pedagogically engaged communities. Our particular focus is on adolescents and their experience of schooling in the so-called 'middle years' where the problems of student alienation, attrition and disaffection seem to be most acute (Dwyer, 1996; Fine, 1991; Smyth & Down, 2004; Smyth & Hattam et al., 2004).

Although our account is based on Australian studies, we believe that the stories of our informants, both teachers and students, will strike a chord with educators in most Western societies. Issues of school completion, engagement and curriculum relevance are universal concerns in an age in which global forces are dramatically changing the ways in which we think about work and the purposes of schooling. Increasingly, it appears that the ideals of a liberal education are being subverted by a discourse of vocationalism, managerialism and accountability as economic rationalist values have gained primacy over social policy objectives of governments (Stilwell, 1994). But for many young people in the United States, Australia and Britain, schooling has become synonymous with boredom and despair, as they find themselves being 'educated and regulated within institutions that have little relevance in their lives' (Giroux, 1996, p. 13). An earlier book in this series, *Dropping Out, Drifting Off, Being Excluded* (Smyth & Hattam et al., 2004), investigated the complex issues through the voices of early school-leavers. We want to build on this account and show the transformative possibilities of schooling through a close examination of the educational ideals and practices in six public schools that have made adolescent education a high priority.

Our approach is informed by three key questions: first related to student's identity, second to teacher's identity and the third, more generally, to whole-school change:

1. What are young people saying about their experience of schooling and its relevance to their lives?
2. How are teachers reinventing themselves for young adolescents?
3. How are schools reinventing themselves as more inclusive and learner-centered organizations?

In the remainder of this chapter, we outline the major perspectives and ideas informing our study, describe the research design and methodology, and briefly introduce the project schools.

Our frames of reference

Our study is situated within a socially critical framework. Accordingly, we want to emphasize the dialectic nature of the inquiry in which we attempt to bring grounded research into conversation with the literature in the fields of youth studies, sociology, curriculum theory and school reform. Our approach to the research issue is not that of 'detached or disinterested observers' (Lynch & Lodge, 2002, p. 2). We neither 'cling to the guard rail of neutrality' (Kincheloe & McLaren, 1994, p. 140) in our efforts to expose the inequitable nature of schooling and the many structural constraints confronting young people as they navigate a pathway from schooling to adult lives, nor do we rest our case on theory alone. As we have already suggested, our book is concerned with the practical possibilities of reform. We have therefore chosen to foreground examples of innovative and, in some cases, quite courageous policies and practices from the project schools that formed part of the study.

We recognize that there are some tensions involved in this process. Those engaged in critique from above sometimes fail to consider the practical difficulties confronting teachers trying to implement socially just practices in a hostile policy context (Cribb & Gewirtz, 2003, p. 15). We hope that we have been sufficiently sensitive to their struggles without presenting an overly romantic view of the enormity of the task. We also acknowledge that any effort to bring about change requires a collective response from a broad range of human services in society. Schools cannot do it alone.

Our study offers a sociological perspective on the issue of youth identity. At a time when the educational field is awash with learning theories and ideas from cognitive psychology, we believe that we need to take a sociological reading of what is happening inside schools and the community at large. Australia is a culturally diverse society today, but a growing body of evidence suggests that it is also becoming a more unequal society with a large number of families suffering from high levels of poverty, social dislocation and insecurity as a consequence of economic restructuring, unemployment and the casualization of the workforce (Fincher & Saunders, 2001; Peel, 2003). Although many Australians have benefited from the globalized economy and mass communication systems, educational disadvantage is reinforced through a 'digital divide' in the realm of information and communication technologies (Angus, Snyder & Sutherland-Smith, 2003). In these circumstances, we need to reassert the importance of social class as well as gender, ethnicity and other markers of student identity and take greater account of their impact on the educational success and failure of students in schools. A great deal of the justification for instituting special provisions for students in the middle years is premised on the need to respond to the so-called 'characteristics of young adolescents', but, as Beane (1999, p. 6) argues so vehemently, we need 'to hear less talk about hormones as explaining behavior and more about the unsavory conditions under which too many of our adolescents live.' (p. 6)

Finally, we want to emphasize the role of teachers in reclaiming what we see as the 'wasteland' of the middle years of schooling. In a geographic sense, the term 'wasteland' conjures up images of a desolate landscape or lifeless environment. Perhaps it is a little harsh to conceive of the middle years as being pedagogically impoverished, but it does appear that many students have 'switched-off' schooling and often regress in terms of their motivation and academic achievement in these years. Although a range of societal factors are invoked to account for young people's experience of alienation, it seems that there is often a mismatch between the organization and curriculum of high schools and the educational expectations, needs and aspirations of young people. Most significantly, subject-based departments, hierarchies of knowledge, teacher directed forms of learning and the competitive assessment practices in these institutions tend to reinforce patterns of exclusion and perpetuate educational inequalities. But there are signs of renewal in the middle years as teachers and school administrators begin to shake off the shackles of the entrenched pedagogies and develop alternative and more fulfilling educational programs for young people.

Teachers in the middle

The title of our book *Teachers in the Middle* is obviously a play on words but we think it conveys some sense of the social, political and pedagogical territory inhabited by teachers.

Teachers are one of the most maligned, frequently criticized, widely misunderstood and grossly undervalued professional groups in our society. They are pilloried by the media and are the butt of ill-informed, poorly conceptualized and damaging policies developed by politicians and the business community, and this is not by any means a recent phenomenon. Part of the problem here is the widely held but misguided public perception that because we have all been students in schools at some time in our lives, this qualifies us to pass judgment on what schools do. This is a view that is being continuously reinforced by the neo-liberal move to construe schools as places of consumption in which we are all discerning 'consumers.' While there is an element of populist appeal to this line of thinking, it is widely astray of the mark. It is one thing to have been a witness of schooling a generation ago, and at best to vicariously experience it through our children now, but quite another thing to legitimately claim a right to know in any kind of meaningful way from a distance many years later.

The problem is that schools are enormously complex social institutions and, furthermore, they are not static social entities. What might have been true about schools at some point of time in the past, rapidly becomes obsolete. Schools are places that are continually in a state of flux as they tangle with the vibrancy of the aspirations and expectations of young lives which are themselves in a state of turmoil in increasingly dangerous and uncertain times. All of these are by way of saying that what it means to be a teacher is not something that can be presumed or even prescribed; it is continually in the process of being worked out daily by teachers in classrooms.

Teachers are caught squarely in the middle of the maelstrom of the shifting tectonic plates of capitalism as schools are increasingly co-opted into the worldwide attempt to redesign them as engines of economic growth and restoration. In an era of de-industrialization and globalization, schools are seen as the new harbingers of 'economic work,' and teachers are regarded as 'key frontline operatives' in delivering enhanced skill formation, vocationalization, value-added, demonstrable performance against world's best practice, international benchmarking and the call for continually raising standards. This is no mean feat for an occupational group that has suffered very significant degradation in real terms in remuneration that has not kept pace with community standards over several decades.

Teachers are also in the middle in policy terms. They have systematically been excluded and silenced in terms of having a say in the school reform process that has been swirling around them. Schools have literally been transformed from the outside without teachers being consulted or meaningfully involved at all. The argument has been that to have involved teachers in the reform process would have been to feed into the very interests of 'producer capture' (Bottery & Wright, 2000, p. 12) that has led to the alleged 'problem' in the first place: falling standards, decline in student achievement, lack of discipline and general moral degeneracy. On the other hand, teachers are the frontline professionals struggling to reconcile the increasingly complex agendas that come into classrooms with young lives: poverty, disintegrating families, cultural diversity, parental expectations of a valued place for their children in the social order, in work and in higher education, along with demands from young people themselves for an authentic, relevant, fulfilling and meaningful educational experience. As Connell (1993) points out:

> Beyond the question of rights, teachers can be a vital resource for change. They, more than any other group of adults concerned with schools, know where the shoe pinches—where things are not working well. Teachers have, among them, an enormous fund of experience and ideas which *if tapped* represents a tremendous asset for progressive reform. (p. 58)

Teachers find themselves in the middle when it comes to mediating the relationships between the school, the home, the classroom and school administration. Although teachers provide a great deal of emotional, social and intellectual support for students, they are also expected to maintain institutional norms and practices that can sometimes damage personal relationships.

Yet another way of thinking about teachers as being 'in the middle' is in terms of making sense of and reconstructing their own identities in working with young adolescents. We think these teachers are so unique that it is not unreasonable to describe them as literally reinventing themselves for young people. To pursue this idea a little further, one of the big issues about youth and young adolescence is the way they are constructed and positioned by the wider society, and in many instances the institution of schooling. If young people are portrayed in ways that make them a 'problem' in adult eyes, then what occurs around them takes on the feel of blaming them. The kind of categories that are invoked is around the notions of 'raging teenage hormones' (Maran, 2001, p. xii), with the implication that when things get complicated, it is somehow young people themselves that are the 'cause,' and the blame should be sheeted home to them. Young people suffer from negative media reports that tend to portray them as threats, victims, dole bludgers and deviants.

There is a sociological dimension to this phenomenon. The most demonized and stigmatized youths are cultural minorities and those in poverty, especially when they live in public housing—so much so that some young people will not even own up to their post codes. Deficit views of these young people can infect teacher attitudes. One of the most common perceptions of students in disadvantaged school communities is that they lack the academic ability and the potential to engage in higher learning (Thomson & Comber, 2003). As a consequence, young people living in poverty are often offered 'a pedagogy of poverty' (Haberman, 1991) as an alternative to a rigorous and challenging curriculum. Teachers reinventing themselves for young adolescents are themselves challenged to counteract these deficit views and to begin to reconstruct their practices around the aspirations, concerns and interests of students in the middle years.

Finally, in terms of school organization, teachers of young adolescents generally work betwixt a primary and secondary divide corresponding to years 6–10 in the compulsory phase of schooling in Australia. But beyond the student cohort, these teachers are caught in the middle of a pedagogical debate about the merits of a broad, integrated curriculum as opposed to a more specialized and subject-oriented approach to learning typically associated with the senior years of schooling. With pressures from top and bottom, they often find themselves having to defend their practices in the wake of stiff opposition from senior school colleagues, parents and conservative policy makers.

Although we do not propose to locate our study exclusively within the middle school movement—indeed we find some aspects of the middle schooling discourse quite unhelpful—we feel it is necessary to explain the relationship of our study to the middle school literature and present an overview of the various conceptual understandings of middle schooling in Australia.

The promise of middle schooling

Most of the recent Australian initiatives to establish alternative educational arrangements for young adolescents have been framed around the category of middle schooling. Indeed, the label 'middle schooling' has come to signify a progressive alternative to the contemporary high school that has largely been endorsed and, to varying degrees, sponsored by state education systems (Barratt, 1998; Eyers, Cormack & Barratt, 1992). However, the concept of middle schooling remains deeply problematic. Broadly speaking, the middle schooling approach might be understood to be about developing pedagogy that emphasizes the student–teacher relationship, engages students in negotiating the curriculum (Boomer, Lester, Onore & Cook, 1992), integrates the personal and the social concerns of students into the curriculum (Beane, 1991), promotes success-oriented assessment, and encourages collaboration between teachers and students in the learning process. A more radical form of middle schooling could be said to carry a commitment to social justice and equity that emphasizes democratic practices, critical literacies and community-minded educational programs. But equally, a more conservative form of middle schooling limited to structural changes simply reproduces existing pedagogies in an organizational unit labeled a middle school.

Given the contested nature of the field, we want to distinguish between the terms 'middle years,' 'middle school' and 'middle schooling' (Chadbourne, 2001). When we talk of the middle years we refer to early adolescence, the age span from 10 to 15 years. Students in this age group occupy the upper primary years (5–7) and the lower secondary years (8–10) in Australia. The term middle school denotes a distinctive organizational unit that caters specifically for students in the adolescent years. Although there are examples of architecturally designed middle schools in Australia (McInerney, Hattam, Lawson & Smyth, 1999), more commonly existing secondary schools have been restructured to form sub-schools or smaller learning communities. However, the point needs to be made that naming an institution a middle school does not necessarily mean that the education principles and practices are consistent with the philosophy of middle schooling (Chadbourne, 2001). In contrast, the term middle schooling carries with it a new orientation toward teaching and learning that is responsive to the needs and concerns of young adolescents (Brennan, Sachs & Meritt, 1998). Although it is difficult to see how this can be achieved without some significant structural and cultural changes in schools, this notion places a much greater emphasis on pedagogical changes of the kind we described earlier in this section.

Our decision to confine our research to schools with a commitment to middle schooling was based on the pragmatic position that if we are looking for some answers to the issues of alienation and disengagement in adolescents, we should look to those sites that are stepping out in terms of curriculum reform and innovation in the middle years. This is neither to deny that some conventional high schools are not making serious efforts to tackle the problems, nor is it to affirm that those schools espousing the virtues of their middle school programs have got it right; indeed, in this book we raise some major concerns about the efficacy of some middle school responses. However, we agree with Wood (1992) that when it comes to school reform 'we are more likely to learn from success than failure.' (p. xvi)

The project schools

The six schools selected for the research project were broadly representative of the student profiles of South Australian public schools in terms of gender, social class and ethnicity. Although they differed in terms of school organization, all were experimenting with middle schooling as an alternative to existing secondary school arrangements. In all schools there were varying degrees of emphases on:

- collaborative approaches to teaching and learning;
- alternatives to competitive assessment and reporting practices;
- integrating information and communication technologies into the curriculum;
- utilizing community resources and inter-agency support teams to support student learning;
- interdisciplinary approaches to the development of literacy, vocational education and higher-order thinking skills;
- social learning, co-curricula activities and programs to develop personal health and well-being;
- promoting student voice and identity;
- fostering belongingness and positive relationships among students and teachers.

What follows is a brief overview of the organizational features of the schools which, for reasons of confidentiality, were given pseudonyms:

- *Plainsville School (R–8)*: A small disadvantaged school incorporating middle schooling in the upper years (6–8), situated in an outer metropolitan area.
- *Broadvale Community School (R–12)*: A large disadvantaged school in an outer metropolitan area with senior (10–12) and middle school (7–8) campuses.
- *New Vista Community School*: A multi-campus R–12 school in rural South Australia with a 6–9 middle school campus.
- *Seachange High School (8–12)*: A rural high school with architecturally designed middle schools (8–9).
- *Investigator High School (8–12)*: A large metropolitan disadvantaged school with an architecturally designed middle school (8–9).
- *Gulfview Secondary School (6–12)*: A purpose-built middle school, incorporating four sub-schools, situated in an outer metropolitan suburb.

Each of these sites is described in some detail through a series of school portraits in Chapter 2.

Research design and methodology

In what could be described best as a 'multi-sited' ethnography (Marcus, 1998), the study began with a single case study in 2000 (Smyth, McInerney & Hattam, 2003) and was followed by studies of five additional public schools between 2001 and 2003. From the beginning, the project attempted to anchor the research in vernacular accounts of teachers' lives and experiences (Goodson, 1991; 1994), and those of students. We took the view that if we want to find out what motivates teachers and what they bring to the classroom, we needed to engage them in purposeful conversations (Burgess, 1988) about their beliefs and practices. We were also keen to talk to young people about their experiences of schooling in the middle years.

Having negotiated access to possible school sites with the education system and with principals, we invited school personnel with a particular interest in, or responsibility for, middle schooling to participate in the project. The kind of questions we pursued with these informants included:

- How is the school reinventing itself around an inclusive agenda in the adolescent years of schooling?
- Who are the teachers who work with young adolescents? Why do they do it?
- How do teachers reinvent themselves as middle school teachers?
- In what ways are they restructuring, reculturing and changing their pedagogy?
- What are the attributes of a successful middle school teacher?
- What do they see as the rewards and frustrations?
- How do they sustain the energy for this kind of work in a policy climate that appears largely inhospitable?
- What are the tensions, contradictions and dilemmas involved in middle schooling?
- In particular, how do teachers handle the policy pressure to institutionalize relationships with students?

The ethnographic research methods used in the research included audio-taped conversations and semi-structured interviews with principals, curriculum coordinators, teachers, school support staff and middle school students at each of the schools, as well as a small number of external agents, including a school superintendent, a teacher educator, a social planner, and a training and development provider. In many instances, interviews were preceded by classroom observations. As shown in Appendix 1, some 104 people were interviewed either individually or as part of a small group. Voiced research (Smyth, 1999) was complemented with field notes and case records of an extensive phase of participant observation, during which time we inhabited classrooms, staffrooms and playgrounds, attended numerous staff meetings, professional development activities, committee meetings and school assemblies, and participated in school excursions, open nights and school reporting sessions. We compiled a portfolio of curriculum documents, school policy statements and artifacts of student learning including learning plans, curriculum audits, course outlines, assessment guidelines and work samples. This process began in 2000 and then occurred continually between 2001 and the end of the 2003 calendar year.

Representing schools and teachers' and students' lives

One of the main aims of this book is to provide the reader with a vicarious experience of school culture and teachers' lives as a basis for developing an empathetic understanding of the issues facing young adolescents. In order to anchor the text in 'the worlds of lived experiences' (Denzin, 1997, p. xv), we have drawn extensively on field notes and interview transcripts to provide a 'thick description' (Geertz, 1973) of school life. (We should add that each of the 104 informants in the study was given a pseudonym to preserve their anonymity.) In a similar vein, portraits of the project schools were developed from information gathered in the project schools. These accounts aim to provide the reader with a geographical and cultural orientation to each school and a context with which to understand the pedagogical reform described in other parts of this book.

Conscious of the importance of honoring the voices of our informants in a way which preserved the language and complexity of ideas, we decided to reorganize and condense a number of the lengthy transcripts so as to produce a two- to three-page narrative portrait from the interviews. Our intention was to capture the essence of what teachers and students had to say in a concise and coherent fashion without losing the tenor and character of the voices. Inevitably, some pruning of accounts has taken place as we have had to make some pragmatic decisions about the content and details of the conversations. This form of textual representation was a distinguishing feature of *The Stolen Generation*, a report into the forced removal of Aboriginal children from their parents (Commonwealth of Australia, 1997), and was used to capture the voices of early school-leavers in a South Australian study (Smyth & Hattam et al., 2004). In total, some 45 narrative portraits, including several dialogic portraits, were developed from the interviews and field notes in our study. Excerpts from these portraits have been inserted as boxed text to capture the voices and experiences of middle school teachers and students. In other instances, the text incorporates direct quotes from our informants' interviews and field notes from participant observation activities.

The organization of this book

Following an orientation to the project schools in Chapter 2, the remainder of this book is organized around three main themes: young lives, adult lives and school lives.

1. *Young lives*: Schools supposedly exist for young lives but there is frequently a mismatch between young people's project of 'becoming somebody'

(Wexler, 1992) and the school's agenda of doing what it thinks is best for young people. In Chapter 3 we focus on young people (their identities, aspirations, interests and concerns) and identify a number of issues and dilemmas around poverty, educational inequality and the sociology of high schools. We explain why adolescence is everybody's business and hear what young people have to say about the attributes of a 'good' teacher. In Chapter 4 we describe programs and initiatives from the project schools that foster belongingness, promote student participation and engage students in worthwhile learning that supports their identity formation.

2. *Adult lives*: What young people gain from schooling depends in large measure on the quality of their relationships with adult educators. However, many teachers find it difficult to shake off the entrenched beliefs and practices associated with subject specialization and the hierarchy of high schools. In the second section, we shift our attention to adult lives and examine the pedagogical struggles and transformations as teachers attempt to reinvent themselves for students in the middle years. The emphasis in Chapter 5 is on the characteristics and pedagogical knowledge required of teachers to improve the education of young people. In particular, we explore the class-based nature of schooling, the importance of developing trusting and respectful relationships, and an inclusive school culture. In Chapter 6, we focus on the practices, school culture and organizational structures of schools that enable teachers to become successful middle school teachers.

3. *School lives*: Both young people and adult educators experience schools as institutions. Historically, these institutions have shown a strong capacity to resist reform, especially when it comes to changing the norms and assumptions about teaching and learning. In the third section, we explore the institutional arrangements of schools and the degree to which they are able to revitalize themselves as pedagogically focused and student-centered organizations. In Chapter 7, we take a closer look at the history of the middle school movement and describe the structural, cultural and pedagogical elements of middle school reform in the project schools. We highlight the tensions and dilemmas involved in the process, the extent of system support and the unfinished nature of the middle school project. Finally, in Chapter 8 we present a set of touchstones or principles to guide the development of the 'pedagogically engaged school' (Smyth, 2003a) and discuss the resources needed to achieve this goal.

CHAPTER TWO

Taking account of the context

Introduction

In this chapter, we provide an orientation to the study that takes account of the regional and global context. Beginning with some general remarks about the research sites, we proceed to an overview of the educational policy environment and then present a portrait of each project school in which we sketch the geographic, cultural and socioeconomic features of the communities and the pedagogical elements of school reform in the adolescent years.

Our research took place in six co-educational public schools that varied considerably in terms of size, location, history, organization and traditions. One was a small K–9 school; two were conventional 8–12 high schools; another was a large K–12 school; one was a campus of a multi-sited community school; and the sixth was a purpose-built middle school. Four were situated in the metropolitan area and two in country areas; three were near the seaside and three in outer industrial suburbs; two of the sites were officially categorized as disadvantaged schools, but all had a significant proportion of students from low socioeconomic backgrounds. Five of the schools were remarkably homogeneous with few students from non-English-speaking backgrounds (NESB) while one school had a much more culturally diverse population and a large number of indigenous youth. However, what these schools had in common was an agenda to reconnect disaffected students to education.

All project schools had a degree of local autonomy in terms of curriculum priorities and resource allocation, but all were part of a public education system and subject to the regulatory controls and policy frameworks of state and federal governments. Before examining the schools in some detail, we want to say something about the national and regional context of this study and the impact of educational policies on the work of public school teachers.

The Australian educational landscape

Although a certain mythology has developed around the role of the 'bush' in shaping the Australian identity, the vast majority of Australians are city dwellers. Despite the vastness of the land and the economic dependence on primary resources, more than 90 percent of Australia's 20 million people live in a narrow coastal strip that constitutes a mere 10 percent of the continent. In fact, half of the population reside in a handful of metropolitan centers on the eastern and southeastern seaboards. There are uniquely Australian lifestyles and cultures, but Australians have a lot in common with people in western industrialized societies. They are beset with many of the environmental, economic and political problems and are subject to the globalizing tendencies of western capitalism. By world standards, Australia is a relatively affluent country, but social indicators, such as gross domestic product (GDP), tend to disguise the great extremes of wealth and resources which exist within the country. Nowhere is this more apparent than in the economic and social conditions of indigenous Australians which are more akin to inhabitants of third world countries.

Over the past decade, neo-liberal reforms and economic restructuring have resulted in a growing gap between the haves and have-nots, a high level of welfare dependency in 'rustbelt' communities, and a large body of unemployed and chronically underemployed people. The patterns of inequality are particularly acute in the capital city of the state in which the project schools are situated. As the region occupies a peripheral position within the overall Australian economy and is highly dependent on a narrow range of manufacturing goods, it is especially vulnerable to the damaging impact of globalization and economic restructuring. According to Spoehr (2004), this has resulted in 'a city divided by socioeconomic fault-lines and entrenched inequality' (p. 7); a place of unequal futures where the rich and poor are divided by the suburbs they can afford to live in. A period of recent economic growth, marked by rising employment (albeit much of it part-time in nature), has done little to alter the unequal distribution of income, wealth and power that is typical of most Australian cities. If anything, a property boom has made home ownership an unattainable dream for low-income earners and has saddled middle-income earners with high mortgages.

Poverty and material inequalities penetrated all the project schools to varying degrees, but the Plainsville and Broadvale communities had exceptionally high levels of financial hardship, unemployment and transience. In these schools, 60 to 70 percent of families were recipients of the school card (something equivalent to subsidized lunch programs in the United States), a government benefit paid to low-income families to offset the cost of school fees and materials. Even in the more prosperous communities of New Vista and Seachange one-third of the families qualified for assistance. We will say more about funding arrangements to disadvantaged schools a little later, but suffice it to say that across public schools there is an enormous disparity in the funding and resources to maintain facilities and educational programs.

Public education policy

As the project schools were all government schools, they operated under the same administrative guidelines and policies with regard to staffing and resource entitlements, occupational health and safety standards, industrial agreements, school leadership structures, curriculum accountability frameworks and credentialing arrangements. Under a recently introduced index of disadvantage, the project schools were differentially funded to take account of socioeconomic disadvantage, Aboriginality and other factors. On a ranking from 1 to 7 (with 1 being the most severely disadvantaged) two of the project schools were categorized as level 2. Educational programs in all schools were based on a state curriculum framework that incorporated essential learnings and areas of knowledge associated with the arts, design and technology, English, health and physical education, languages, mathematics, science, and studies of society and environment. At the senior school level, this learning culminated in a certificate of education. Within these broad guidelines, schools were free to develop local priorities, areas of curriculum specialization and special projects.

For more than 100 years, constitutional responsibility for the provision of public education in Australia has been vested in state legislatures and administered through centralized bureaucracies, but some significant changes are taking place in public schooling today—changes which are having a major impact on teaching, curriculum development and school organization in all the project schools. In what follows we want to say something about the increasingly powerful role of the federal government in setting the education agenda, the impact of funding cuts and shift toward local school management and marketization of education.

The Commonwealth government has sole authority over taxation collection in Australia and in recent years has begun to exercise a much stronger influence over

educational policy through an extension of corporate federalism. State education systems that have traditionally exercised a high level of curriculum autonomy now have
to comply much more rigidly with national guidelines and accountability requirements in order to qualify for federal funding. Among other measures, the
Commonwealth Schools Assistance Act 2004 stipulates that state education systems must certify that schools are reporting to parents on literacy and numeracy
attainment against national benchmarks, that reporting on student achievement is
in plain English, and (as a gesture toward citizenship education) that the national
flag is displayed in all schools. Many of these measures are in conflict with curriculum practices in state education systems; for example, some states have moved
toward outcomes-based education, but schools are now being required to assign
grades (A, B, C, D and E) specifying student achievement in every curriculum area
from K–12. As if this fetish for measurement was not enough, schools are also
required to assign quartile rankings to students within the instructional groups.

With the ascendancy of neo-liberal ideas, there has been a retreat of governments from the funding of public education and human services and a consequent
shift of responsibilities to parents and school communities. In the state in which the
study was conducted, school fees or levies are now compulsory and principals are
legally authorized to use the services of debt collectors to retrieve fees from parents
and caregivers. Due to the shortfalls in Commonwealth and State government funding, school councils are now busily engaged in raising funds through fees, levies and
corporate sponsorship—a process that reinforces the disparity between the well-
endowed schools in middle class suburbs and those situated in poorer suburbs like
Plainsville and Broadvale, where the capacity for parents to supplement school budgets is markedly reduced.

Coincident with this funding reversal has been a movement by state authorities to devolve educational responsibilities to school councils and to promote the
concept of the self-managing school. All of the project schools had entered into local
school management agreements under which principals and governing councils took
on major responsibilities for managing global budgets and administrative tasks
once handled centrally. Most disturbingly, accelerated moves toward devolution have
been accompanied by a withdrawal of centralized curriculum services and advisory personnel to facilitate school reform. Under the new arrangements, much of the
responsibility for the professional development of staff has been pushed back to
schools.

The combined influences of globalization and neo-liberalism have generated
a market-driven approach to education with an emphasis on competition and efficiency. In the new scenario, education is increasingly viewed as a commodity with
students/parents positioned as clients, and teachers/schools as providers, while
principals in many instances have become 'managers' rather than 'educators.'

Establishing a market niche through special interest and highly specialized programs has become a major preoccupation for principals and school councils in this competitive education environment. There was little doubt that these pressures had impacted on all project schools, especially in those communities where private schools were major players in the competition.

School portraits

Having described the broader policy context, we now turn to the localized features of each of the project schools. Our portraits begin with Plainsville School, a rather unique educational site that has stepped out of the traditional mold when it comes to student-initiated learning.

Plainsville School[1]

When it comes to outward appearances, schools can be notoriously deceptive places. On entering the grounds of 'Plainsville' School, the visual impression is of nondescript 1960s pebblecast building that is not different in appearance from hundreds of others in this struggling de-industrialized part of an Australian capital city. This is not a school that is larded with resources—it exists in a swathe of this city that has been ravaged and dealt with harshly by economic globalization. Unlike many of its equivalents in other parts of this city and state, this school has seen a paintbrush in the last decade, but the extensive asphalted grounds, and the perimeter of the school looking out onto government rental housing, give us more than a hint of the circumstances the school is struggling with. Plainsville is one of almost half of the government schools in this state officially classified as 'disadvantaged'—the local euphemism for communities suffering from poverty, low income, high levels of unemployment, high incidence of family dysfunction and disintegration, high levels of transience and low levels of parental education. Almost 70 percent of the students at Plainsville qualify for government assistance. But, it is what is going on inside this R–9 government school of 300 students and 30 staff that sets it apart.

Impressions change rapidly and dramatically once inside the school reception area where we are greeted by a sandwich board proclaiming: 'Plainsville is delighted to welcome Professor John Smyth and Dr. Peter McInerney and hope you have a pleasant stay in our school.' The school offers this level of personalized welcome to every one of the several hundred visitors who come through its doors each year. This is part of the notion of respectful relationships that are at the center of everything the school does. More often than not, the visitor is greeted by a student rather than an adult behind the reception counter, for in this school students know in intimate detail what is going on and can inform, or even usher the visitor, to wherever they need to go in the school. On any morning the visitor is likely to be greeted as well by the smell of freshly made toast, for in this school almost half of the children provide themselves with breakfast from food subsidized by the school.

It is not so much the structure of the school that hits the eye either, even though Plainsville is divided into three open *learning areas*, each with its own identity: *junior primary* (reception to grade 2), *primary* (grades 3–5) and *middle school* (grades 6–9). Our particular interest is in the 88 young adolescents in grades 6–9 and the 4 adults who work with them in their *learning areas*, *learning teams* and *talking-circles* that are part of the complex process in this school—a school where students construct and pursue *individual learning plans* in a context of what the school refers to as *student-initiated curriculum*.

What goes on, or more accurately what is missing, reveals much that is radically different in this school. There is a palpable absence of stress or anger, and there is a subdued atmosphere of relaxed calm about the place, something that becomes even more apparent once we enter the learning areas. Missing is any notion of a conventional classroom, with its rows of desks facing the front, and a teachers' refuge behind the obligatory desk that so often in most classrooms acts as boundary between the teacher and students and signals in unmistakable terms where authority lies. Instead, there is no identifiable teacher domain in any room at Plainsville; it is as if teachers have been made invisible, and as we rapidly found out, to even speak of the personage of 'a teacher' is likely to raise a curious eyebrow among the students at Plainsville. All adults here, no matter what their status, are regarded as *resource persons* available to all students. This might include adults who are formally trained 'teachers,' but it also includes as well adults who are School Service Officers (SSOs) (professional teaching aides), parents, community volunteers, and the school janitor or grounds person. All are addressed by the students using whatever name they prefer—Mr., Miss., Mrs., or simply by their given name, or some abbreviation of it.

Not only is there an absence of conventional classrooms here, but the walls that previously separated rooms and acted as corridors or conduits for channeling the movement of students have disappeared to create additional space for clusters of tables or simply open spaces in which adults and children sit on the carpets at the beginning of each day in *learning circles* to share and discuss everyone's *learning plans*, sessions that were usually chaired by a different student each day. This notion of adults sitting on the mats at the level of the students seems to convey a very subtle but profound message about who has power in this school.

Attention is soon drawn to the many colorful posters around the school that loudly 'talk up' important messages for students about rigor, expectations, personal possibilities and a commitment to learning—words like 'Courage,' 'Risk,'

'Teamwork,' 'Concentrate' and 'Challenge.' These words seem to fit neatly with the school motto which is displayed and uttered everywhere: 'Live on the edge and be the best you can be.'

A large white board with the names of 30 to 40 students in each of the learning areas tells us another part of the unique story at Plainsville. It is here that each student registers their whereabouts next to their name during the course of the day, when they are not in the learning area—the library, the art room, another specialist area, one of the computer areas or out in the school grounds. Even more perplexing is the fact that this does not appear to be a surveillance or policing device but rather a quick and convenient method by which an adult can locate a student to provide resources or to check on progress toward the completion of a learning plan.

This is only the start of the incredible story about a school that has brought on a revolution in the way they place learning in the context of respectful relationships, at the center of everything they do. It is a theme that we will revisit in later sections of this book because it seems to us to get to the very heart of the middle schooling project. We will also consider the importance of pedagogical leadership and the ways in which the school has attempted to improve school completion (graduation) and engagement in a community that has traditionally suffered from a poor image.

Broadvale K–12 Community School

It was rather a drab winter morning when we first made our way to Broadvale Community School on the northern outskirts of the city. Leaving the busy highway, we journeyed through the public housing estates and mix of industrial and commercial businesses that make up the local neighborhood. This is a district that is very similar to Plainsville where the stains of the rustbelt are very much in evidence in the form of derelict factories, vacant lots and 'for sale' signs.

A siren heralding the start of a school day had just sounded as we drove into the school grounds and students, with varying degrees of haste, were making their way across the oval and asphalt paths to their home group classes. We were struck by the contrasts in the landscape. In the distance, some rather functional two-story red brick buildings dominated the senior and middle school campuses while in the foreground a stunning galvanized iron and timber administration center stood out in the architectural desert. Near the entrance our attention was drawn to the school motto 'Achievement for all' which stood out boldly on a welcoming board. It appeared again in the school foyer and in the bundle of school newsletters strategically placed in the visitor reception area. What does this mean in practice we wondered?

With a current enrollment exceeding 1000 students and 73 full-time equivalent teaching staff, Broadvale K–12 Community School is by any measure a large and complex school. Built in 1979 to serve a rapidly growing population on the urban fringe, the school has a long history of involvement in the federally funded Disadvantaged Schools Program (DSP) and a reputation for curriculum innovation and social justice. More than 65 percent of students are recipients of a school card and some 10 percent are on individually negotiated educational programs. Many of the students come from an Anglo Saxon background, although in recent years the school has become a much more culturally diverse community with an increasing enrollment of indigenous and Asian students.

Our initial conversations with teachers confirmed the intrusion of social concerns into school life and the high level of disadvantage experienced by many students in this community. Although the area has a strong sense of history and social capital associated with the post-war economic development, the district has fallen on hard times following the decline of manufacturing industries in the deregulated industrial environment of the 1990s. In a case of 'global meets local,' escalating unemployment and growing casualization of the workforce has exacerbated the level of poverty and welfare dependency. Teachers have to deal on a daily basis with the 'fractured lives' of students and the intrusion of violence, resentment and anger in their classes. It seems that a great deal of their time is invested in counseling students, brokering inter-agency referrals, and monitoring and managing student behavior matters. So severe was the stereotyping and negative images of the community that school leavers were unwilling to own up to their postcode address.

Following restructuring in 1995, Broadvale is now organized into a K–6 junior primary and primary school, a 7–9 middle school and a 10–12 senior school. A building program resulted in a new administration center (replete with a well-furnished staffroom), a K–12 resource center, junior primary classrooms and an extensively renovated middle school center. Although a few staff, including student counselors, special education and English as a Second Language (ESL) teachers work across the primary/secondary divide, most operate exclusively within a particular school. A Cambodian youth worker supports Indo-Chinese students and Indigenous students have access to an Aboriginal Education Teacher (AET) and an Aboriginal Education Worker (AEW).

Since our particular interest lay in the educational arrangements for the 400 young adolescents in grades 7 to 9, we soon made our way via a covered walk way to the middle school complex adjacent to the canteen. Janet, the assistant principal, pointed out the features of the multipurpose building, which comprises a staff preparation and meeting room, offices for the middle school coordinators, a large, flexible space for team teaching and more conventional classrooms. In a deliberate attempt to create small learning communities, class sizes are kept to a maximum of 24 students and the 16 classes are organized in two sub-schools. In year 7, home group teachers have their students for a pastoral care session and four subjects. This is reduced to two subjects in grade 8 and one subject in grade 9. The intent is that students develop positive relationships with a core group of teachers, but one teacher pointed out that the aim is to gradually 'wean them off the primary school model.' Although integrated curriculum is not a priority at Broadvale, teachers are encouraged to develop a thematic approach and two primary trained teachers have managed to sustain a team teaching arrangement with their home groups. Professional dialog among staff is fostered through fortnightly meetings of grades 7–9 teachers and weekly leadership team meetings. As we were to discover in subsequent visits, these are opportunities for teachers to discuss the concerns and progress of particular students, share insights from professional development conferences, plan middle school activities and deal with nuts and bolts issues.

Broadvale's middle school priorities are nested within the broader school goal of improving attendance, engagement and participation. A transition program aimed to ensure greater continuity in schooling from the primary to secondary years, and a good deal of staff development was focused on middle school teaching methodologies. Literacy and numeracy were given special attention. As part of an effort to promote inclusivity and improve student welfare, an anti-bullying program was initiated and additional time was set aside for pastoral care in the timetable. A major initiative involved an extension of student voice through a revitalized student representative council and class meetings. Together with student-run assemblies, they helped to maintain a sense of identity and promote student achievement.

During our time in the school, we saw much to admire about the school's efforts to foster 'achievement for all.' Whether it was in the sporting, social, cultural, artistic or academic fields, it was apparent that much had been done to promote a culture of success through school newsletters, middle school assemblies and open days. But it is difficult to carve out a space for middle schooling within the confines of conventional high schools. In spite of structural support, many teachers were struggling against a culture of privatism and entrenched practices associated with subject specialization and competitive assessment and reporting practices. As it will become more apparent in this study, efforts to promote a middle school ethos were highly contingent on the efforts of a few strongly committed teachers.

New Vista Community School

It was a cool morning in late autumn when we made the first of a many visits to the school. As we meandered through picturesque hills and valleys, we began to take in the freshness of the countryside and the diversity of the land use: dairy farms, vineyards, cereal crops, open paddocks and the occasional pockets of native scrub. The mist had lifted as we reached the small township of Scottsville where we joined a queue of yellow school buses on the main road to the local school. New Vista Community School serves a rural community some 60 kilometers from the metropolitan area. More than 70 percent of students live outside the town, so bus travel is a daily occurrence. As if we needed any further reminders of the rural connection, the northern perimeter of the school was dominated by several large grain silos and a flour mill.

When we stepped into the school foyer and signed the visitor book our attention was drawn to the large display cabinets replete with trophies and pennants. They seemed to convey a powerful message about the importance of sporting and academic achievements in the community.

For much of its history, New Vista Community School has been a secondary school, but following a review of regional education arrangements in 1996, it was developed as a multi-campus K–12 school with special middle schooling and senior secondary provisions. Four of the seven campuses (K–2, years 3–6, 7–9 and 10–12) are in Scottsville and three smaller K–6 campuses are in outlying townships. The school now draws students from an area of 1000 square kilometers and has a current enrollment of 1200 students, one-third of whom are school card holders. The relatively small proportion of students in low socioeconomic circumstances means that the school does not qualify for additional funding under DSP criteria but we were told that rural poverty is a growing concern in this district. With just a handful of Aboriginal and NESB students, this is very much a mono-cultural community.

The idea of a multi-campus school has challenged many of the long-standing administrative, industrial and educational practices associated with public education. The school has 120 staff members, including SSOs. Leadership positions comprise a K–12 principal, 7 heads of campuses, 12 coordinators, 5 advanced skills teachers and a director of finance and administration. While sites retain their own sense of identity, whole-school planning and curriculum development is a feature of the new arrangements. There is one consolidated budget for the school and a set of shared priorities for the seven campuses. Many teachers, school assistants and school leaders work across campuses. A whole-school dialog is sustained through K–12 staff meetings and professional development activities, leadership programs and cross-campus committees. These cooperative arrangements are complemented by a K–12 Governing Council and five campus advisory committees that involve a broad cross-section of parents in formal decision-making processes. As we will relate later in this book, the changes have not been without tensions and some staff resistance (especially on the part of senior school subject specialists), but for the most part the restructuring has won considerable community support, especially the creation of the middle school unit.

The middle school campus occupies the same site as the senior school and students share many of the facilities. Accompanied by Josie, the Head of the 7–9 campus, we made our way to the middle school unit in the southwestern corner of the school. Opened in 1997, this red brick building consists of an administration block, a teacher preparation area and eight classrooms, two of which can be opened up for meetings and team teaching purposes. It says something about the appeal of middle schooling (or a lack of foresight on the part of planners) that enrollments have grown so rapidly that students can no longer be accommodated within the unit. Two of the grade 7/8 home groups now occupy a double unit weatherboard classroom, and year 9 groups are somewhat more dispersed about the campus. Nonetheless, there is a strong sense of middle school identity in the campus. Teaming arrangements enable two teachers (one of whom is a home group teacher) to present most of the curriculum to small classes of vertically grouped 7/8 students. Students receive certificates for sporting, cultural and academic achievements at whole- and middle school assemblies. Their birthdays are recognized, and there is an 'Aussie of the week' award nominated by a student to acknowledge a peer who is a thoughtful and helpful person.

'Middle schooling here works on the "why not" principle' said Josie. As we made our way around the unit, there was some evidence to support this spirit of innovation. We observed teachers integrating curriculum and working in teams. We saw some outstanding examples of projects addressing the question of sustainable energy. We heard about the annual presentations to a community panel by the grades 7 and 8 students. Posters depicting 'six thinking hats' and charts showing Bloom's taxonomy highlighted the emphasis given to cooperative learning and a 'thinking curriculum.' It was apparent that much had been done to make learning areas as comfortable and stimulating as possible. The walls of most rooms were covered with artifacts of student learning in the form of charts, assignments, projects and models. Even the normally drab desks had been given a makeover, thanks to the initiative of an art teacher who encouraged and taught students how to design and decorate their own desktops. 'It just gives kids a sense of bonding' exclaimed Lisa, the chief architect of the project. For a fee of $20, students could purchase the desk and keep it for the duration of their school years. It was apparent from the creative and colorful designs that this decoupage activity had generated much personal pride and ownership on the part of students.

We could say much more about the vision, achievements and struggles of the middle school campus of New Vista, but our purpose here is to give the reader a brief glimpse of the remarkable changes that have taken place in this rural school. As this book unfolds we will explore in some detail the pedagogical elements of schooling and the ways in which the school has developed as a collaborative networked community to better support the needs and aspirations of young adolescents.

Seachange High School

It is a beautiful spring morning, an ideal opportunity for Macca to take his year 8 home group outdoors for an environmental activity. The destination is Hadley's River, more a small stream than a river, that flows conveniently along the northern boundary of Seachange High School. There is an abundance of flowering plants this time of the year, but the streams have become polluted from sewerage and storm water as the town's population and demand for housing has grown. Macca's students are doing something to restore the environment. For the past year, they have been involved in a re-vegetation project, and today they are investigating the microscopic life in the murky waters. Working in pairs, they collect water samples in phials from the creek and puddles. Jokingly, Macca tells them to watch out for snakes in the high grass. As they wander along the flood plain, he quizzes them about the landscape. 'Why are the trees so tall here but stunted further away from the river? What kinds of trees live near the river? What stresses are they under?' he asks. His passion for the environment rubs off onto the kids. With considerable pride they point out the fledging trees that they have planted earlier in the year. It is obvious they feel some ownership of the area. Back in the laboratory students analyze their samples under a microscope. Some find tiny forms of life and begin to speculate whether it is flora or fauna. Those who do not find any specimens begin to ask why—was the water too pure? . . . did it lack nutrients? Macca is on the move most of the time. He gets to see how each pair is going with the task, asks critical questions, encourages some students to analyze other samples or to increase magnification and reminds a few boys about sticking to the task.

Meanwhile, Colin has his year 9 home group for science. The topic is simple machines, and the task is to make a catapult out of cardboard from instructions downloaded from a web site. They have already viewed a film on the topic and are now going to do some experiential learning. Colin is very enthusiastic about the venture and shows the class a model that he constructed the previous evening at home. He tells them it is similar in design to that used by the ancient Romans. A little bit of history creeps into the science lesson. Most students seem to be familiar with the technology and a few boys comment about the destructive capacity of catapults. This is to be a cooperative activity and the class is organized in groups ranging from 3 to 5 students. Colin goes over the instructions and reminds them about sharing the tasks within the groups. Most students are familiar with this kind of activity, and they have little trouble cutting out the sections and assembling the parts. 'I'd rather make a catapult than just read about it in a book,' a student tells me. Not surprisingly, this is a rather messy and noisy activity as the students check out the guidelines, allocate jobs within the group, cut out the parts and construct the catapult. Discarded paper begins to pile up on the floor, and there is a considerable movement as students collect materials and inspect the models of adjoining groups. Like Macca, Colin is not a passive observer as he moves about the groups clarifying instructions, offering advice and praising the students' efforts. Gradually the catapults take shape and the works are put on show at the front of the class. But these artifacts are not just for display purposes. They will become a point of entry into deeper investigations into technology in the following weeks.

At first sight these pedagogical encounters may seem unremarkable, but they are indicative of moves toward a more student-centered approach to learning at Seachange. Some teachers talk about this as 'constructivism,' others simply refer to it as 'hands-on learning.' In practice, it means that students often work as members of groups rather than individuals. They still use textbooks but have access to many other resources. They learn by doing real things. Teachers build on what students bring to the classroom. The work is rarely quiet. Macca and Colin now spend much of their time in a specially designed middle school as members of teaching and learning teams that deliver the curriculum to grades 7 and 8 home groups. The change has not been without some trauma. For most of its history, Seachange has been a conventional high school with a strong academic focus. Teachers have tended to see themselves as subject specialists with strong faculty affiliations. But concerns about falling school completion rates, lack of student engagement (especially in the middle years) and the relevance of studies to the world of work and the lives of kids led to a major curriculum review. The ensuing change resulted in the formation of a separate middle school for grades 7 and 8 students, an extension of Vocational Education and Teaching (VET) programs, moves toward greater subject integration and an emphasis on pastoral care and relational learning. In 2002, the school was acclaimed as one of the top ten schools in Australia by *The Australian* newspaper for its music department. Plans are afoot to offer an integrated studies course around the theme, 'Gone fishing,' for 20 students in grades 9 and 10 who are having difficulties in meeting expectations of traditional schooling.

To some extent, curriculum reforms were also prompted by demographic and socioeconomic changes within the community. With its beautiful beaches, bays and headlands, Seachange has always been a popular seaside resort and retirement center, but in the last decade the population of the town and district has expanded rapidly. Much of the local economy is based on tourism, hospitality and community services that are skewed toward the aged. According to data from the Australian Bureau of Statistics, the mean age of the population is 50.6 years. At first glance the community seems affluent and stable, but, as Joan, the middle school assistant principal, pointed out, pockets of poverty and a transient population tend to belie Seaside's comfortable image. Approximately 30 percent of the school's 750 students receive government assistance and a growing proportion of students are on negotiated educational plans because of diagnosed difficulties with literacy and numeracy.

With rising enrollments and a more complex curriculum, there has been a proliferation of school buildings and amenities. Today the school consists of a mixture of solidly construction buildings, including an administration center (built in the 1930s) and a recently constructed middle school, as well a score of prefabricated structures deposited in a haphazard fashion across the school grounds. Walking through the maze of dilapidated classrooms, one gets a sense that this is a school that needs more than a fresh coat of paint. Unfortunately, proposals for a Technical and Further Education (TAFE) center senior high school complex have not come to fruition as the state government has changed priorities and political directions. This has left staff and parents angry and frustrated. Like many secondary schools, Seachange competes for enrollments with private schools and has to deal with unfavorable media images of public education. Having to put up with second-rate facilities does not help.

In contrast to the rather drab and uninspiring architecture of surrounding buildings, the middle school is an impressive two-story brick and glass structure with a central staircase, flexible learning spaces, laboratories, offices and seminar rooms. Though most learning areas are fairly small, some can be opened up for team teaching purposes, and all are reasonably well equipped with display boards and storage spaces. Teachers share offices with team members and have ready access to information and communication technologies and teaching resources. Other structural changes have helped to promote a middle schooling ethos. Firstly, there has been a reconfiguration of leadership roles to include an assistant principal and coordinator with middle school responsibilities and hard-fought timetable changes have led to longer lessons (3 × 110-minute block per day) and more flexible teaching arrangements. Secondly, in a concerted effort to promote the idea of learning communities, year 8 teachers take groups for 4 classes per day and a pastoral care session and move with the class into grade 9 where possible. Class sizes are kept to maximum of 22 students. Thirdly, there has been a large investment in professional development that has enabled teachers to participate in international middle school forums, visit innovative middle school sites and engage in action research projects.

It appears that these changes have been broadly accepted by the Seachange community, but as we will reveal later in this book, sustaining a commitment to middle schooling within the confines of a traditional high school is quite problematic. In this context, a core of dedicated middle school teachers have to tangle with indifference and downright resistance on the part of some senior school colleagues as well a lack of system support for the ideals of middle schooling.

Investigator High School

It is a bitterly cold autumn evening, perhaps not the best time of year to schedule an open day. Nonetheless many parents and students brave the elements to tour the school and meet the staff of Investigator. As darkness closes in, most seek refuge in the school hall and adjacent classrooms where there is an opportunity to view displays of student work and chat informally with teachers and students. For many parents, middle schooling is the big topic of conversation, and Linda's grade 8 students are on hand to tell them about their own experiences. Some have acted as tour guides and are now rehearsing their talks as they munch their way through pizzas. A group of 25 prospective parents and upper primary students make their way into the classroom. Linda gives a lively 5-minute introduction to middle schooling and then it's over to her students. The good things are 'getting lots of rewards from Linda . . . being in small classes . . . having 6 teachers . . . doing technology studies . . . organizing our own assemblies . . . having a peer support program . . . lots of sporting activities.' The not so good things are 'not having lockers . . . having to carry bags around all day . . . not being allowed into the library at recess time.' The students are well organized and confident. They answer questions from parents about school uniforms, discipline and the subjects they study. Parents seem to be reassured with their responses and warmly applaud their presentations.

Linda teaches in a school that has undergone a remarkable transformation over the past decade. Located on the outer margins of an Australian city, Investigator High School is a large educational complex of 1000 students, 55 percent of whom are supported by school cards. A small minority of students comes from an NESB and 15 percent operate on negotiated educational plans. A Special Unit supports students with disabilities and the 40 Aboriginal students have access to a Nunga Resource Center, an AET and AEWs. Investigator High School is an adult re-entry school, and students are able to access a broad range of TAFE courses through a vocational education college.

Like Seachange, Investigator High School is bound up with the culture and lifestyle of the beach, but poverty cuts much more deeply into the community. The district has a diversity of land use ranging from petrochemical works, manufacturing industries and commercial complexes on the seaward margin to grape-growing and horticultural enterprises on the gently sloping hills. Although the regional economy is relatively strong, unemployment figures are high in some neighborhoods and poverty is a significant social issue for the community. The proportion of youth is twice the average of the metropolitan area with some 39 percent of the population less than 25 years of age. Not only is youth unemployment exceptionally high, but also according to the local council there is an urgent need for youth accommodation in the district and a four-month waiting list for youth counseling services. Like Broadvale, the school and community has had to contend with negative media publicity about the incidence of crime in the area, although a joint project involving local schools and youth groups is working to counteract these images. But more positive images of the physical and cultural landscape surfaced in our conversations with students, many of whom spoke of their love of the sun and the surf and the recreational activities of the area. This lifestyle was captured quite evocatively by student artists through the murals in the school grounds.

All schools have a history—a legacy of traditions and customs that is reflected in the architecture of the buildings, educational programs, the ceremonies, rituals and events that characterize school life and the values and messages conveyed to the community. These tend to give an air of permanence to the institutional structures and culture of schools. Tyack and Cuban (1995) remind us that schools are quite resistant to change, perhaps for the very good reason that much reform is of a 'faddish' nature and unlikely to make a real difference to student learning. Continuity in schooling may be desirable, but entrenched practices and inflexible structures can act as major barriers to school improvement. Such was the case at Investigator High School. Established as a dual campus secondary school in 1967, the school expanded rapidly during the 1970s, reaching a peak enrollment of 2000 students. But during these years, an east/west divide created by the geographic separation of the senior and junior secondary schools helped to reinforce a culture of isolation and privatism that did little to promote educational innovation or debate.

The opening of other secondary schools in the region relieved some of the pressure on educational facilities at Investigator High School and allowed for some major restructuring. In 1998, the development of a $6.7 million building project enabled the school to be located on the site of the eastern campus, thus removing the barrier to access that was an unsatisfactory feature of the original school site. The consolidation of the school represented more than a geographic shift; it also involved a fundamental change in the structural arrangements for schooling in the middle years. The construction of an architecturally designed middle school center certainly helped this transformation. Peter, one of the middle school teachers, commented to us 'it certainly helps to be able to see a middle school.' Students also appreciated having a place to call home, even if they do not have lockers in which to store their possessions!

At Investigator High School, middle schooling is organized through four sub-schools—two at grade 8 and two at grade 9—which function as discrete organizational units and learning communities each with its own coordinator. Sub-schools are further divided into four home groups of approximately 22 students with each class having a core group of teachers responsible for the teaching program and pastoral care. Each sub-school is located in a separate building with its own classrooms and teacher preparation areas, thus reinforcing the idea of a self-contained learning community. Flexible teaching areas accommodate team-teaching practices and sub-school assemblies and withdrawal rooms for small groups. All teaching areas are equipped with gas and running water to allow for some arts and science activities (normally carried out in specialist rooms) to take place in the sub-school. There are no corridors in these buildings, thus allowing students easy access to play grounds and outdoor spaces.

'Make the timetable fit the curriculum,' say the middle school advocates. At Investigator, the teaching day is organized into three 105-minute time blocks which are further divided into two lesson periods of approximately 50 minutes. At year 8, each curriculum area is allocated four lessons per week, but the possibility of subject integration, and team teaching, is enhanced by setting classes on the timetable in the 105-minute blocks. This commonly occurs in English and Society and Environment. Sub-schools have considerable autonomy with regard to curriculum planning and the day-to-day running of the school. Middle school team meetings are programmed each week and alternate between gatherings of the whole group of sub-school teachers and home group teachers. The latter is much more focused on immediate issues and concerns of students and the day-to-day issues of middle schooling. In one of the sub-schools, part of the meeting is commonly referred to as the 'gossip' session, but the conversations go beyond mere speculation about the complexities of students' lives to discussions about strategies for addressing problems that frequently arose out of home life, for example, how to support these students to improve their literacy, how to tackle low self-confidence or how to engage them in curriculum activities.

In common with Seachange and Broadvale schools, a middle school ethos at Investigator has been developed within and often against a prevailing high school culture. As we will relate further into the study, the tensions are never far from the surface.

Gulfview Secondary School

It is a bright October morning and the siren signaling the end of morning recess has just sounded as we make our way to Cockatoo sub-school to join Lauren's middle school class. As we enter the classroom our attention is drawn to the colorful posters, charts and students' assignments which adorn the walls. Lauren makes us welcome and invites us to move about the room and talk to her students. The class consists of twenty grade 9 and five grade 8 students. Desks and tables have been arranged to accommodate small groups. According to the timetable, today's 90-minute lesson is scheduled as English, but Lauren's students are studying an environmental theme that crosses curriculum boundaries. Students can choose from a range of tasks that are intended to promote creative writing, informed research, higher-order problem-solving and multimedia presentation skills. Lara, a grade 8 student, tells me that she has chosen to write an essay on the water cycle, to investigate how rain is produced and to write a creative piece on rainbows and moonbeams. She says that some of this work will go into her portfolio, which will be shown to parents in reporting sessions. Pedro, a grade 9 student, is busy designing an information package to promote 'Clean-Up Australia Day' at the school. He says that students can borrow the school's digital camera and are taught how to write an essay on an environmental issue.

These brief glimpses into Lauren's classroom reveal a little of the pedagogical features of Gulfview. As a purpose-built middle school, Gulfview is quite a unique place. To begin with, visitors are likely to be impressed with the architecture of the buildings, especially the break with convention in the design of classrooms and the innovative use of iron, steel and glass. Curved walkways connect the various learning centers and facilities, and there is feeling of spaciousness about the place that is often missing in inner-city schools. The dreary asphalt is far less dominating and one's gaze is invariably drawn to the pleasantly sloping grassed mounds, the newly planted gardens, the extensive playing fields and panoramic views of the nearby gulf and hills.

This is a 'switched-on school' that prides itself at being at the 'leading edge' of technology. Staff and students have access to an extensive network of computers in workrooms, classrooms, specialist technology centers and the library. Whiteboards have replaced blackboards. Students can borrow laptop computers to complete assignments at home. They can communicate through cyberspace. Many facilities, including the library and recreation center, are shared with the community, and it is not uncommon to see parents and young children occupying the same territory as students.

Situated betwixt gentle rolling hills and the sparkling waters of the sea, Gulfview serves a rapidly growing population on the fringe of a large metropolis. The attraction of the coastal environment, coupled with the sale of large tracts of rural land, has contributed to an influx of new residents, many of whom commute to the city to work each day. At first sight, the newly constructed homes, shopping centers and civic amenities convey the impression of a prosperous community. But while poverty of the kind described at Plainsville is largely missing, many families are struggling to meet home repayments in this 'mortgage belt.' Regional unemployment is fairly high and some 30 percent of students are school card holders. The school lacks the cultural diversity of Broadvale Community School with the vast majority of its students coming from English-speaking backgrounds.

What attracted us to Gulfview was its reputation for middle schooling. A little history lesson is required at this point. Following a major review of the educational arrangements for young adolescents (Eyers et al., 1992) several Australian states experimented with the idea of specialist middle schools to cater for students in an age range from 11 to 15 years. Gulfview was one of the pioneer schools in this bold venture. The foundation principal had a strong background in middle schooling and was passionate about its possibilities of modifications to staffing policies enabled the school to select a core of committed middle school staff members, some of whom had experience in the upper primary years. These teachers were given time and resources to meet as a team and develop a middle school curriculum in the latter half of 1995. An architecturally designed middle school, consisting of three sub-schools was opened in 1996 to accommodate 350 students from grades 7 to 9. A center for students with severe multiple disabilities was added in 1998, and the major building program was completed with the opening in 1999 of an additional sub-school, a senior school for year 11 and 12 students, and a recreation center.

From its inception, Gulfview attempted to create an ethos of middle schooling around a constellation of ideas and practices, including sub-school learning communities, integrated and negotiated curriculum, collaborative teaching and learning, student participation and an emphasis on relationships. Currently, sub-school consists of five to six home groups of approximately 25 students who are vertically grouped in grades 7 and 8 and grades 8 and 9. Within each sub-school, a coordinator and a team of five to six teachers are responsible for the development and delivery of a curriculum based on eight areas of study (English, science, mathematics, health and personal development, design and technology, the arts, studies of society and environment, and Japanese). Students can access an extensive range of extra-curricula activities including sports, a tournament of minds, musical and drama activities. The school day is organized in three 90-minute teaching/learning blocks that facilitate a thematic approach to learning. Support across the four sub-schools is provided through a middle school assistant principal, a school chaplain and a school counselor. Originally, teachers taught largely within one sub-school— often taking students for three to four areas of study and pastoral care. However, this practice has been undermined in recent years following the addition of the senior school and the adoption of a line timetable.

We will relate more of the Gulfview story in the following chapters, especially the school's efforts to promote integrated curriculum, authentic forms of assessment and reporting and student voice. We will take a closer look at the structural and cultural changes to support middle schooling practices and consider how teachers learn to become successful middle school teachers in the context of a secondary school. We will also consider the problematic of school reform at Gulfview and the difficulties of sustaining middle schooling in the absence of ongoing system support.

Closing remarks

Before we close this chapter, a few caveats are in order. Firstly, we do not present these schools as model places that have all the answers to the concerns and issues raised in the introduction to this book. To do so would be to over-romanticize the difficulty of the task involved. Nor would the teachers in these schools want to be represented in this way. However, these schools are courageous places that are struggling to develop an ethos of middle schooling in an unsupportive policy context. They may not offer recipes to be copied in an uncritical manner, but they do offer resources of hope to those engaged in the task of making school more relevant and inspiring for young adolescents. Secondly, we do not claim that these are the only sites that are worthy of study. There are many other committed individuals and schools working to improve the education of young adolescents in Australian education systems. Our choice of sites was necessarily limited by geographic boundaries, financial constraints and time. Thirdly, we do not limit our vision of what is possible in transforming teaching and learning for young people to the practices and policies that we have observed in our studies. Although the study is anchored in grounded research, our analysis involves a critical engagement with the literature in sociology, youth studies, curriculum and pedagogy, teacher development and school reform. In re-imagining the possibilities of schools as more inclusive and student-centered organizations, we have stepped outside the boundaries of the project schools to address matters of educational policy, community capacity building and democratic curriculum.

Note

1.   Some of the ideas cited in this portrait come from and are elaborated upon further in Smyth and McInerney (in press), especially the italicized terminology used there.

PART TWO

Young Lives

CHAPTER THREE

Making adolescence everybody's business

Introduction

We now turn our attention to young people and their experience of schooling. Schools supposedly exist for young people but some students are far more advantaged than others in the education stakes. Falling high school completion rates, poor attendance and participation figures, combined with a lack of engagement and alienation of youth, especially in the middle years, are a clear indication that schools are not working for a significant proportion of students, especially those from disadvantaged backgrounds (Smyth et al., 2000). Not only are these young people 'at risk' (Fisher, 1993) of not acquiring a passport to satisfying and rewarding employment, but also they risk being trapped in a cycle of poverty, with attendant health problems, welfare dependency and homelessness. This is not just a problem for individuals and their families. A nation is culturally, intellectually and economically deprived when it fails to develop and utilize the knowledge, skills and resources of all young people.

Adolescence is everybody's business not only because young people are a large proportion of the population but also because they represent the hopes for building a better world. All our futures depend on having a well-educated and politically engaged group of young citizens. In the circumstances, we have a moral obligation to ensure that resources are directed to the benefit of all students, not just the privileged elite. The question of adult responsibility is especially pertinent.

To a large extent, the fate of young people rests with adults and the governments they elect. Since young people, especially those below 16 years of age, are constituted as 'non-citizens' (Davis, 1999), they enjoy few of the entitlements of adults. Such a status connects, in part, to the idea that they are vulnerable and hence in need of adult protection (Bessant, 2004), but it also says something about the ways in which adults and adult institutions exercise power and control over children. The reality is that most young people are financially, socially and emotionally reliant on older people, and the rights and privileges they enjoy depend largely on the discretion of those charged with their care.

Unfortunately, far too many young people are the victims of institutional abuse and the neglect of human services that masquerades under the banner of market economics. With the ascendancy of neo-liberal governance, education is increasingly being construed as a consumer product, with schools having to compete for parent and student clients in a marketplace. But as Furlong and Cartmel (1997) explain, 'the illusion of choice created by the marketization of education masks the continued entrenchment of traditional forms of inequality' (p. 11). In a post-industrial society where young people have to strive for the credentials needed for entry into the workforce, class and gender remain important determinants of educational pathways and achievements.

The old adage, 'as we sow, so shall we reap,' seems to be particularly apt when it comes to our commitment to the education and welfare of young people. There can be little doubt that if we do not address the causes of alienation and educational disadvantage we will bear the consequences in terms of escalating crime rates, substance abuse, community disorder, youth homelessness, intergenerational unemployment and entrenched poverty (Davis, 1999; Social Inclusion Board, 2004). But the issue is not just about the future. Adults can learn so much from youth and the passion which many of them express for global peace, environmental sustainability, acceptance of cultural difference and social justice. We need to find ways of harnessing this energy and commitment in our communities rather than driving young people away. This is an issue that cannot be resolved by coercion or simplistic political measures such as raising the school leaving age or mandating national testing programs. It requires a far more sophisticated strategy that places the needs, concerns and aspirations of adolescents at the center of educational policy and practice. For far too long curriculum has been developed at arm's length from the very people that schools are supposed to serve. In the following chapters we will hear what young people have to say about their hopes, expectations and concerns of schooling as we explore a number of sociological and pedagogical issues around the topics of adolescent identity, inequality and school reform in the middle years. Specifically we ask:

- What is the nature of young adolescence?
- How are youth identities constructed by teachers, schools and society at large?
- How do these constructions influence education policy, curriculum and school organization?
- How are young adolescents treated in contemporary contexts and schools?
- What do young people tell us about their experience of schooling?
- To what extent does schooling ameliorate or reinforce existing inequalities and injustices experienced by young people?
- How can we steer educational reform back to students?
- How can teachers and schools assist students to successfully navigate a transition from school to adult life?

In this chapter we identify key concerns and issues regarding the education of young adolescents, particularly those associated with the persistence of educational disadvantage, and the damaging effects of economic restructuring and neo-liberal policies on public schools and students' lives. We argue that we must make adolescence everybody's business if we are to create the proper conditions for a just and sustainable society. In essence, we must steer reform back to students. In the following chapters we draw on empirical data from school ethnographies and narrative portraits to illustrate whole-school programs and initiatives that foster belongingness, encourage student voice and engage students in challenging and worthwhile learning.

A young person's perspective

For the most part, young people experience schooling as something which is done to them. They are the objects of government policies, testing regimes, curriculum frameworks, behavior management codes and school regulations that govern the content and conditions of learning. The idea that they might have something important to say about curriculum, pedagogy and school organization or that they have the knowledge and skills to shape the directions of their own learning has not found much favor with policy makers. In the first instance, we need to listen respectfully to what young people have to say about their schooling. In the following portrait, a former student of Plainsville School gives us an insider's view of life in high school. Categorized as 'a failure' and 'a trouble-maker' by many of his secondary school teachers, James reveals himself as a thoughtful and articulate student who is able to describe the culture of high schools and the ways in which these institutions work against those who do fit the system.

THE SYSTEM IS ALWAYS RIGHT

Since leaving Plainsville I've been to two high schools. High schools are all really the same house, just decorated differently. The biggest problem is the lack of individuality. If they've got a middle ground and you don't fit into that, then the high school is going to fail you. I don't really like to use the term 'above' the rest of the kids in the class but if you're a bit faster than they are then you're going to be expected to stay back with them and do that work. Then you get bored and muck around. On the other hand if you're having difficulty, if you've got a learning disability and you can have trouble keeping up, you're going to get left behind. There's no individuality in what you need to learn and what, how, what is the best way for you to learn it. If you're not capable of sitting there with a pad and a pen, and copy and doing what you've been told, then you're not, in their eyes you're not learning ... you're going to fail.

I had a problem with my care (home group) teacher. We have some garden sheds in the courtyard outside our corridor where our class is and there was a special education kid locked in the garden shed. Someone had locked him in there and he was getting rather distressed so I went out and took two seconds to let him out and my care teacher has come up the corridor and seen me mucking around by the garden shed. Automatically he's come ripping out, 'James, what are you doing? Get in the class right now!' I said, 'Well, actually Sir, I'm just letting this kid out of the shed.' Some heartless s—' you know so-and-so, had locked him in there so there is no need to yell and get agro about it. 'Don't you start with me ...' ra, ra ra. 'You're already having arguments with all the other teachers, don't you start with me;' and um we were talking about that. I said, 'Why didn't you just come up to me and say, James' what are you doing?' I could have said 'Well, letting this kid out of the shed. Someone has locked the special ed. kid in there' and then he should have found out who'd locked him in there instead of having a go at me. He said 'Oh well, I interact with 300 students' blah blah and all their lies, and if I was to do that, that would take a lot of time because it would be individual.'

I've been at high school for two years and I've not once been involved in any major projects. Their peer mediation program is a joke. When I went there in year 8 we thought it would be a good opportunity for us to show them what we've got, where we're coming from. But they told me 'No, there's no way. You're only year 8,' I said 'Yeah, but I was doing this in year 6.' They tried to re-teach us everything. We were in year 8 and there was no way that we could have this vast array of knowledge and they were bringing in people from other places, other organizations, to train us how to mediate with your peers when the resources are there—the teachers and students. The problem at high school is that here's no teacher–student relationship at all where they can come in and work together to achieve a common goal which is the student learning. It's 'I'm the teacher, you're the student, I've given you this.' A fine example of that, Miss P, who's the maths teacher in our school, I never interacted with her in my life, didn't even know her. I had never said hello to her, and one day I was walking around and she goes, 'Oh get to class,' ra, ra. 'I'm on a free period [non-instruction time].' 'Oh you don't have a free period.' 'Yeah I do because I do a personal development course on Fridays and you have a free period.' 'Uh uh,' and she goes, 'Hang on a minute, I know you, you're James Y.' I said 'Yeah, I don't know you though.' and she goes, 'Oh no, I've heard a lot about you from other teachers' and I said—she goes 'Oh, they say you've got atrocious behavior and an attitude problem but you've got a lot of potential.' I'm like 'Well, hang on a minute, don't come and tell me I've got atrocious behavior if you don't even know me.' But they . . . must sit around and talk about you or something.

The other problem is that the lack of individuality. They're not really interested in individual learning. The whole culture would really need to change just even physically. They're all classrooms, a corridor with classrooms, chairs in rows, a teacher and a whiteboard up front, which isn't really an area, which is going to engage students in learning. It needs to be more open, more resources readily available, also um, yeah—it's really hard because the teachers would need to change their whole attitude and perception as well. If a student says, 'Well, I can do this,' actually saying well, maybe they can, instead of just saying, 'Well, no you're only in year 10, there's no *way* you can do that.' I'm in year 10 now, and this is the first year that I've even come into contact with computers. The government is talking about truancy and people leaving school but the problem is that there's nothing there to keep them at school. There's no reason to be at school. I was at a meeting yesterday and was told that I 'undermine the teacher's authority,' that I have 'a reckless disregard for teacher authority.' I could just sit there and be like every other student and I still would fail at the end. I've got to wonder how many people are out there that went before me that had the potential to be rocket scientists and they're now on the dole because the school failed them.

But kids at Plainsville want to be at school. They don't want to wag [truant] and go off and muck around. They don't want to come here and just sit back and muck around with their friends. They actually want to come here . . . and use every learning minute that they have to actually get something out of school. No one at our high school wants to be there and that's why the truancy rate is so high, that's why the grades are so low, that's why you've got people misbehaving, 'undermining teachers' authority'—as they would have you believe. That's why they've got people leaving early—because they don't want to be there but still the teachers don't see that as being their problem, it's the students' problem and there's nothing wrong with the system. I think they're scared to say 'Well we were wrong, we failed these kids.' The biggest problem isn't that students are failing schools and getting Es, it's that the school is failing the student but they don't want to see it that way. The student failed school; the school never fails the student. The system is always right. The system is never wrong. That's the problem.

(James, February 25, 2003)

The anger and frustration in James's voice are palpable. Having experienced a much more learner-centered approach to education at Plainsville, he feels devalued and powerless in high school and expresses his dismay at the absence of student voice, the unchallenging nature of his learning and the lack of trust between teachers and students. Above all, he is deeply troubled by the school's failure to treat him as an individual with something worthwhile to contribute to the school.

According to James, the system is failing the student. Perhaps he is right. Traditional high schools have not always served adolescents particularly well. Learning is often fragmented into subjects and insulated from the emotional lives of young people. In many instances students don't have the time or opportunity to develop close relationships with teachers and peers. Many feel lost and out of place in large schools where hierarchical arrangements often inhibit student voice. Technologies of exclusion operating through sorting and streaming practices and inflexible behavior management policies tend to reinforce the practices of exclusion that are writ large in the lives of many students. Many of these concerns have been brought to the fore in reports on early school leaving issues (Smyth et al., 2000; Social Inclusion Unit and the South Australian Department of Human Services, 2003). Students in these studies expressed concerns about their lack of involvement in school decision-making, the limited degree of personal and academic support, the regressive nature of behavior management policies and the inflexibility of schools when it comes to dealing with part-time students and those in the workforce. Lacking the social capital of middle-class Australians, many indigenous or working class students, like James, experience the 'deepening divide' (Gilbert, 2000) of an education system which still tends to favor the rich and the powerful through the maintenance of a hegemonic curriculum (Connell, 2002a), inflexible pedagogical practices and discriminatory testing regimes. This is especially evident in secondary schools where hierarchical relations of power operate through university selection processes that help to sustain stratification of educational opportunity (Teese, 1998).

James's painful experience of high school cuts to the quick when we contemplate how schools can reinforce patterns of educational disadvantage rather than opening up new horizons and opportunities for young people.

Becoming somebody: adolescent identity

Another way of reading James's story is to see it from the point of view of identity formation. 'Becoming somebody,' as Wexler (1992) puts it, is a complex process that involves a tension between agency and restraint. Although James has much to offer his school and community, his efforts to generate and maintain a sense of self-worth are being restrained by the hierarchical and disempowering culture of the high school. He feels trapped in a place that refuses to treat him as a young adult or to provide him with the opportunities and resources to express his ideas and encourage him to become a more independent learner.

Young people like James are the subjects of a powerful discourse about adolescent identity and development. Cormack (1996) reminds us that the notion of the adolescent is a social construction, a late nineteenth century invention constituted through discourses in the human sciences which have sought to map and distinguish human populations on the basis of age, gender, sexual orientation, culture and ethnicity. Typically, adolescence is viewed as a transition phase between childhood and adulthood, a state of becoming an adult but not quite being an adult (Wyn & White, 1997). Such thinking often assumes a strong link between chronological age, physical growth and social identity and has given rise to commonly held views about the essential needs and characteristics of young adolescents (Carnegie Council on Adolescent Development, 1989; Cormack, 1991; Hargreaves & Earle, 1990). Indeed, the call for a separate phase of schooling for adolescents is often based on the assumption that these students have 'special' needs that distinguish them from older and younger students.

To pursue the idea of generic traits, adolescents are said to experience irregular spurts in their physical development, have ravenous appetites, mature at varying speeds and are highly disturbed by body changes. Supposedly, their intellectual development is marked by a heightened sense of curiosity, a preference for active learning that is related to real-life experiences and a capacity for metacognition, seeing the bigger picture. A tendency toward erratic behavior, sensitivity to criticism, moodiness, and search for identity and peer acceptance are among the commonly perceived psychological attributes. Adolescents are often portrayed as being rebellious toward parents and authority figures, fiercely loyal to peer group values, often aggressive and argumentative, but also in need of affirmation of love from adults. With regard to their sense of morality and ethical behavior, young people are said to be idealistic, have a sense of fair play and are prepared to ask ambiguous questions about the meaning of life (Forte & Schurr, 1991). According to popular thinking, adolescents, as distinct from young children, have a greater need for peer friendship and sexual relationships, express a growing sense of independence, want to establish their own identity, and are keen to explore alternative lifestyles and values. However, because they are not fully mature people, they still need boundaries and controls set by adults.

Overriding the social construction of youth identity is a common perception about the instability and unpredictability of young people—traits that spill over into the ways in which they are represented in educational discourses and the media. The notion of the adolescent as 'a problem to be solved' is embedded in *Turning Points* (Carnegie Council on Adolescent Development, 1989), one of the most influential studies on the education of young people in the United States. Media coverage of issues relating to young people often focuses on the negative aspects of youth behavior and lifestyle, particularly drug abuse, sexual activity, welfare dependence, mental health and school violence (Colman & Colman, 2004). A tendency for mainstream media to demonize adolescents as rebellious, delinquent, unreliable or socially irresponsible human beings has been well documented by Cormack (1996), Roman (1996) and more recently by Panelli, Nairn, Atwool & McCormack (2002). An investigation by Panelli into the representations of youth in public spaces as reported by the *Otago Daily Times* (New Zealand) concluded that young people were commonly associated with alcohol, unsupervised behavior and disorder. A clear inference of parental failure was built into these discourses together with a view that young people ought to be excluded from public spaces for their own as well as the public good.

Evidence of a lack of trust and a reluctance to accept young people as citizens in their own right is widespread. Writing about the position of youth in American cities, Giroux (1996) observes:

> Youth as a self and social construction has become indeterminant, alien and sometimes hazardous in the public eye. A source of repeated moral panics and the object of social regulation, youth cannot be contained and controlled within a limited number of social spheres. Youth cultures are often viewed in the popular press as aberrant, unpredictable and dangerous in terms of investments they produce, social relations they affirm, and the anti-politics they legitimate. (p. 11)

Giroux calls attention to the moral panics generated by the demonizing discourse of youth and reminds us that social relations are embedded in discourses of politics, power and exclusion. The process of adolescent construction is neither natural nor neutral (Cormack, 1996). Moreover, what is often missing from the view of adolescent development described previously is a sociological perspective that takes account of the gendered, radicalized and classed location of young people. It is almost as if young people inhabit a space that is devoid of social and cultural influences, and that identity formation is a purely individual phenomenon. However, as Wyn and White (1997) point out, many young people are marginalized and placed at risk because of economic and political processes, not just because of their youth.

Growing up in a risk society

The idea that youth live in a risk society has been explored by numerous writers, including Davis (1999), Bell and Bell (1993), Hamburg (1992) and Giroux (1996) in the United States, and Furlong and Cartmel (1997), Beck (1992) and Giddens (1991) in the United Kingdom. As used by Davis (1999), the term 'risk' denotes not just the chance misfortunes, instability and unpredictability that characterize human life but the 'excessive risks' and 'extreme risk' conditions that plague adolescents. She argues:

> high risk conditions stem from many sources—dysfunctional families, poor schools, lack of rights, drastic cutbacks in funds for education and welfare; poor physical and dental health; insensitive and brutal caregivers; and, simply the levels of stress and aggravation of living in a society that provides little direction of values for youth outside of materialistic success goals. (p. xiii)

Young people have to navigate a set of risks such as environmental disasters, terrorism, nuclear war and the AIDS epidemic that were virtually unknown to their parents (Furlong & Cartmel, 1997). Although many of these risk conditions are universal, some are more directly connected to the inequitable and oppressive structural elements of an economy and society which has made life more difficult and disabling for particular groups of young people, notably the poor. Beck (1992) reminds us that 'poverty attracts an unfortunate abundance of risks . . . [but] the wealthy can purchase safety and freedom from risk' (p. 35). According to Davis, inequality and oppressive social relations have now reached the point where many adolescents are succumbing to permanent social and economic disadvantage, victimhood, deviant behavior and criminal lifestyles.

During our time in the project schools, we were constantly alerted to the damaging impact of poverty, homelessness, intergenerational unemployment and social dislocation on the lives of children. In the Plainsville community, a considerable number of students came from families in crisis and frequently arrived at school hungry and emotionally upset. As many students and their families had little or no experience of a work ethic, they were inclined to have low aspirations of schooling and future pathways. Hence, as we will explain, in Chapter 4, a major task of educators in these communities was to challenge the deficit thinking about working class students and develop a pedagogical response to poverty and social exclusion.

There is a real danger that the notion of 'youth at risk' becomes yet another negative construction of youth identity that can be used as a blaming category instead of a useful social construct (Smyth, 2005). As Furlong and Cartmel (1997) point out, an intensification of individualism means that the crises confronting young people are often attributed to the shortcomings of individuals rather than deficiencies in institutions such as schools. As with the demonizing discourse described earlier, popular perceptions of the innate instability of youth and their tendency toward risk behaviors tend to reinforce the view that young people need to be protected from their own destructive tendencies. The 'youth at risk' discourse has entered the realm of education policy and practice through notions of 'students at risk' and 'at risk behaviors.' Particular cohorts of students, usually those from disadvantaged backgrounds, are deemed to be 'at risk of not completing schooling,' 'at risk of remaining illiterate,' 'at risk of criminal behavior' and/or 'at risk of domestic violence.' In turn, this discourse has given rise to early intervention programs in schools and communities as a means of reducing or eliminating the risks for particular groups. How schools address these issues will be considered in other parts of this book, but for the moment we want to explore an aspect of adolescent identity concerning cultural difference.

Confronting difference

In the process of 'becoming somebody,' young people have to negotiate territories of class, gender, sexuality, ethnicity and race. In the school context, students' identities are constructed with and against prevailing norms of social behavior, religious beliefs, gender stereotypes and school policies. The following dialogic portrait highlights the added pressures confronting young people who do not fit the pattern in a conservative rural community. Johnny and Annabelle are 13 years of age and members of cooperating year home group classes at the New Vista middle school campus. They are close personal friends and are both passionate about the performing arts. As representatives of the student forum (the grades 7–9 decision-making body) they play an active role in school affairs. In the following excerpt from a dialogic portrait, they talk about some of the highs and lows of their adolescent years of schooling, particularly Johnny's experience of homophobia and harassment.

EVERYONE HAS THEIR DIFFERENCES

'My hobbies are dance, singing and acting,' says Johnny. 'I enjoy learning to play the piano and the trumpet and I do dance, and netball and that's about it,' says Annabelle. I'm interested to hear whether the school curriculum enables them to follow their passion for the performing arts. Johnny explains, 'We did this whole unit on music through the decades and I really enjoyed that, but I know that the boys in the class that are only interested in going out and playing 'footy' (Australian rules football), didn't really like it.' 'So your interests are a bit different from some of the other boys,' I suggest. This seemingly innocuous comment prompts a forthright response from Annabelle. 'Yeah. That's another thing, harassment in our classes.' 'So do you get paid out for having different interests', I ask Johnny, 'Yeah, a lot,' he says, 'They say stuff like 'Only gay guys do dance and different activities to football' because for all the other guys, it's just football, football that, football this, soccer that. But everyone has their differences.' What began as conversational starter turns into a much deeper discussion about Johnny's experience of harassment. 'So how do you handle that stuff?' I ask. He replies 'Um, I ignore them . . . and then if it gets worse then I go to a teacher. If it kept going, then I'd go to the principal.' In what becomes a feature of this interview, Annabelle begins to build on his story. 'Or here, we go to the student counselor. I don't have to go there because I don't get harassed, but the other day Johnny was being harassed but he sat there and did his work and just ignored . . .". Rather abruptly I cut her short and inquire, 'Have either of you seen the film *Billy Elliott*? It tells the story of a ballet dancer in England. Billy's father was a coal miner and he was brought up in industrial community in Wales or northern England. He had a lot of harassment, for a long time. His father couldn't accept that his son wasn't going to become a soccer player and rugby player and so on.' I am trying to draw a parallel between the homophobic experiences of Billy and Johnny. Annabelle has seen the film and makes some interesting comparisons about the relative levels of fitness of ballet dancers and footballers. 'Yeah, that's what we were saying to this boy that was harassing Johnny the other day. He didn't realize someone like Johnny is so strong that he can do the splits, they'd probably do better at kicking a football than someone who just runs.' 'Do you reckon the school is handling your harassment adequately or do you feel sometimes that a bit too much is left to you?' I ask Johnny. 'It depends who you go to,' he says, 'Some people say you can deal with it, some people talk to you about it. The student counselor comes around into the classroom and sorts them out. Some teachers say, "I'll be with you in a minute" and "I've got better things to do than sort something out." I ask, 'How do you think it would go if people had an opportunity to watch the film, *Billy Elliott*.' Annabelle replies, 'That would be a good idea but there's lots of swearing in it, and stuff, though.' Johnny is less enthusiastic. 'Yeah. Well, if the guys had to watch it, they'd just fall asleep and rot away, but the people that enjoy movies like that, with music and dance . . . they'd be pretty interested.' Undaunted, Annabelle pursues an optimistic line; 'If they watch that I think they'd realize what they're saying to people is wrong.' Keen to explore the sources of this homophobia I ask, 'Where are the boys getting those sorts of ideas from?' Annabelle retorts, 'Television and advertising of like boys playing football.' Johnny simply says, 'I suppose their dads.'

Our conversation shifts to other aspects of harassment in the school. 'Some guys think it's cool to pay out someone so they can be like popular and stuff to pick on somebody,' claims Johnny. 'Yeah, and then the rest of the class laughs,' adds Annabelle. They then go on to talk about other things that people get 'paid out' for ... 'like physical appearance ... glasses ... not having Adidas socks,' says Johnny and 'girls who put hair tails in their hair,' comments Annabelle. They agree that image is a big thing for kids in the teenage years. I ask them whether these matters are ever the topic of class discussions. Annabelle says, 'Our home group teacher did a big thing on harassment and what we thought was a "nerd" and what we thought was a "square." We made all these notes in our reflection journals about what was a "nerd" and what was a "square." People call me a square just 'cos I got all VHAs (very high achievement levels) but then in the yard, I'm not a square, not like I sit down and do my homework at lunchtime or whatever, and study. Just 'cos I got all the highest marks, I don't think that's fair.' Both Johnny and Annabelle reckon that too little recognition is given to high academic achievers at the school assemblies. Annabelle tells me about a unique award given at school assemblies. 'The "Aussie of the week" award is when friends nominate you for doing something nice for them or giving them good advice, nothing about the academic, and all the other awards are about sport achievements, like getting into the state team. I haven't seen one award for getting a VHA for science or whatever. There's never any of them except like at the end of the term when we're given our things and then they say the list of people that got at least four VHAs, but that list goes on and it's not really—just 'cos you got four VHAs doesn't mean you're a square really get more. Yeah, there could be a few more awards for academic achievement.'

(Johnny and Annabelle, September 3, 2003)

Like a long-standing couple, Johnny and Annabelle seem to be able to read each other's minds, so much so that they frequently finished off each other's sentences! Annabelle's supportive relationship with Johnny seems to be a crucial factor in maintaining his self-confidence and belief in a hostile environment. As Johnny says 'everyone has their differences,' but those students whose behaviors, lifestyles and interests do not match community norms and stereotypes often find themselves on the outer when it comes to peer acceptance. What's 'cool' is a big topic of conversation in schools. The pressure to fall in line with a narrow range of identity types and lifestyles is particularly strong in a consumer-oriented society. But more significantly, the emphatic masculinities which seem to prevail in the community draw on a reservoir of homophobic attitudes that are a resource for identity formation and protection (Epstein, Hewitt, Leonard, Mauthner & Watkins, 2003). For Johnny, this means sustaining his love for dancing against a prevailing discourse of hegemonic masculinity which tends to deride artistic and cultural pursuits. Although some of his teachers attempt to challenge the homophobic behavior and stereotyping of individuals, it is apparent that others are rather dismissive of his complaints. This pattern is consistent with research by Epstein et al. (2003), which indicates that even schools which have well-defined guidelines for dealing with sexism and racism often find it most difficult to deal with homophobic abuse and tend to ignore its occurrence in schools. An absence of school policies and a reluctance to challenge community attitudes mean that students like Johnny continue to be subjected to harassment and ridicule by their peers.

Class rules okay?

Johnny and Annabelle show how cultural oppression can have a damaging impact on students' schooling. The same is true for students from low socioeconomic backgrounds. It has become somewhat fashionable to downplay the significance of class in theorizing youth identity formation, but it was quite apparent from our study that class inequalities had a profound effect on schooling and social relations. Despite the widely held view of Australia as an affluent and egalitarian society, there is evidence of growing inequalities and welfare dependency in post-industrial times. In fact, Australia is now a more unequal society than at any stage in its past (Grieg Lewins & White, 2003). In spite of the much-trumpeted prosperity of the past decade, some 700,000 children live in jobless households, and at least 1 million Australians are living in poverty or extreme economic hardship. According to the Luxembourg Income Study (2002), Australia has a higher poverty rate (measured by half median income) than most European countries.

Of particular concern is the fact that Australia's level of child poverty is currently estimated at 14.9 percent (Harding & Greenwell, 2001) and some 50,000 to 70,000 young people are homeless. A national housing census in 2001 calculated that there were some 12,230 homeless secondary students in Australia, of whom 1020 (approximately 11 per 1000) were in the state in which our research was undertaken. To put these figures in context, 93 percent of homeless students are in the government school system, and the vast majority is concentrated in disadvantaged schools (MacKenzie & Chamberlain, 2002). In some schools as many as 5 to 10 percent of senior students may be homeless or living independently in dire circumstances. This means that a significant group of students in our schools has to negotiate a complex and demanding curriculum in the absence of family support and the resources to maintain a decent standard of living. Students in single parent households have an additional burden to carry.

They call them 'povs'

Our conversation with a group of year 8 students from Investigator High School revealed some of the ways in which class differences impact on social relationships in schools. As outlined in the school portrait in Chapter 2, Investigator High is a disadvantaged school with a high proportion of students from a low socioeconomic background. When it came to harassment, it was apparent that students from the poorest neighborhood, Greytown, were often stigmatized and disparaged by fellow students because of their 'shabby' appearance and poor economic circumstances. 'Greytown is where all the poor people live. It's all housing trust,' remarked one of our informants in reference to the high proportion of public housing tenants. 'People from Greytown live in "pov,"' said another. 'They call them "povs" and they get beaten up,' added a third voice. Certain character traits and dispositions were ascribed to these students. 'They're all the psycho types and gang leaders,' said one, while another remarked, 'They don't try hard enough in school.' The common perception was that these students were 'losers.' 'They're like drop-outs at year 10 and become homeless,' claimed one student.

We were told that this sense of class difference was acted out in the school grounds with the so-called 'povs' occupying the margins of the recreational areas. But there was also an aged, gendered and ethnic dimension to territoriality. 'Everyone has their own area of the yard. The older tougher kids get the best spots, like the shady areas and we get the middle of the oval,' said one of the boys. 'It's gang related,' suggested another boy. 'A whole group just sit down in a spot—you get 30 people—if anyone comes along you go yaaagh!—it's more like if you come on my territory I'll beat you up—we have the best spot.' Belonging to a gang was an important identity marker in the school and the community, and the year 8 students were eager to share their knowledge with us. Jason began by decoding the acronyms of the various gangs in the district. 'FWAs are females with attitude,' he explained and added as an afterthought 'that's a girl one.' He continued, 'MAS is modified arts style—they're into spray cans and big pictures; AWS are anarchists with style but they don't do pictures; COA stands for constantly on attack; then there's Afghan Warriors and Dado Boys who drive Datsuns. Dado Boys have some 300–400 members within the area. They're not just school groups; they have 25-year-olds as well and come from all over the city.' Identity, lifestyle and class factors all seemed to be involved here. However, for some students the imperative to join a gang was quite straightforward—peer pressure. 'If you don't belong to them and you're a guy, you are likely to get bashed,' said Jason.

Although there may have been a degree of exaggeration about these claims, the issue of a safe space was clearly a concern for newly arrived students. When we accompanied them on a walk around the school grounds, they pointed out the territories occupied by various groups. The smokers sit in a large circle on the margins of the oval, near the out-of-bounds area. Some groups hang about near the canteen and others near the middle school buildings. Senior school students congregate near their own building. There is some mixing of senior and junior school students but they mostly stick to their own spots. According to one of the girls, the senior students were responsible for most of the bullying because 'they got it done to them when they were in year 8.'

The issue of social class surfaced again in an interview with a group of year 10 and 11 students—young people in the senior school. What triggered the connection was the age-old topic of school uniforms. Although Investigator had a school uniform policy, it was more a dress code specifying adherence to school colors and the logo rather than the formal dress items typically associated with private schools. Nonetheless, the school administration was in the middle of a compliance campaign during our time at the school. 'The school is toughening up on uniforms,' said one of our informants. 'It's part of the image of the school but I don't see what clothes have to do with it,' he added. This prompted a lively conversation about the rights of students to wear what they chose. 'People should be able to express themselves; we all look like clones,' said one. But the discussion soon turned to the role of school uniforms in promoting the school's image in a highly charged atmosphere of public versus private school debate. Several students expressed the view that uniforms were regarded as an indicator of a school's reputation, but they also pointed out the shallowness of this claim:

> Just because Investigator doesn't have the uniform we're all seen as rejects and people that stuff up all the time. But every other single school is the same. You've got all the same amount of people doing drugs and stuffing up but because they wear a uniform they are not seen in the same way. (Ruby, September 16, 2003)

A girl questioned the middle-class respectability of private schools and the inequitable nature of funding arrangements for public education:

> When I was choosing a high school it was a toss-up between Investigator and Mount Repose [a private school]. My parents said I should go to Mount Repose because they wear a uniform so it's got to be a good school. But they have worse problems than our school. Sure, we've got less money than them in our school, so we have to be more frugal with our spending—they get computers and everything—but because they have more money they have more of a drug problem, a gang problem, more violence and basically they don't get along as well. Just because we're public and we don't have all the money, we get labeled. (Trish, September 16, 2003)

Although our young informants did not use the term 'social classes,' they were aware of the stratified nature of their community and their place in the social schema. They also acknowledged that many of their teachers were doing their best to support students with special needs. A student explained:

> There is support for kids who are struggling, especially in the lower years. We have a STAR (STudents At Risk) program. You get a little star put next to your name and a

teacher comes in to help you if you chose to do the program. As far as I know this sort of help is not available at Mount Repose. (Michael, September 16, 2003)

Not all students shared this perception. One of the students remarked:

I know a girl who goes to Mount Repose and she says that the teachers are actually better because they're not as slack as here. For a private school you have to have higher qualifications to get in as a teacher. (Lisa, September 16, 2003)

In general, these students were remarkably loyal to their school and very supportive of a public education system that they perceived as catering for all irrespective of wealth or social standing. Two of the students even spoke of the threat to public schools as a consequence of a shift toward local school management. Otherwise known as 'site-based decision making' or 'school-based management' the move involved a shift in responsibility for the management and delivery of educational services from the educational bureaucracy to school councils. 'It's about letting the government off the hook for funding schooling and making parents pay more,' said Damien. Somewhat emphatically Michael exclaimed 'Yeah, they did it in Victoria [another Australian State] and it was a "stuff-up." ' By way of explanation, under the leadership of Liberal premier, Jeff Kennett, the state of Victoria moved toward a marketized version of local school management in the mid-1990s. Popularly referred to as 'Kennett's revenge' the radical shift was accompanied by a massive reduction in funding for public schools, the closure of 300 schools (many serving working class communities), staff reductions, increased class sizes and the dismantling of centralized curriculum services for schools. The havoc wreaked on schools and communities in Victoria continues despite the demise of Kennett's government.

Poverty and educational disadvantage

Our conversations with students brought home to us the realities of poverty and educational disadvantage for many young people. We were reminded that 'not everyone has a perfect life' (Hattam & Smyth, 2003) and that many students lack the security of a middle-class childhood and arrive at school with very few of the economic and cultural resources needed to successfully navigate a pathway to adulthood and financial independence. Young people's accounts from the project schools suggest that social class remains a powerful generator of educational advantage and disadvantage. In their study of equality and schooling in Northern Ireland, Lynch and Lodge (2002, p. 183) claim that students from working class and welfare-dependent backgrounds are unable to access, participate or achieve on equal terms with more materially advantaged students. Moreover, parents on low incomes are unable to exercise the same degree of choice available to middle-class families, and their children are more likely to be concentrated in low-ability streams and special needs programs. The net result is that the rewards of the education system remain unequally distributed (Furlong & Cartmel, 1997). This was very much the case in the majority of the schools that formed part of our research.

The harsh reality is that vast numbers of young people do not have access to the basic resources and services that will enable them to lead productive, satisfying and fulfilling lives. This has probably always been the case, but over the past decade their hopes and aspirations have been dealt a savage blow by neo-liberal regimes that have largely sidelined principles of social justice in favor of a market-oriented approach to policy making and the delivery of human services. In a recent submission to an Australian Senate Inquiry into Poverty, the Brotherhood of St. Laurence (2003) commented on the vulnerability of many young people who face a precarious labor market which offers them few opportunities for rewarding work. To make matters worse, these young people have to deal with a social security system which punishes them for minor breaches of unemployment allowances. These realities are not unlike the ones reported by Kozol (1992, 2005) especially in the urban areas of large US cities.

Blame the victim

In the current political climate, social policy has taken a back seat to economic policy, as governments at state and federal levels in Australia have moved to privatize government utilities and implement user-pays approach to education, health and welfare. Meanwhile, governments have targeted welfare dependency and shifted the blame for poverty to its victims rather than acknowledging failures in economic policies and structural inequalities. In recent times a rationale for school reform has developed around the logic of the marketplace as governments seek to promote national economic goals in a competitive global environment. Now the purposes and goals of education are being reframed in narrow utilitarian ways that threaten the democratic and egalitarian goals of public schooling. Young people are caught up in a discourse of parental choice, individualism and vocationalism that appears to take little account of their aspirations, concerns and circumstances. The real winners in this game are those students and their families with the wealth, power and social capital to purchase the educational goods and services needed for academic success and personal fulfillment. Meanwhile those students whose lives have been fractured by poverty and oppressive social relations continue to struggle in an under-funded and increasingly residualized public education system.

The persistence of educational disadvantage remains one of the great blights on Australia's social landscape. Education is crucial to young people's life chances, but students from low-income families continue to struggle when it comes to participation and success in schooling. An analysis of school completion rates clearly indicates that indigenous students and children from low socioeconomic backgrounds are most likely to 'drop out' of school (Smyth & Hattam et al., 2004). However, the problem of student engagement is often attributed to individual failings and weaknesses rather than faults within the institution of schooling or the political system. As Dei (2003) points out, the pathologizing of families and communities for youth failures at school has the effect of shifting responsibility for the problem away from schools and governments to the victims themselves. Meanwhile, a shift in funding arrangements from public to private schools has meant that public schools in Australia are fast becoming sites for the concentration of social and educational disadvantage (South Australian Council of Social Service, 2002). With the adoption of a user-pays approach to higher education and the residualization of public education, the notion of equality of opportunity is little more than hollow rhetoric.

We will return to the issue of social class in Chapter 4 when we discuss at some length the pedagogical responses to poverty and social deprivation at Plainsville School, but for the moment we want to emphasize two key points about the nexus between poverty and educational disadvantage from the project schools. Firstly, teachers in all schools had to deal with the distressing effects of financial hardship and personal suffering on the lives of students. In the absence of well-connected family networks, many adults took on the roles of carers and provided a great deal of social and emotional support for students. Teaching in this context demanded more than knowledge of subject matter and technical competence; rather what was required was a capacity to develop and sustain trusting and respectful relationships with students. Secondly, there was a view, especially in the most disadvantaged communities, that efforts to ameliorate educational disadvantage demanded a whole-school curriculum response. Due to the enormity of the task, this was not something that could be left to individuals. What this looks like in practice will be discussed at some length in Part III, but we also want to emphasize the crucial role that teachers play in assisting students to make sense of their lives and identities. One of the lasting impressions of our conversations with young people was the appreciation they had for those teachers who went the extra yard in nurturing their aspirations, supporting them through tough times and creating a challenging learning environment. Before we close this chapter we want to return to our interviews with students to hear what they have to say about the qualities of a 'good' teacher.

Who is a 'good' teacher?

A group of year 9 students from Seachange High School described the qualities of a good teacher as someone who is 'happy, lenient and not strict;' who 'doesn't treat you like a little kid that knows nothing;' who 'gives you second chances;' and who 'understands like all your problems and what you're going through and stuff.' They went on to say, 'If you're having a bad day they won't take it out on you like some teachers do;' and 'they'll actually listen to you and not just say,' 'Yeah, I don't want to know about it.' 'No one really listens to the strict teachers much, unless they scare them,' remarked one of the students. 'Yeah, because they're boring,' added another. 'Students who don't really want to work will work because it's fun and interesting and they want to learn and understand,' commented one of the students.

Having fun was important but they also acknowledged that good teachers knew their subjects well. 'It's fairly important because otherwise you can't learn very much if they don't know the answers and stuff. If you're asking for help and they don't know that's not very good,' explained one of our informants. 'But they still need to be friendly and understanding,' cautioned another. It seems that students could be bribed into working. Speaking of one of her teachers a girl remarked 'When he really wants us to buckle down and work, he'll come in and give us lollies [candy].' He makes deals with the people that like don't do as much work, like he'll say, 'Okay, if you really try and if you get an 'A,' I'll buy you like a packet of Mars Bars [candy] or something like that and he motivates us.'

The Seachange students agreed that good teachers are flexible in the way they approach school rules and sanctions. One of the students expressed it as follows: 'They still want you to operate on the same procedures as you would in a normal class but when they're more lenient, if you just want an easy lesson they'll mainly do some easy work that you can quickly finish in the lesson relatively easily.' They admitted that they looked to push the boundaries with teachers, even the good teachers. 'We test and we push them as far as they can go,' said one. 'They get a bit angry and they yell at you but afterwards it's all okay. But you have to find out where that line is.'

A group of year 10 students from Investigator High School shared similar stories about supportive and understanding teachers and, as the following comment suggests, age was no barrier when it came to good pedagogy:

> Mr. X is an old teacher but he's really great. He takes his time when he explains things to the whole class and he allows us to put it in our own words to each other. He seems to care about you and makes time for you; everyone is an individual. He doesn't compare you with others; it's the work that you've done that counts and not what someone else has done. (Student, September 6, 2000)

Students explained that good teachers seem to be able to personalize learning for students to the extent that they are able to individualize instruction and make connections to their own lives. Having a friendly teacher was not enough according to one of our young informants:

> Mr. Y was friendly but he was a shocker of a teacher. You'd ask him for help but he would put too many things in his answer. He never took the time to explain things. Often he would do it for you. Then you'd say I didn't want you do it I just wanted some help. (Student, September 6, 2000)

At New Vista Community School we spoke with Rachel, Brendan and Susie, student members of middle school decision-making group known as the Student Forum. In Rachel's words, 'Good teachers socialize with you and explain things really well before they start teaching you. And then if you have trouble with it, they just give you a bit of one-on-one teaching.' Brendan added, 'Being able to be friendly to the students but not being too strict when they don't have to be—like being strict when you *have* to be like when people are playing up, but not too strict when you're not.' Susie summed up her thoughts in these words: 'I reckon someone who's fun and someone who can teach the subject well and they know what they're teaching; someone who can teach in their own way that's different to like normal teaching— someone like Mrs. N, who can think of really creative assignments that are fun to do.'

At Broadvale we talked informally to individual students in a year 9 society and environment (S&E) class. Josie remarked 'teachers must be nice to students . . . they need to be understanding . . . they should have a sense of fun . . . be fairly lenient . . . they should teach you about the curriculum . . . what you need to know . . . they should tell you in advance what is to be assessed.' Josie explained that she was keen to do further study, possibly at university. Science was her best subject. She said that good teachers know how to 'demonstrate ideas' and 'explain things to students in different ways.' Jamie said good teachers 'spend time with individual students.' He told us that he does not like teachers who 'make you copy stuff from the board because it's boring and doesn't help you to learn.' 'It's better for teachers to have a conversation with you,' he explained. According to Sam 'Good teachers do different things in class . . . like in society and environment we have learnt a lot about the law and done interesting work on [forensic] identity kits. Good teachers are funny and nice . . . they listen to what you say. Some teachers don't like students . . . they don't talk to them. Good teachers help people . . . Mrs. S spends a lot of time with individuals.'

What these young people were consistently telling us about their expectations of schooling and their teachers can be summed up as follows. In the first place, they want to be treated fairly and respectfully by their teachers. One of their major concerns is for their own safety and welfare. They look to their teachers to maintain a safe learning environment. They do not like being treated as 'children' and especially resent the arbitrary use of authority and recourse to petty rules and sanctions. They can accept the need for rules and sanctions but only if they are fairly and consistently applied. Students dislike constant surveillance and monitoring of their behavior in school. They place a premium on trust and have a high regard for teachers who place them in positions of trust and responsibility. Students want to be treated as individuals and not just as members of a class or some amorphous student body. When it comes to matters close to their own heart they want teachers and those in positions of authority to take their concerns seriously, especially in matters of harassment. They want to be involved in decisions that affect them at school. They want to be taught by teachers who are knowledgeable about their subject field but also have an understanding of students as people.

Young people like their teachers to have a friendly manner and to be able to share a joke with them. Most students say they enjoy opportunities to relate to their teachers outside of the classroom setting. They appreciate teachers who are flexible in their thinking and willing to give them a second chance. However, they do not like teachers who shout at them and refuse to give them a right of reply. They especially dislike teachers who are sarcastic or humiliate them in front of their peers. They acknowledge the curriculum expertise of teachers but want to have some say in negotiating aspects of their learning. They dislike didactic teaching approaches, especially the overuse of hand-outs, blackboard notes and exercises—'these teachers give us the sheets' was a common complaint. Students enjoy the opportunity to work in groups and to learn outside of the classroom. Most resent being labeled and categorized according to perceived abilities and aptitudes. They do not like to be compared with other students, especially other family members.

Students want teachers to challenge them in their learning and expect them to push them along when they slacken off. But they want to see some purpose in their learning and expect to receive constructive feedback on their assessment tasks. They admit that they like to test the boundaries when it comes to classroom norms but recognize the need for fairly applied behavior guidelines and consequences. Most importantly, they want to be recognized as a person and not just as a student. When it comes to the purposes of schooling they want schools to recognize and value a much broader range of attributes than mere academic achievement. They do not like being summed up in terms of a grade—'I'm just a "C" grade student,' lamented one of our informants.

Students have high expectations of their teachers but from our discussions it was apparent that many appreciated the extraordinary lengths to which many teachers went in supporting their educational aspirations and needs. How this occurred in practice will be discussed in some detail in Chapter 4, but it is worth recording the transformative role of teachers as described by students in two of the project schools.

Mossy, a year 8 student from Plainsville, has something of a checkered history having been expelled from his previous school because of his aggressive behavior. This is how he describes the transformation in his learning at Plainsville:

> This school has helped me to plan my own work and school is a lot easier for me. The teacher helps me to read and I'm pretty good at maths so I don't need any help with that but I do in English because I'm not very good at that. I get a lot of help from every teacher. I've been in a couple of fights with my friends but the school helps me to manage my anger with a lady called Leah and Dawn, the school counselor. (Mossy, November 20, 2002)

Nichole and Amy, members of the Student Representative Council at Gulfview School, spoke of the opportunities for student participation in their school. In the following excerpt from their dialogic portrait they explain how they were encouraged to join the student decision-making body.

TEACHERS TAKE YOU SERIOUSLY

'Teachers at our school take you very seriously,' says Nichole. 'As long as you can back up your idea, or try, or get some information from somewhere, our teachers are very willing to help.' 'Many of the teachers understand you,' says Amy. 'They listen to your problems and they don't give up on you. They push you along and they get behind you to get an "A" for that subject. They want to make you want to go to school.' Amy support's Nichole's views: 'Yeah, they make you achieve and they open up so many doors to things,' she says. 'You think, "Oh, I'd never be able to do that," and because it was my first year here, everyone sort of got to know me and they're like, "Oh, why don't you go for SRC?" and I'm thinking "Oh, I don't want to do that. No one even knows me." But they say "Oh yeah, just go for it. I'll put your name up and just see what happens" and by the end of it you're elected, you know, and it's a really good feeling. But yeah, they open up so many different things for you, in your first term or whatever.'

(Nichole and Amy, November 7, 2002)

Conclusions

In this chapter, we have deliberately foregrounded the perspectives and ideas of students regarding their schooling and identity formation. We have taken the view that if we want to understand the issues confronting young people, we need to listen respectfully to what they have to say and be willing to involve them more directly in discussions about school organization, curriculum and pedagogy. Adolescence, as we have suggested, is a social construct that exercises a strong grip on educational policy and practice. Unfortunately, much current thinking is based on an uncritical acceptance of the universality of the biological and psychological states of young people to the exclusion of sociological understandings. For young people the process of 'becoming somebody' takes place in social territories marked by boundaries of class, culture, gender and race. Inequalities, class differences and the prejudices of adults penetrate schools. We heard from students about the 'povs' and the impact of poverty on student's lives. In their comments about public and private schools, students reminded us that education is not a level playing field where all students have equal access to resources and opportunities. Students recognized the injustice of this situation. Johnny's experience of homophobia revealed that inequality in education is not generated solely by economic relations; political, sociocultural and affective relations all contribute to the oppressive conditions under which many students live out their lives (Lynch & Lodge, 2002).

We have sought to locate young people's experience of schooling within the framework of neo-liberal policies which have enshrined parental choice and individualism at the expense of public good. In its submission to the Senate Inquiry Poverty, the Catholic Social Services Victoria (2003) argued that the test of how well a community is doing is not answered by the question, 'How well is the average Australian doing?' Rather the test is answered by the question, 'How well are the least well off doing?' To draw a parallel in education, the test of how well a school or education system is doing is not answered by the question, 'How well is the average student achieving?' but by answering the question, 'How are the most marginalized or disadvantaged students achieving?' Increasingly, it seems that the responsibility for education and well-being of children is being pushed back to families and local school communities under the banner of parental choice. However, as Furlong and Cartmel (1997) explain, 'the illusion of choice created by the marketization of education masks the continued entrenchment of traditional forms of inequality' (p. 11).

During our conversations students told us how important schools and teachers were in their lives. They reminded us that schools are significant sites in the identity formation of young people, not only in terms of socialization and intellectual development, but also as places that create a sense of community and belongingness for students whose lives are fractured by financial hardship and neglect. Schools can create opportunities for personal growth and development of students, and they can broaden students' horizons and play a significant role in determining young people's life chances. However, we were also told how some schools can stifle individuality, blunt creativity, suppress student voices and switch kids off education through uninspiring pedagogy.

How can schools promote more inclusive curriculum? How can schools become more learner-centered communities? How can students become more involved in school decision-making? How can schools respond to, and engage with, their local communities? In Chapter 4 we will provide illustrations from the research sites of the ways in which schools have addressed these questions.

CHAPTER FOUR

Steering school reform back to students

Introduction

In an age of consumerism where media culture penetrates most aspects of daily life, at least in Western societies, it has become rather fashionable to downplay the influence of schools on young people's identities. Nonetheless, schools remain significant sites of social and cultural formation, which help to shape student's lives and assist in their socialization into the Australian and global community (Smyth, Hattam & Lawson, 1998). For many students, schools are safe havens—places of stability and security that offer protection, comfort and hope in their otherwise fractured lives. For all their flaws, schools have valuable resources to assist young people to make sense of their world and to navigate pathway to satisfying and rewarding adult lives. However, as we have explained in Chapter 3, these claims need to be tempered with an acknowledgment of the persistence of inequality and educational disadvantage that continues to plague our society. There can be little doubt that under-funding of public schools coupled with a neo-liberal policy obsession with standards, testing and accountability measures has reinforced the damaging effects of the competitive academic curriculum (Connell, 1993) that has long held sway in traditional high schools. Now more than ever it seems that the interests of dominant groups are preserved at the expense of the most marginalized students.

Addressing these concerns is a task that stretches beyond the perimeter of schools and education systems, but as a starting point we want to argue that school reform needs to be steered back to students; we need to put their interests, concerns and aspirations at the center of the curriculum and not at the margins. In particular, we need to look at this issue from the perspective of the most disadvantaged students, as we re-examine the nature of the student–teacher relationship in schools, the relevance of the officially sanctioned curriculum, the educational merits of dominant assessment and reporting practices, the extent to which students participate in school decision-making and the appropriateness of the school structures in supporting students to become more autonomous learners. Perhaps more than anything, we need to rethink the fundamental purposes of schools and the degree to which contemporary programs, policies and practices promote the development of educative relationships and critically literate citizens.

The question of what young people learn and how they learn is a matter of crucial importance. Rejecting the apolitical nature of schooling, Connell (1993) maintains that 'a curriculum necessarily intersects with the relationships of inequality in society that constitute social interests' (p. 35). As such, it can serve to domesticate students by working to preserve the *status quo*, with its entrenched inequalities, or it can be an instrument for liberation and a referent for progressive social change (Freire, 1993; Giroux, 1985). It cannot be emphasized too strongly that if we want young adolescents to become active and politically informed citizens, then we need to foster and model democratic practices in schools. If we want them to develop respectful relationships, a concern for the environment and an appreciation of cultural diversity, then we must enact a curriculum that values these sensitivities. If we want students to achieve a measure of economic independence and personal fulfillment, we have to provide them with the resources and knowledge to read and act on their world. Above all, if we believe that schools are sites that can transform the class-based, racist and sexist attitudes and ideas which students (and adults) bring to the classroom, then we need to develop a curriculum that challenges taken-for-granted beliefs, and engages students in the acquisition of critical literacies (Luke, 1993).

In the previous chapter, we heard from students about their perceptions of schooling. We gained some insights into transformative work of teachers and their capacity to open doors for students. But we were also reminded that not all students experience schools as caring and supportive institutions; that for some students, a deep sense of failure is etched into their memories of their school days. In this chapter, we provide specific instances of curriculum support for the identity formation and educational development of young adolescents within the project schools. We have chosen to represent much of these data in the form of vignettes and narrative portraits of students and teachers around six major themes, which we consider to be at the heart of transformative schooling:

1. Supportive relationships: nurturing an ethos of care and trust
2. Broadening horizons: opening doors for young people
3. Negotiating the curriculum: student-centered learning
4. Having a say: student voice in action
5. Engaging with the community: capacity building
6. Critical literacies: reading the word and the world

Supportive relationships: nurturing an ethos of care and trust

In the many conversations we had with young people, the importance of developing trusting and supportive relationships with teachers was a recurring theme. Unfortunately, a significant proportion of students experience schools as alienating and inhospitable institutions. Many socioeconomic, individual, cultural and school-related factors (Farrell, 1990), often around quite pronounced 'deficit thinking' (Valencia, 1997), are invoked to explain the 'non-inclusive' nature of schools. Among these following can be cited:

- an incompatibility of school goals with youthful interests;
- irrelevant curriculum and inflexible learning environments;
- personal and family history of failure at school;
- inability of schools to envisage an expanded range and horizon of skills and abilities;
- disjuncture between the values of school and the home;
- communities that are fractured and fragmented by poor health, sub-standard housing, single parenting and high levels of poverty;
- young people with diminished career aspirations;
- absence of positive role models and supportive individuals to provide guidance;
- a peer culture that portrays school success as being 'uncool;'
- class, ethnic and racial oppression;
- harassment, bullying and stereotyping;
- unhelpful 'put-downs' by teachers;
- an inability of schools to understand or respect family history and background;
- absence of care by schools;
- corrupted, corroded, distrustful and unfulfilled relationships with peers and teachers;
- schools incapable of listening seriously to student' and community' problems.

Many of these factors lie outside the realm of schools, but others are directly connected to the culture, organizational arrangements and instructional practices in schools, especially high schools. Meier gets to the source of our concerns when she states:

> We've invented schools that present at best a caricature of what the kids need in order to grow up to be effective citizens, skillful team members, tenacious and ingenious thinkers, or truth seekers. . . . The older they get, the less like 'real life' their schooling experience is—and the more disconnected and fractionate. . . . We've cut kids adrift, without the support or nurturance of grown-ups, without the surrounding of a community in which they might feel safe to try out various roles, listen to the world of adults whom they might someday want to join as full members. (Meier, 2002, p. 12)

For Meier, the real issue here is 'the distrustful distance that the young experience towards the adult world' (p. 13)—a distance that she attributes to the standardization and bureaucratization of education systems and to the complex nature of high schools and their incapacity for developing, let alone, sustaining intimate and educative relationships between teachers and students. The challenge, as she sees it, is to break down some of the institutional barriers that work against the notion of learning communities and cultivate a school culture where young people learn from, and in, the company of mature adults. Kaplan (2000) also regards the mutuality of the student–teacher relationship as a crucial element in student engagement but argues that teachers need to strike a balance between personal and professional relationships.

During our research, we heard from students about the uninviting and impersonal nature of high schools—James's story in Chapter 3 perhaps being the most evocative—but we also recorded a particularly moving account from a parent whose faith in schooling was restored by a group of compassionate and thoughtful teachers. In the following portrait, Janice contrasts her son's unhappy experience of schooling in a large and inflexible metropolitan school environment with that at New Vista School where, in her words, 'he was treated as a person.'

THE TEACHERS TOOK AN INTEREST IN HIM AS A PERSON

My son, Simon, is a year 9 student at New Vista School where I'm employed as the Director of Finance and Administration. Our family has moved around quite a bit—mostly in country areas. Simon started his secondary schooling in a large metropolitan school where the two older children were attending. Early on he ran into problems. He didn't feel like people knew who he was. I know that happens in big high schools, but it did become an issue because he was having trouble attending school. Last year he would have been away, on average, about two days a week for the whole year. But I didn't get one phone call saying, 'We're concerned, your son is continually being away for two days a week.' He wasn't achieving anything. His grades were going down and he didn't care about it, which was a concern as a parent. It wasn't an easy decision to pull him out because he's been to about six schools. When I spoke to the teachers at New Vista they supported Simon and came up with a program that would meet his initial needs. It has been *absolutely fantastic*. I think it's because of the flexibility of the teachers and their ability to understand and to look into a situation rather than pigeonholing a kid. I really appreciate that.

Simon felt the teachers knew who he was and took an interest in him as a person. Because there are people you can talk to here—like the counselor and his home group teacher—he doesn't feel uncomfortable about that. I think too, the fact that you don't change classrooms a lot—like today his home group is also where he spends his science and his maths lessons—means he doesn't waste a lot of time moving around and he's become more comfortable in his home group environment. I think another really positive thing that's happening here is that they work hard to give the kids the opportunity to move around and be with other teachers, whilst appreciating the fact that some kids actually don't cope with that really well. The other thing that was extremely complicating for Simon was that he had a meningococcal infection and was in hospital for a week. It's taken him a *long* time to recover both physically and mentally. Now I'm *extremely* grateful: one that he's still here, two that he didn't have any limb disfigurement because that often is a side effect of meningococcal. He didn't have the ability to cope with a lot of what was happening at his previous school, but they took that on board here and have dealt with it really well. I *know* that they do that for a number of other students here.

The counseling processes are really good here. Usually if somebody is enrolling in the middle school, the counselor shows them the layout of school, talks about the programs and works out what is best for that child. Then there is usually a meeting with the head of middle campus. I feel as though I can contact them at any time to speak about concerns. I think that's the other good thing here. I won't say all—but the majority of the teachers, especially in the middle campus, are approachable and are more than happy to speak with you at *any* time. They don't mind being interrupted and I give them credit for that. The fact that they do things down in their class that invite you in and that is so important, so you actually feel a part of the school. I don't think we do that well enough on the senior side of the school because the kids are older and they actually get embarrassed when their parents come. However, on the middle schooling side, it is a really inviting place and I think that's got a lot to do with the teachers, themselves, and the way that the campus head organizes it. I believe that one of the reasons why middle schooling works so well here is because of the good communication. I had an interesting comment from a staff member when Simon first started coming here. She said, 'Gee, that's a pretty good rap for the school if you bring your own son here.' I said, 'There's no comparison.' He feels really comfortable in his new school. Not so long ago when we were driving past his old school he said, 'That's an evil school.' I said 'Simon!' He said, 'Mum, I just wasn't happy,' you know. The change in him has been absolutely phenomenal. At one stage he was talking about doing Home School because he didn't want to go to school anymore. He said it was a waste of time. He hated it. Now he really enjoys coming to school.

(Janice, August 26, 2003)

Creating a place that students want to belong to may not be sufficient to ensure academic success, but it is surely a precursor to student engagement. As Janice recounts, the turn-about in Simon's attitude toward his schooling was quite remarkable when he moved to New Vista School. In contrast to his previous school where his medical concerns and anxieties were largely ignored, Simon encountered a group of empathetic and caring teachers who treated him as a person and went out of their way to adjust the curriculum requirements during his period of rehabilitation. But what does need to be emphasized here is that the support Simon received did not just depend on the goodwill of a few teachers. Rather, it was nurtured in a school environment where a great deal of attention was paid to the relational aspects of learning. At New Vista, counseling processes, pastoral care programs and the home group arrangements all assisted Simon to make a smooth and happy transition to his new school during a very stressful period of his life. Above all, Simon felt a sense of identification and belonging in a learning community that put just as much store on his emotional and social well-being as his academic learning.

At Plainsville the development of trusting, non-coercive and respectful relationships was also regarded as the foundation for learning. Since this was not always the norm in the community, teachers saw that they had a responsibility to 'walk the talk' in modeling appropriate behavior for students. 'We don't shout at kids,' said Stephanie (February 11, 2003). 'When adults raise their voice to the children they apologize,' explained Leanne (November 20, 2002). Whole-school structures and programs supported educative relationships at Plainsville and helped to break down hierarchical arrangements. Learning teams allowed students to interact with a range of adults, thereby maximizing the extent of curriculum and emotional support. Valerie, a middle school teacher, explained the importance of this adult support for student:

When you come from a primary school of only 300 kids to a large high school of 1300, you don't get known. You're just a number at that school. It would be interesting to see if one teacher could identify your name throughout the day. You might have *one* good interaction through that day. And it's not saying that the high schools are the only problem. Kids need to have someone that they can come and talk to whether it is about family, work or whatever. That's probably why we have six or seven adults working with them, so that they've got someone they can feel comfortable with and I think that's the most important issue, especially for our kids. They do need to feel that they can come and chat about how mum's pissed him off, or whatever. (Valerie, February 25, 2005)

Within each learning team, smaller groups known as talking-circles ensured that each student had access to one staff member who took a personal interest in their well-being and monitored their progress. Students met in talking-circles, chaired by students, at the beginning of each day and at other points during the day. According to one student, these arrangements promoted a bonding relationship:

We can talk to an adult easier in the way we work now from a traditional school. We have a bonded relationship. It's more like a family. They help in all different ways. A two-way trust relationship we have built up. Adults are easy to access and easy to talk to. We can access the adult we need in the area of need. (Sonia, November 20, 2002)

There was a lot of emphasis on outdoor education activities, excursions and community-based studies as a means of promoting bonding between adults and students—indeed, in the first two weeks of the school year all formal learning was suspended. Teachers recognized that cultivating personal relationships with students was crucial to their work:

One thing I've found working with the year 6–7 class is talking to them on a personal basis has a *huge* impact because sometimes they'll sit down and open up, and tell you things—which sometimes you don't want to hear but, you know, it's really good to sit down and just even if it's just a five-minute conversation, it can have huge ramifications just sitting down and talking to them about . . . different things that are going on in their life. (Greg, March 9, 2003)

Recognizing the centrality of relationships was seen as crucial to understanding what adolescents were experiencing:

. . . they're learning how to perform in groups . . . it's a lot about the maturity thing . . . them becoming individuals and learning how to function . . . I don't know how to describe it—it's just growing up . . . These students are still learning how to manage their behavior. (Greg, March 9, 2003).

What Greg and his colleagues were saying is consistent with what Tanner (2003) says about the need to fundamentally reconfigure what we consider to be important in our lives, by 'putting relationships at the center' (p. 109). It is to acknowledge the point made by Connell (2002b) about 'the crisis of ideas' in public education being around our collective failure to see the core problem as being 'social:'

> Education is inherently a social process acting through social relationships. Education involves the development of the capacities of the person as well as the development of society. (p. 30)

How students choose (and in the end it is a choice they make) to relate to learning is crucial to engagement and success; equally, failure is usually a clear indicator of an inability to establish and sustain a workable relationship. Student alienation and subsequent behavior management problems have their origins deeply embedded in an absence of agency in which knowledge, content and processes are labeled by young learners as irrelevant to their lives and aspirations. Plainsville started by acknowledging this glaring inadequacy in the way that many schools operate and instead worked at putting students' relationships to ideas, knowledge, their learning and the organization of schooling at the center.

This thinking was evident in the school's approach to matters of discipline. Students at Plainsville were encouraged to manage their own behavior. There was no detention room nor were students suspended except for acts of violence, which endangered other students' welfare. The school took the view that many behavioral problems could be averted by a proactive approach that encouraged cooperative learning, student participation in curriculum development and conflict resolution, rather than disciplinary or punitive measures. A peer mediation program operated across the school. Instead of invoking the notion of logical consequences and the withdrawal of services, emphasis was placed on the provision of learning services. Students who did not meet learning targets were expected to make up learning time outside of normal school hours. As with other aspects of the curriculum, teachers assisted students to develop a behavior management plan.

In assessing the relative merits of strategies to reduce school violence, Gladden (2002) claims that preventive programs that emphasize anger management and conflict resolution skills are ultimately far more effective than deterrence measures based on zero tolerance, suspension and school surveillance practices. Furthermore, 'schools that possess an engaging curriculum and operate as communities characterized by respectful and supportive relationships tend to be safer' (p. 274). In this regard, Plainsville's efforts to focus on the relational aspects of learning seem to be paying dividends, as attendance and participation rates improved and previously disenchanted, angry and frustrated students found a voice and a reason to stay at school. Our research confirmed that positive social relations can create powerful incentives for students to persevere with schooling when the going gets tough, especially for socially disadvantaged students (Croninger & Lee, 2001; Smyth, 2004a; Smyth & Hattam et al., 2004).

Broadening horizons: opening doors for young people

Steering school reform back to students involves not only rethinking the relational norms of schooling but also reconfiguring the pedagogical norms that influence teachers' perceptions of students and their communities. This necessarily means 'challenging teachers' understandings of children's 'ability' to learn (Quartz, 1995, p. 246), especially in the so-called disadvantaged schools. According to Dei (2003, p. 251), one of the major challenges confronting educators is how to help students to develop a sense of connectedness and belonging to their school. Dei is not talking just about physical connectedness but an emotional, social and intellectual sense of connectedness. His argument is that success for students at school is contingent on much more than the provision of space, resources, personnel and a syllabus. What is fundamentally important is that educational practices are anchored in the multiple cultures, histories and experiences of students. Hargreaves (2001a) makes a similar point when writing about the importance of emotional understandings and 'the emotional geographies of teaching.' He argues that a combination of sociocultural, moral, professional, physical and political factors—increasingly embedded in policy—helps to distance teachers from parents and students. However, if teachers are to make a difference for their students, they must be given the freedom and opportunities:

> to develop and exercise their emotional competencies of caring for, learning from, and developing emotional understandings among all whose lives and actions affect the children they teach. (Hargreaves, 2001a, p. 1076)

In the following dialogic portrait we get some sense of what this looks like from the perspective of students. Amy and Nichole are members of the Student Representative Council at Gulfview School, and both are actively involved in the peer mediation programs. Here they talk about a number of facets of middle schooling, including sub-schools and home group arrangements, the school's extra-curricula program and strategies for dealing with harassment.

OUR HOME IS OUR SUB-SCHOOL

'I'm a year 11 student and I've been here for five years,' says Nichole. 'During that time the school has changed dramatically. We've had the senior school built for the year 11 and 12 students, a new gym and a fourth sub-school to accommodate year 10s. When I came here, I was put into a sub-school with a lot of my friends. The good thing is that you get to know students very well in your sub-school. You mix with the same people in the same sub-school. You get to see other friends at lunch time. You don't swap classes between sub-schools unless you're going with the whole class. I think that's a very good idea. The younger kids don't feel intimidated by the older kids who are in a totally different sub-school and have their own space to do what they want when they want.'

'I'm a year 7 student,' says Amy. 'Coming from primary school you had a teacher that took you for Japanese and another that took you for music and so on. But for every other subject, you're with this one teacher in the one room and that's where you stayed for the whole day. But here, you've got heaps of different teachers. If you have dance, you go to the dance room. If you're having visual arts, you go to the arts room; and in science you go and do practical work, and you get to do things that are different to what you usually did and yeah, it's just great. Yeah, they've got different personalities. You're not sitting down at a table for the whole lesson, writing out stuff. So you're in the sub-school, like your little place that you go to, but having all the different teachers just makes it more fun and they're all different, which is really good.'

'Our home is our sub-school,' says Nichole. 'Our teachers go out of their way just to make you feel like you're someone and that you, you know, they give you help and guidance along the way.' 'You know, you're important,' adds Amy. 'I have a cousin who's in year 8 and she used to be really shy and timid, but she's fine now. Like if you're coming to the school and there are year 8s and 9s that have been here before, they make you feel welcome. Most of the students at our school are willing to help.' However, Amy suggests that some kids experience bullying in the middle school. 'I suppose in the middle school, they were thinking "I'm a year 9, I've got the run of the—I'm a year 9 so I'm at the top, I've got the run of it." When they go over to like senior school, it's sort of a bit different because now you've got year 12s there so they feel like the little one again, you know, like you were in primary school.'

'So does the school have a harassment policy,' I ask them. Amy responds: 'We're very lucky because if something is happening, you've got your home group teacher and other home group teachers as well as your sub-school coordinator. You can come down here and speak to Mr. R. You've got people to go to instead of just having to go and see the principal about it. We've actually got people that can talk with you and help you.' Amy supports Nichole's views, 'We've got a chaplain and school counselors that we can talk to.' With some emphasis Nichole continues, 'In some schools, like if you tell the teacher that somebody is bullying on you that say, "Yeah, yeah, we'll follow it up, what they're doing." But at our school they do something about it. They do try to make our learning enjoyable so that we want to learn, rather than leaving school in year 10.'

Our discussion turns to the issue of peer mediation. Nichole explains, 'In my primary school I never got to be an SRC rep., although I always wanted to be because they were so cool. When I got to Gulfview last year, I actually nominated myself and got voted in. I had *so* much fun that I nominated myself again this year but I didn't get voted in this year. It's basically a popularity contest in the middle school. So Mr. J, who's the coordinator of the SRC, came up to me and said, "We're thinking of doing a peer mediation like peer helpers program. Would you like to sign on?" ' Amy comments, 'Mr. J does a lot of things with students and he organizes the SRC and all that.' Nichole continues, 'He came up to me and said "Would you like to help? You're the one that you can basically be the chairperson because you've got knowledge of the school and every student and things." ' We found somebody from Kids' Help Line that does a peer skills program and 17 of us went down to the local surf lifesavers club for a two-day training session. We learnt about how to listen and give advice and things. Elsie, our Chaplain, was the one who sorted everything out.

Amy and Nichole are involved in a lot of school sporting and performing arts programs, including the Rock and Roll Eisteddfod. 'Not all schools . . . do Eisteddfod,' says Nichole, 'and that's a great experience. There were about 90 students in the Eisteddfod this year and it's so fun. There's year 12s mixing with year 7s and we were all just a huge family. It was really cool.' On the question of school participation, Amy remarks: 'Kids can get involved in lots of things. We've got regional and state sporting competitions, and different things that everyone can get into.'

(Nichole and Amy, November 7, 2002)

Amy and Nichole present a rather rosy a picture of their school life as they speak in glowing terms of the sub-school teaming arrangements, the range of curriculum offerings, the affection they had for their teachers and the sense of community at Gulfview. Obviously, they are successful students who are actively engaged in the life of the school, and it may be their account is somewhat atypical. However, they do offer some interesting insights into the ways in which schools like Gulfview foster a sense of belongingness through sub-school learning communities. This is not achieved simply through an ethos of caring on the part of teachers; it also comes about by encouraging students to take on responsibilities for sustaining respectful relationships within the school community. In this instance, a peer mediation program was perhaps the most fruitful strategy for dealing with harassment issues.

Our conversation with Amy and Nichole affirms the role of teachers in 'opening doors' for students when it comes to broadening their horizons beyond the narrow confines of academic learning. In this case, the school's dance and drama programs created opportunities for them to participate in activities. It is interesting to note how students' recollections of their school experiences revolved around their participation in performing arts, sporting activities, school camps, excursions and out-of-class learning. One of the defining features of all of the project schools was a concerted effort to expand and diversify the school's co-curricula program and to incorporate recreational, vocational, social and cultural interests into the main-stream curriculum. The following examples from the project schools give some indication of the scope of this learning and its potential to hold the interest of groups of students who might otherwise leave school.

At New Vista School, where there was a major emphasis on technology and ecological sustainability, students were involved in a solar car project—a venture which entailed the design, production and trialling of a solar-powered vehicle. In fact the school had built up such an outstanding reputation for the quality and performance of its vehicles in international competitions that a good deal of its image was built on this achievement. Although the high-performance vehicle may have been the pinnacle of learning in this area, many students were involved in environmental projects as a normal part of their learning. Motivated in part by a core of 'green' activist teachers, students investigated alternatives to fossil fuels, participated in a pedal prix event, developed and maintained a school recycling depot, and were engaged in a national tree planting project, Greening Australia. The school had developed a long-term plan to change the renewable sources of energy based on the latest research and technology and was committed to reducing water and energy consumption and implementing principles and practices of organic gardening.

Not surprisingly, the sea plays a big part in the lives of students at Gulfview and Seachange schools, and enterprising teachers were quick to incorporate marine themes into the curriculum. This had been taken to the most innovative edge at Seachange through the introduction of an integrated studies course called 'Gone Fishing.' The course was the brain child of a teacher who was wrestling with ways of engaging a group of 'switched-off' boys in grades 8 and 9. About the only thing that seemed to interest 'the lads' was 'hanging around fishing,' so armed with this insight the teacher proposed a program of learning around the topic of the sea with a special emphasis on fishing. He explained to interested students that they had to be able to demonstrate how the new program would cover important aspects of maths, English, studies of society and environment, science, arts, home economics and technology. With the teacher's support, the students made a submission to the school curriculum committee showing how the course would meet all the learning outcomes specified in the state curriculum framework. The committee was impressed with the submission and agreed that the course could fit within the school specialization on marine studies. With the support of the curriculum committee, the course was developed as an elective for the following year and was almost immediately oversubscribed!

At Broadvale, the school was an important recreational and cultural resource for a community that lacked much of public infrastructure and social services associated with middle-class suburbs. The school's extensive sporting amenities and programs were especially attractive to students and much was made of their participation and achievements in local and state competitions via the school newsletter and assemblies. Although the school offered special sporting programs for students with athletic potential, the emphasis was on participation for all. With some pride, the school boasted that it entered more teams in inter-school sporting competitions than any other school in its zone.

We will say more about 'out-of-class learning' later in this chapter, but for the moment we want to make the following points: firstly, that the significance of learning of the kind described above is often missing from policy frameworks, but is a crucial element in building relationships and a sense of connectedness between students, their communities and their culture; secondly, that schools which are willing to step outside the straight jacket of a competitive academic curriculum can open doors for marginalized students. All of these raise the question of curriculum relevance and the degree to which students are involved in negotiating their learning.

Negotiating the curriculum: student-centered learning

> True learning—learning that is permanent and useful, that leads to intelligent action and further learning—can only arise out of the experiences, interests and concerns of the learner. (Holt, 1970, p. 3)

Some 35 years on, Holt's words about the importance of student-centered learning still ring true, although progressive educators today are more likely to talk about constructivist approaches to learning. Yet, it seems that the ideal is far from reality in many high schools where a great deal of learning is still structured around topics decided by teachers with reference to syllabi decided by external boards and policy-makers. We have chosen to foreground the ideal of student-centered learning in our account because the term has a long lineage in the education literature (Dewey, 1963), and because we believe it still remains an important indicator of how well schools are responding to the issues of youth alienation and engagement outlined in Chapter 1.

For the sake of clarity, we should explain what we understand by 'student-centered learning,' and perhaps, just as importantly, what we think it is not. Drawing on Macedo (1994), we suggest that a move toward student-centered learning implies 'developing pedagogies that speak to the reality of culture produced by students' (p. 171). That is, subject matter and learning activities are oriented toward students' interests, concerns and aspirations rather than exclusively toward those selected by the teacher or some external agent, although, as we point out later, this does imply that the teachers' curriculum knowledge and interests are unimportant. This orientation positions students as constructors of their own culture and agents of change, rather than passive objects or empty vessels. From a practical perspective, it implies that students negotiate significant aspects of their learning with teachers, including the choice of content, approaches to learning, forms of presentation and assessment criteria. In contrast to teacher-directed instruction, the emphasis tends to be on dialog rather than content and on supporting students to become more independent learners. However, we do want to make a distinction between a liberal version of student-centered learning that is primarily focused on the individual and a socially critical approach which is much more strongly tied to collective emancipatory goals and to political action for change.

What is student-centered learning? It is not *laissez faire* pedagogy and it is not student-determined curriculum. As Boomer (1982) was at pains to point out, negotiation is a process involving a number of partners, including the teacher. As teachers are 'curriculum experts,' they have a responsibility to bring their own knowledge to the process so as to stimulate critical thinking and broaden students' view of the world. Moreover, as Steinberg, Kincheloe and McLaren remind us in their introduction to Freire's (1998) *Teachers as Cultural Workers*:

> Children are not taught and empowered by caring alone; children are taught by good teachers who do not abrogate their responsibility to teach, provide students with an agenda, and correct students when necessary. (p. xxii)

However, the need for structure, purpose and rigor needs to be balanced with open and democratic practices, so that while:

> The teacher brings lesson plans, learning methods, personal experiences and academic knowledge to class, [the teacher] negotiates the curriculum with the students and begins with their languages, themes and understandings. (Shor, 1992, p. 16)

In all six project schools, we saw evidence of student-centered curriculum, although what this looked like in practice varied considerably from school to school.

Generative themes: Investigator High School

At Investigator High School, youth issues were incorporated into the curriculum and students had opportunities to broaden their social and cultural experiences through generative themes decided by teachers in consultation with students. Students in Linda's year 8 sub-school began with the topic 'Animal World,' a five-week unit with a focus on the habitat, distribution and ecological issues relating to native animals. Aspects of the topic were integrated with studies in English, science and Indonesian, and a great deal of initial interest was generated through excursions to the city zoo, the botanic gardens and the IMAX cinema. According to Linda, a large number of students had never visited these places. Despite the relative proximity of their suburbs to the central business district, it seemed that some students never ventured far from their local shopping centers and entertainment venues. In addition to broadening students' geographic horizons, these out-of-school activities promoted bonding and helped to break down some of the institutional barriers of schooling.

In Bernard's sub-school, the first topic of study was based on an orientation activity which involved students navigating their way around the metropolitan area of the city using public transport system. With reference to maps, timetables and information brochures, students had to plot a route from the school to a particular destination and make their way there and back within a designated time period. A student in Bernard's class explained what happened as follows:

> We got given a destination and we had to find out how to get there and get some proof of being there. We got to the city center and then had to make our way to a beach suburb. We got to walk around the foreshore, go on the jetty and get to McDonalds. It was wicked because the teacher gave us an hour free. We had to bring things like business cards to show we had been there. (Student, September 6, 2000)

This was an activity involving a high level of trust, if not some risk taking on the part of the school. Although no formal presentation to class was required, students had to write how they got there, what the trip was like and what they had collected. For many students, this was an adventurous activity in which they learnt a lot about the public transport system and the geography of suburbs that lay outside familiar territory. They obviously appreciated having some free time to shop and to do things by themselves, as opposed to being closely supervised by teachers.

Student-initiated curriculum: Plainsville School

The ideal of student-centered learning had been pushed much further at Plainsville School through the recent adoption of a student-initiated curriculum (SIC) and a strong commitment to student decision-making. The reasons behind this shift are important. As explained in the school portrait in Chapter 2, Plainsville is a disadvantaged school community. With an unemployment rate of 17 percent (almost 10 percent above the state average), the region has suffered more than most from de-industrialization and economic restructuring. More than 30 percent of families have a household income below $400 per week and only 25 percent of families own their own home. With restructuring has come a reduction in the number of reasonably well-paid skilled and semi-skilled blue-collar jobs. The work previously available to working-class students no longer exists. Now school leavers have to compete for white-collar jobs with middle-class students or settle for low-paid, casual and part-time work often negotiated through labor-hire firms. Few companies take on apprentices, preferring instead to employ trained workers. There are opportunities in the information technology area, but only one in five students has access to a computer at home. There are many young unemployed people in the district who are less physically mobile than their employed counterparts. Substance abuse and petty crime are major social concerns for the community. A significant number of students come from families in crisis, and they often arrive at school hungry and emotionally upset. In the absence of well-connected support networks, parents look at the school to provide a safe, secure environment for their children. Lacking the economic, social and cultural capital of middle-class communities, it is not surprising that the life experiences of these students are very limited. The principal explained:

> Seventy percent of our students had never been to the beach when I came here—learning comes from experience—they haven't been anywhere nor done anything. They have incredibly restricted boundaries. (Leanne, November 20, 2003)

Since many students and families have little or no experience of a work ethic, they are inclined to have low aspirations of schooling and future pathways. A senior teacher commented:

> Many of their parents never finished school either, so they don't see a huge value in education. I remember [the principal] saying she took her class to a university—and as they went into there the kids are saying, 'Oh wow!' and she said, 'Well, you know, you might come here one day,' and they said, 'Oh, nobody in Plainsville goes to university.' (Stella, February 25, 2003)

Staff explained that their greatest challenge was to break the cycle of failure and low expectations, and to broaden the students' horizons—in Stella's words 'to give them an idea of what's out there without actually telling them' (February 25, 2003). 'Our kids need to look forward to the future,' she explained. Many parents were also concerned about their children's future, especially the poor school completion rate of students once they left Plainsville. We were told that less than 50 percent of students continued schooling beyond year 8. This was one of the major factors driving the development of middle school arrangements at Plainsville.

Assisting students to become 'architects of their own education' (Eisner, 2002, p. 582) has been a longer-term project at Plainsville, but one which has ultimately transformed an industrial model of teaching into an SIC. In the new arrangements, all adult educators on the site are referred to as adults. As mentioned earlier, an educating adult might be a teacher, a school support officer, a parent, an older student or a community member. Teams of adults work with students to facilitate and plan their learning. There are no 'self-contained,' teacher-led classrooms as such. All available spaces are called 'learning areas' and students make decisions on a daily basis about which spaces inside and outside the school best suit their learning needs. Adults do not program learning for groups of students. Instead, students have their own individual learning plan for English, mathematics, 'issues' and 'out-of-class learning.'

Prior to preparing a learning plan, students work with adults to audit their own knowledge and to make decisions about what and how they want to learn. They have a user-friendly version of the state curriculum guidelines to ensure that they address key concepts and learning objectives across the curriculum. As a general rule, teachers do not engage in whole of class instruction; rather, students negotiate learning meetings with adults who have specialist knowledge of a particular topic or subject. With reference to a key competencies framework and other curriculum guidelines, students collect evidence of their learning to share with others. A permanent record of their achievement is kept in a 'learning folder.' When a student has completed a learning plan and satisfied criteria set out in the curriculum standards framework, they receive formal recognition in the form of a 'knowing card' which is signed off by an adult. Finally, when the topic is completed, they arrange to meet with an adult and three other students to talk about what they have learned in the form of a '- round-table assessment.'

What kind of learning is involved in SIC? Kate, a year 8 student with an interest in building design, discussed with us the main features of her issues about learning plan on architecture. She explained that she had prepared a concept map of the topic and met with her home group teacher to discuss her research questions and how she proposed to address specific curriculum objectives and undertake the research. Kate recorded the following challenges for her fifth week study on architecture:

- *Society and environment*: find out about a well-known building in the community.
- *Languages Other Than English (LOTE)*: find out about 10 different buildings and their styles.
- *Design and technology*: learn how to design a house using a computer-assisted design (CAD) program.
- *Imagination*: think of possible designs to replace the Twin Towers.
- *Maths*: work out how much it would cost to build the walls of a double-layer brick house.
- *English*: find out what it is like to be an architect.

Among her research strategies, Kate planned to interview an architect, design a house using CAD, investigate building styles and features using the Internet and library resources, go for a tour around the central city area and sketch the features of buildings in her local community.

What did students have to say about this form of student-initiated learning? We begin with a former student, James, who gave us the powerful critique of the teaching and learning environment in high schools in the previous chapter. Here he reflects on the change in his attitude toward schooling at Plainsville, where he was encouraged and supported to take on responsibilities in the SRC and school curriculum projects.

I DIDN'T MUCK AROUND BECAUSE I WANTED TO BE HERE

I was always in trouble with teachers and students. I was just misbehaving, being naughty and fighting. I really hated school. Even when I came to Plainsville, I still hated school. It was better but I was going because I had to. Then a new principal, Leanne, came in and all of a sudden all these small changes began to occur. I started thinking, yeah, yeah, this is getting somewhere where I might actually want to come every day; I might want to be here. When our school was chosen as the primary school for the key competencies project, Leanne saw some potential in me and slotted me in there even though I was failing. I wasn't failing academically but I was failing in school. I wasn't really getting along with people and I was still mucking around. I was accelerated and I went into the key competencies research team. Then I was put into the conference team. I went around with them. I was learning how to do public speaking and how to set up conferences and facilitate workshops. A couple of the students that Leanne chose were shy and didn't really get along with kids, but they had the potential to really be good leaders and excel in school. They were a bit 'nerdy,' if you know what I mean. And then there were students like me who really hated school and didn't want to be there. She could see that if she could make the learning relevant to kids like me, we would want to come to school. And if she could show the shy kids that they could be leaders and teach other kids, then their self-confidence and self-esteem would be boosted and they'd really want to learn more and become better people.

Along with the other chairperson of the SRC, I was chosen to interview the students and find out what was most significant in their learning and what the staff needed to change in the school to make it better for them. That meant interviewing students, putting up tallies analyzing the information and presenting it to the staff. Then we all talked about it and made recommendations as to what the staff was going to do from there. So it brought about major changes within the school from the SRC to students. I know it sounds really bad but there's no such thing as a teacher at Plainsville. There are 300 learners and the teachers are learning, the adults are learning and the kids are learning. The teachers are really just there to facilitate the students' learning rather than to teach them or keep them in order, for finding information, and they're really like: 'Well, this is what you've got to learn. What's the best way for you to learn it?' It's really individual. And so they'll say, 'Well I'd like to research on the Internet, make a PowerPoint . . .' and they go off and they do it and so the teachers are doing more than just teaching them about science, they're teaching them about learning. So for every day of their life, if they want to know something they're going to know how to go about getting the information and then presenting it to somebody else. I think that's the most important thing.

Generally when kids are displaying bad behavior a school will say, 'Right, well you're suspended.' I could go home for five days. I'd win. Whereas at Plainsville, they try to look at alternative consequences, which are going to make the kids turn their behavior around but at the same time, keep them in school. See a lot of the kids want to be here. They know a suspension would be a real punishment because they want to be here, they don't want to be at home. You've got kids that get here at seven o'clock so they can work on assignments before class, and are here until nine o'clock some nights. I was one of those kids. I'd be here till ten o'clock at night typing up speeches and different workshops. I didn't muck around because I wanted to be here. I wanted to learn so I tried to stay on task, and yeah, there were fewer temptations to muck around and stuff like that.

(James, February 25, 2003)

For James, one of the most powerful features of SIC at Plainsville is the fact that he has ownership of his learning and a capacity to influence curriculum priorities. In an environment where everyone is a learner and anyone with pedagogical knowledge and ideas can become a teacher, the power differentials become less apparent than in conventional schools. Formerly disengaged students, like James, are less inclined to 'muck up' because they see some purpose in their learning and no longer view their teachers as the enemy.

Other students described the benefits of the SIC as follows:

The 'old world' [the style of learning that existed before this innovation] didn't work out for me . . . I was waiting for others to catch up, but in the 'new world' [the term used to refer to SIC] I can work at my own pace . . . We've got learning plans. We chose the topic and we set the challenge. (Kate, November 20, 2002)

We have a bonded relationship. It's more like a family. Adults help in different ways, a two-way trust relationship we have built up. At the work level they [adults] are easy to access and easy to talk to—it's because we have access to every adult in the school. We have more opportunities because we chose what we learn—it's more interesting. In the traditional high school the teachers decided what we will learn. Here we want to learn because we're the ones deciding what we learn. (Sonia)

I've been here since kindy [reception year]. I was not too good in the 'old world.' I understand it more now and the teachers are much more friendly toward me. Instead of calling them Mrs. blah blah blah you can call them by their first name—like they are your friends. They teach you more about right and wrong. I had an anger management [problem]. I was always being suspended and things when I was 8. It's much better. Now I don't have that problem. I was helped with this at the start of the year. We go on 'bonding' excursions ... bushwalking and things like that and it helps everyone be friendly. If you go on without doing activities, people just don't understand each other and it's harder ... They encourage you to reach your targets in your learning plans ... do other things and come back to it. I was doing bits of maths and bits of English. The adult said I could just work on maths. I negotiated. And when I feel like it I can work on one thing at a time. You have to negotiate. They won't understand if you don't negotiate. It just gets harder if you don't negotiate. (Andy)

What are the implications for teachers? Steering school reform back to students requires a concerted effort on the part of schools, teachers and administrators to place students at the forefront of curriculum and to tangle with the complexities of students' lives. In his first year of teaching at Plainsville School, Mark offers a novice's perspective on school life and the issues confronting young adolescents. Apart from some exposure to middle school theory in his undergraduate days, his learning has been profoundly shaped by his experience in a disadvantaged school. For Mark, middle schooling is about putting students at the center of the curriculum.

PUTTING STUDENTS IN THE CENTER

Our kids bring in so much learned behavior from outside. You don't want to discredit that as less valuable than the other learning which is going on here, but you need to try and set up the understanding that there are certain ways of talking and acting. I don't like to say you hear it *all* the time here, but it is something that the kids will let off and like some of the children here are reasonably volatile and a lot of them come from, I guess—I don't really like to use the word 'violent'—but ah, volatile, I guess, home lives. And because of the nature of the community here, we've got emergency housing out the back and a women's shelter, and I think 18 percent of the students here at any one time are coming from emergency housing facilities. A lot of them have seen just about everything in regard to domestic—again I don't like to use 'violence' but I guess domestic issues with ah, some with substance abuse and issues of the like. It's hard to understand how the children must feel when suddenly their family is torn apart and they're taken with mum or whatever, or dad in some cases. They've literally got no place to go except for these shelters and emergency housing, and some of them turn up at those with no more than the shirt on their back and they have literally no possessions, no money and in some cases they don't know where the next meal is coming from. And so I guess they bring these worries with them and they're probably foremost in the children's minds rather than learning and some of the relationships that they're building here.

Some of the students simply don't have a lot of stability, or I guess a lot of support, from those home structures. A lot of them literally have to get themselves out of bed, pack their own lunch, some of them organize brothers and sisters, and they don't really have the driving force that actually gets them to school in the morning. Yeah, and some of them don't have anyone pushing them out the door or even out of bed in the morning and motivating them to get in school, so a lot of them actually do make it here on their own steam. In spite of these difficulties, we don't have a real large number of absences. Most students *do* look forward to coming to school even if a lot of them literally do have to get themselves and their brothers and sisters to school and pack lunches in some cases. Some of them come to school without lunches and they have the emergency breakfast program—the breakfast club in every morning. Most learning areas have their own loaves of bread and a toaster, and that sort of thing; so if students come without lunch they can make themselves an emergency lunch with toast; most of them have jam and Vegemite and that sort of thing which is, which we haven't really been able to establish in our learning area yet because we're only in our temporary learning space.

Building relationships is really important. I have found myself in that sort of situation in the first two weeks where you don't necessarily initiate the confrontation, but the students will stand their ground and you almost end up in a no-win sort of situation with some students. Sometimes you do just have to back away and say, 'Look, now we can't speak reason or give you my reasoning at this point. We can perhaps reason it at a later point.' So I think in a sense the focus on relationship building which was put through at university was important and I think that here they do that really well. And that was partly the reason behind me taking eight boys on the fishing trip last week. It was aimed at a bit of a bonding for me and those boys. These boys are sort of recognized as being pretty challenging, but get them to build a positive relationship with someone in the learning area, and try and establish that throughout the year so that maybe they will come along a little bit and engage a little more in their schooling. Building good relationships is not something that's going to happen in the first two weeks of term or maybe even the first term of this year. It's something that builds up over time.

I guess another focus of the middle schooling program that we looked is integrated curriculum and how to integrate learning and transfer learning across curriculum bands or the actual subject areas: for example, a theme like cars. They might be integrating learning from language and maybe investigating things, researching things like history and maybe transferring some of that into maths when looking maybe at the speeds of cars—if they're looking at car racing—and transferring knowledge in these sort of averages of speeds and even in technology and stuff where they might actually build models of cars or things like that. So I guess it's working out an area of a student's particular interest—like the issues learning plan, where students come up with an issue of particular interest or relevance to themselves and it has to be something which affects the lives of them or the lives of others. Some people are doing issues learning plans on things like hairdressing and while you might say, oh how does that affect your life or the life of others, they're actually investigating a career in hairdressing.

There's not a committee in the school which doesn't have student voice in it from the governing council, right down to the most basic things like talking-circle decisions and class decisions. It gets even more basic when you talk about negotiating learning plans. Students here even have 'behavior learning plans.' So you identify with the student an area of behavior which has been an issue over an extended period and come up with a plan of how they can actually work on and improve certain aspects of the behavior. At university you hear a lot about student-centered learning but here they take it right to the edge. They put students right at the center of literally everything that they're involved in.

(Mark, February 11, 2003)

'Making the curriculum fit the child' seems to be the main intent of school reform at Plainsville. Adults facilitated students' learning by: assisting them to develop organizational skills; posing challenges; encouraging them to utilize all opportunities for learning; monitoring their progress; assisting them to evaluate and report on their learning; providing them with a range of ways of learning about topics under study; and, generally, assisting them to become more independent and confident learners. This is how Greg, a beginning teacher, explained what was involved:

> Our school is very heavily focused on student-initiated curriculum—giving students a range of different choices and out-of-school learning. It's not a matter of us saying, 'Do you want to do this?' and then them coming back and saying, 'Oh, can I do this?' They elect what they want to do and it's up to the staff to provide them with the opportunities. The curriculum is based on the state curriculum framework even though it's student driven. It's a matter of identifying how learning outcomes fit within the official curriculum. For example, one of our year 6/7 girls is investigating dancing bears and the unethical practice associated with that. She has worked out how she can address different curriculum areas like health, physical education, science and maths. Our students all have a copy of the state curriculum framework to help them in this process.
> (Greg, March 7, 2003)

One of our grade 8 informants explained that letting go of power was not easy for some staff members:

You can't go half way. You can't give us some choices and then take it away from us and take a little of the power back. You have to jump those few steps. It's hard for adults and teachers to give some of their power. We don't use the word power much because it is shared equally among the parents, teachers and students. It's shared. I've got just as much power as an adult. We help each other so we all have the same amount of power. (Gabriel, November 20, 2002)

Having a say: student voice in action

According to Shor (1992), participation is the key to empowerment because 'it challenges the experience of education as something done to students' (p. 20). In the previous section, we described how students were involved in negotiating classroom learning with adult members of the school community. We now want to explore the issue of the participative aspects of their learning.

Often schools pay lip service to student voice, but at Plainsville teachers spoke of the importance of 'walking the talk' (Leanne, November 20, 2002) when it came to sharing power and involving students in the 'core business' of schooling—the curriculum. A review of the school's decision-making processes in 1997 tackled two difficult questions: 'How many authentic decisions do students make in our classrooms and in our school?' and 'How many authentic decisions do families make in our school?' Alarmed at survey findings, the school began to overhaul its decision-making processes. Beginning with out-of-class learning, which was regarded as less confrontational for teachers, the school invited input about the directions and goals of the school from all members of the community. Giving more power to students was not achieved without some angst on the part of adult educators, however, as the following teacher's comments suggest, the impact has been quite dramatic:

[I]t's a lot about student voice and giving them the power to express themselves, to choose their own learning, to make decisions on what they want to do and where they want to go . . . giving them a range of different choices and out-of-school learning . . . building up their own power . . . not just telling them what needs to be done. (Greg, March 9, 2003).

Susie, Brendan and Rachel are members of the student forum, the year 7–9 decision-making group, at the New Vista Middle School Campus. In this account they discuss the ways in which they are involved in negotiating curriculum and offer some perspectives on student voice and their experiences of schooling in the middle years.

WE GET TO HAVE A SAY

'In class meetings we get to vote on things we want to change, like uniforms and things,' says Rachel. 'And then a student forum member in that class would take that issue to the student forum meeting where it would be discussed and a decision brought back to the class,' adds Brendan. 'Also, when we choose our subjects, we can choose what sort of things we want to learn and get told what teachers we learn it with,' says Rachel. So far as negotiating the curriculum is concerned, it appears that students have some say but it is rather limited. 'Well, in English this term we got some free choice but basically the teacher tells us what to do, like what things we are going to learn about. In some subjects we get to choose what we can research about and what interests us—yeah, within the topic we have choices as to what we do.' Brendan supports Rachel, 'In science, Mrs. C gives us choice assignments where we have a certain number of things and we decide what ones we want to do.' In the earth forces assignment, you could present the information and I made a model of a volcano. 'But,' he continues almost apologetically, 'there's a set curriculum; the teachers are given a set curriculum by the Education Department. It's hard for the teachers because some people are a fair bit ahead of the others in sort of—like there's a group of people in the maths class that includes me and Allan, and some of the year 8s that do some extension work because we know what we're learning.'

'At the start of the year anyone who wants to be on the student forum can get an application form and fill it out and then give it back to the head of the middle school, and she picks the people that she wants,' explains Brendan. 'Oh, I think she just chooses the *best* people,' says Rachel. 'Normally there's at least one person for every class that is involved in the student forum, so the class can put their input into the school.' 'We try to have meetings once a week during our pastoral care lesson,' comments Brendan. 'We usually talk about what happened at student forum but we also discuss issues someone else might want to bring up. I think one time we talked about having a lawn bowls team, but I don't think we decided to do that. And we talk about things we want to do to make the classroom better.' At this point Brendan holds up a notebook and remarks, 'This is my student forum book where I write down the matters that we talk about in our meeting. I keep a record of things I have to take back to the class for discussion. We organize most of the casual days which are fund-raising events; we talked about a PE uniform and the disco, and we asked students their opinions about getting a school scarf. We decided not to. And something I brought from the class was to fix the drinking taps on the way through the building. We also discussed getting a PA system because the only way to get the message to the whole school is by calling an assembly.'

'In the meeting last week we had a big discussion about whether we should or not get homework,' says Brendan. 'Kids were saying that they go to school and that takes up a lot of their social life and on top of that they have to do schoolwork at home, which takes up more of their social life. The school counselor tried to explain why we needed to have homework; that it's hard for the teachers because they've got a set curriculum that they have to do in the year and they don't actually get that many lessons with us. In the end I think we decided that it was necessary to have homework, but not quite as much as we had.' (The students' efforts bore fruit in the following school year. In a surprise move, the school principal announced that homework was no longer part of the school policy. The rationale given was that students already spend considerable time on their studies and should be free to spend more time relaxing with their families outside of school hours. The statement made media headlines and generated a good deal of debate about the pros and cons of homework within the educational community.)

'If you had a magic wand to make some improvements in school, what sort of things would you do?,' I pose. As usual Brendan is quick to respond. 'I think we need more money. Most of our money is taken up by paying staff. They don't have much money to carry out improvements and they rely on us for fund-raising.' Susie joins in, 'yeah, because this year, they're having to get another middle school classroom.' Brendan offers another suggestion: 'Well, I think if they had more teachers they could categorize people into skill levels and make smaller classes. The smaller your classes the better you can learn because it's easier for the teacher to extend people who are better at subjects and help people along who aren't as good at subjects.'

(Brendan, Rachel and Susie, September 3, 2003)

Engaging with the community: capacity building

The six project schools in this study were community-oriented schools that were engaged in a process of capacity building with local organizations and groups. Rather than seeing the school in isolation from the community, they understood the school as being integral to the community in three significant ways: firstly, they recognized the need to develop educational experiences that were responsive to local concerns and issues; secondly, they saw the community as a significant educational resource that could complement and enhance learning for students; and thirdly, they sought to involve students in community-based action programs. In what follows we want to illustrate a number of aspects of school/community dialog and development at Plainsville and Broadvale schools.

Tapping into 'funds of knowledge': insights from Plainsville School

One of the ways in which schools can promote inclusive and participatory forms of education is to value the knowledge and resources which students bring from home and to capitalize on the social networks of communities. Moll, Amanti, Neff

& Gonzalez (1992) argue that the 'funds of knowledge' embodied in households and communities can support educational goals of schools and improve classroom instruction. They use the term 'funds of knowledge' to refer to 'those historically accumulated and culturally developed bodies of knowledge and skills essential for household or individual functioning and wellbeing' (p. 134).

If Australian Bureau of Statistics (ABS) data is the sole reference point for describing communities like Plainsville, it is not surprising that negative perceptions and deficit views of working class households prevail. There is no denying that Plainsville is an economically depressed community, but statistics tend to conceal those community assets: the individuals, groups and institutions that enhance individual and community well-being. Many families have lived in Plainsville for two or three generations, and there was considerable pride in the school and its achievements. Not only was the school a meeting place for community groups, but it was also an important contributor to cultural capital through the transfer of valued knowledge and skills from adult education programs, arts and craft courses, and recreational activities.

At Plainsville, there was a view that pedagogical knowledge did not reside exclusively with teachers, and we were constantly reminded about the importance of 'bringing the community into the school.' This occurred in several ways. Firstly, all students were involved in service learning which engaged them in community development projects in conjunction with the local council and other organizations, such as aged care homes and child care centers. We gained some insight into this during an interview with year 8 students, Andy and Kate. Andy, an avid skate boarder, commented:

> I'm a member of the district student representative council. There are two of us from Plainsville School. Recently we met in the council chambers and told the councilors about the damage in the area. The skate park needs to be pulled down and replaced. We held an environmental expo where we learnt about trees and stuff. The district let us express our views about things that need to be done in the area. (Andy, November 20, 2002)

Kate went on to explain that her service learning involved a tree planting project in the school and the town center—an activity which engaged her in a lot of learning about the natural environment and the community. Talking of the value of public service projects, Eisner (2002) argues:

> Students need to learn that there are people who need services and that they . . . can contribute to meeting these people's needs. Service learning . . . affords adolescents an opportunity to do something whose scope is beyond them. (p. 583)

While the intent of this learning was to encourage the idea of voluntarism, to give something back to the community, it also brought students into contact with other significant adults who could support their learning about vocational education, child care, local industries, retail trade, and health and welfare. It also shifted the focus of their learning away from the notion of an individual benefit to that of being a collective good.

Secondly, parents and other community members organized and conducted sporting, cultural and craft activities as part of an experiential learning program. A teacher related how parent involvement brought other tangible benefits as well:

> One of our parents can't read and write, and she has seven children. We found out she was really good at arts and crafts. She said, 'Why would anyone want to talk to me?' but she stayed and brought another friend, and now there are four of them. She comes to governing council because of her confidence. She has started to go to the learning groups here and asked if we can start an adult learning group here. (Leanne, November 20, 2002)

Not only did the students gain from the arts and craft initiatives, but also as the parents grew in confidence they began to see that they had the capacity to make a worthwhile contribution to school governance.

Socially disadvantaged students have limited access to all forms of capital in their lives (Croninger & Lee 2001; Smyth, 2004a). Although Plainsville School could tap into locally produced funds of knowledge, there was a general recognition that students needed to enlarge their views of the world beyond the boundaries of the neighborhood. The school saw itself as a major resource for building social capital and getting students to strive toward a more optimistic future. To this end, the school established extensive networks of support for students that reached into the business community, social welfare groups and educational institutions; funds were allocated for camps and excursions; successful former students were invited to speak to present students about their life experiences; and a major investment in information technology enabled students to choose and use a wide range of learning technologies not available in their homes. Much of the learning was 'future oriented.' Work perspectives were included in all learning programs and students were assisted to develop a pathway planner as part of their personal portfolio. Middle school students were able to study vocational education courses through a local Technical and Further Education (TAFE) college, and were involved in enterprise education programs, a work placement scheme and a wide range of service and out-of-school learning activities.

These learning experiences broadened students' cultural and geographic horizons. They assisted them to plan for future work and study options and helped to break down some of the negative attitudes and low aspirations engendered by poverty and social exclusion. In short, the school went some distance in nurturing a transformative habitus by giving a voice to traditionally marginalized students, authorizing locally produced knowledge, supporting students to become architects of their own learning and encouraging them to think creatively about their futures. However, the innovative approach to curriculum at Plainsville created some dilemmas. As the school was 'living on the edge' of officially sanctioned curriculum, it was constantly having to demonstrate the merits of a radical alternative to the education system. Moreover, many school leavers experienced a difficult transition to high schools, where they often found the forms of instruction and hierarchical arrangements out of kilter with their experience of SIC at Plainsville. This meant that the school leadership had to maintain an ongoing dialog with neighboring schools in promoting school reform around social inclusion—in effect, 'walking the talk' with the broader community.

Community connections program: Broadvale R–12 Community School

Community capacity building at Broadvale School involved a high level of cooperation with the state and local government agencies. A key component of this endeavor was a community development model that sought to build a more integrated and holistic approach to the provision of community services. Marcus, a social planner with the local council, offered a community orientation program for teachers in the district which took the form of a bus tour of the area and a talk which emphasized the cultural, economic and environmental assets of the area, not just the socioeconomic concerns. He explained that it is very important for schools to enlist the support of significant individuals who know the neighborhood, have the respect of the community and can act as advocates for young people, and promote the value of education.

The Broadvale principal argued that strengthening the links between the school and the community was a major priority, and he offered the following appraisal:

> Last year we ran a successful trial with community policing. If this school is going to do anything about bullying and harassment that's going to be sustainable, we actually have to engage the community in the process. What gets you stuck there is of course, there isn't *a* community but several communities to engage. So somewhere along the line, if we're going to be building the social capital of this area, it's got to be schools working with the council and the other agencies that are here. We have to have a more coherent means of all working together. (Garfield, April 4, 2003)

We will explore the idea of educational partnerships in Chapter 7, when we consider the notion of schools as collaborative networked communities, but we want to reiterate the need to forge educative relationships between schools and communities and to promote participatory forms of decision-making within the community.

Critical literacies: reading the word and the world

In their provocative book *Teaching as a Subversive Activity*, Postman and Weingartner (1969) argue that 'schools must serve as the principle medium for developing in youth the attributes and skills of social, political and cultural criticism' (p. 2). Using a more colorful turn of phrase, they go on to suggest that that young people need to be experts in 'crap detecting' (p. 3) if they are to navigate their way through the minefields of information and propaganda that confront them in their daily lives. What they are talking about amounts to 'schools cultivating in the young the most "subversive" intellectual instrument—the anthropological perspective' (p. 4) as a means of investigating their own lives and culture both from within and from the outside. Such a view invests students with a sense of agency in the construction of knowledge. Unfortunately, classrooms are often managed in such a way that students never get to ask critical questions or to engage in social and political action arising from their own concerns and investigations.

Making a case for an inquiry (or problem-oriented) method of learning, Postman and Weingartner claim that knowledge is produced in response to questions and issues generated by students rather than teachers—an idea popularized in the notion of constructivist learning with its emphasis on negotiated curriculum, hands-on learning and student voice. But do the student-centered pedagogies, described earlier in this chapter, necessarily promote critical literacies? Even when teachers operate under the banner of democracy or 'constructivist' learning principles, students are far from autonomous beings constructing their own knowledge. Power differentials operate in all classrooms; in the gendered, radicalized and classed experiences of students; in the sanctioned authority of policy-makers over practitioners and students; in the choice of topics, texts and perspectives for classroom learning; and, as Klein (2000) claims, 'in the ways in which language is used to position students in sometimes limiting and sometimes enabling ways' (p. 64). The latter point is particularly significant when we consider the persistence of stereotypes and myths about boys and girls in relation to mathematical practices; for example, the notions that 'women need only low-level maths' and 'girls are hard workers but boys are clever.'

Despite moves toward cooperative forms of learning in most of the project schools, there was still a disposition toward individualized instruction and competitive assessment practices. Constructivism in practice seemed to mask hegemonic practices of exclusion by glossing over power differentials. Arguing for a critical constructivist approach, Zevenbergen (2004) claims that:

> [Constructivism] is limited by its failure to acknowledge that the schooling system recognizes only particular constructions of meaning. Students who come from social and

cultural groups, whose culture is not that of the dominant culture, are at a distinct disadvantage when entering the school system. (p. 111)

Not all teachers in the project schools were willing to accept the *status quo* when
it came to the selection of course content. Concerned about the Eurocentric and
colonialist version of Australian history in her school, a Broadvale teacher lamented:

> There's got to be more relevant stuff for our kids than studying Captain Cook for five
> years in a row. I mean no wonder they get tuned out. I would be too. It's boring, it's irrel-
> evant and it's crap. I think there needs to be a total overhaul of what we do in terms of
> our curriculum. (Monica, March 19, 2003)

Some school texts still refer to the English explorer, James Cook, as the discov-
erer of Australia, despite archeological evidence that Aboriginal people have occupied mainland Australia for some 50,000 years. The racist and sexist nature of
teaching resources became a topic for discussion during a society and environment
faculty meeting at Monica's school. Susan, the Faculty Coordinator, claimed that
much of the audiovisual material in the school library was outdated and offered a
stereotyped, sexist and culturally exclusive view of Australian society. With the support of her colleagues, she initiated a review of the resources and argued for a more
critical and thoughtful approach to the purchase of new texts. In the same meeting she spoke of the resources to support students' learning in sustainability and
social justice at the Global Education Center.

To what extent were students in the project schools involved in learning that
engaged them in a critical reading of their world? What opportunities did they have
for political and social activism in support of that learning?

Some instances of this learning in the area of environmental studies have been
described earlier in this chapter, so our focus here is on cultural and social issues.
We begin with some insights from Katrina about the approach to an Aboriginal education program at Investigator High School:

> There are about 39 Aboriginal students at the school and two staff members have
> responsibilities for their education and welfare. I'm the Aboriginal Studies Teacher
> (AET) and we have an indigenous person who is an Aboriginal Education Worker
> (AEW). Apart from supporting indigenous students, I also act as a resource teacher for
> the staff in developing Aboriginal studies courses. Presently Aboriginal studies is avail-
> able in the senior school but in years 8–10 we are looking more at Aboriginal perspec-
> tives across the curriculum. This is in accord with the education department policy and
> it happens here fairly well. Instead of having the traditional days to celebrate Aboriginal
> Cultural Week, we have a whole-school program operating throughout the year. All the
> year 8s will have some exposure to some Aboriginal performances and story telling, story
> writing and music. This will continue to years 8 and 9. We are putting together a fold-

er which we're hoping will become a permanent record of year 8 students' learning about Aboriginal cultures, societies and perspectives in whatever subject they study. The idea is that by the time they get to year 11, they will have a resource folder which will show their development as a person and their attitudes and values. When they get their folder in year 8, the first thing we're going to get them to do is to write themselves a letter beginning 'I am in year 8 . . . the things I know about Aboriginals are . . . the things I know about reconciliation are . . .' When they get to year 11, they can read it and go 'I've come a long way because now I know this, this and this . . . I feel totally different to what I did then.' So it can actually be measured in a fairly loose sort of way but there hopefully should be some change in their knowledge at least. Next Monday we are being presented with an Aboriginal flag. On special days when we fly the Australian flag we will also fly the Aboriginal flag. We have invited elders from the area to attend. It's something we have needed to do for a while. (Katrina, September 16, 2000)

Katrina was under no illusions as to the difficulties of implementing a cross-curriculum program on Aboriginal perspectives. She spoke of entrenched racist attitudes in a mono-cultural community and reluctance on the part of some staff to give up pedagogical territory for the task. Challenging prevailing stereotypes and prejudices about indigenous people had been made all the more difficult in a political climate in which many of the advances toward reconciliation and recognition of land rights had suffered setbacks under conservative Australian governments. Indeed, since the events of September 11 those who dare to speak out against government policies on border protection, the detention of asylum seekers and Australia's participation in the Iraq War are often vilified for their so-called 'unpatriotic' behavior.

Students too are often discouraged from participating in acts of resistance by the education system. When a national youth group organized an anti-racism rally in the city center, schools were asked to discourage student participation because the loss of school time could have a damaging impact on their studies. However, from time to time we witnessed examples of student action for peace and reconciliation. During a learning area meeting at Plainsville in March 2003, two girls announced that they were involved in a campaign against the possible war in Iraq and spoke of a highly unsatisfactory response they had received from a local politician concerning the reasons for Australia's commitment to the American task force. The 13-year-old girl student spoke passionately about her concerns and of a forthcoming protest rally. To draw attention to the cause they had stuck a poster on their backs promoting the rally. Rather than castigating them for their actions, the principal asked the students if they would like to present their views on the issue at a middle school assembly later in the week. They duly did so and with the encouragement of teachers organized a bus to take students and parents to the protest rally. Not only was this kind of activism tolerated in this school, but also it was encouraged in an educative atmosphere where they had to make a reasoned case for their stance. This was not always the case in other schools. In one instance, a group of students left their classes to assemble on the school oval to protest at the war in Iraq. While for some it seemed to have been motivated by genuine concerns about the war, others simply joined the exodus to be part of the fun. Although some teachers had made a concerted effort to encourage debate and discussion on the Iraq War with their classes, others seem to have seen it as a distraction to the set curriculum. As a result many students were either confused or ignorant of the political issues involved in the war. Not surprisingly, the protest became a rather disorganized and divisive event.

The selection of curriculum content and learning activities is clearly important in promoting critical literacies among students. During our observations in one of the project schools, it was apparent that several students were not very enamored with the Real Game, a joint Canadian/British interdisciplinary project, which supposedly engaged students in learning about the 'real world.' The program was being trialed at Investigator High with a view to developing a more authentically Australian version based on feedback from teachers and students. According to the authors, the aim of the project was to encourage students to stay on at school with a view to making informed choices about their careers. In the game, students adopted an occupational role from 40 job profiles and made decisions about budgeting and disposal of their income, especially in relation to financing a house, motor vehicle and household goods. Initially, students were told that they could choose whatever house and material possessions that they wanted. Only later in the game did they take a 'reality check' of their financial situation where they matched income with expenditure and were encouraged to make any necessary adjustments in their spending habits.

The game may have been designed to simulate real-world situations, but for some students it simply did not match the reality of their own life experiences. A student told us that the homes illustrated in this kit—mostly two-story dwellings in middle-class suburbs—were far too 'posh' and looked nothing like the places around Investigator High. Aside from these criticisms, the unquestioning acceptance of materialist values and lifestyles was somewhat disturbing. In spite of the so-called 'reality check,' there was little or no analysis of class, gender, ethnicity and other factors which might influence employment opportunities, identities and lifestyles. Although this activity was being marketed as the 'real game,' it seemed to a number of students to be a very 'unreal game' in terms of its social context and the unrealistic expectations regarding the accumulation of wealth and material possessions. This was yet another reminder that texts are cultural products which embody what Williams (1989) refers to as a 'selective tradition' in which certain meanings, values and perspectives are privileged over others. In this case, it seems that the life and circumstances of working class students were largely devalued or ignored.

Closing remarks

This chapter has focused largely on students' expectations and experiences of schooling. Young people are often disparaged in the popular press and society at large; the thought that they might have something worthwhile to contribute to dialogs about school reform is rarely acted on by policy-makers. However, one of the things which stood out in our conversations with students was their knowledge and understanding of their society and their ability to reflect on their own learning and the broader purposes of schooling. Many students in the project schools offered remarkable insights into the qualities of a 'good' teacher, practices which promote effective learning, the relevance of their high school curriculum and inequitable arrangements in education.

The enormous talent and creative energy of young people shone through in the outstanding drama performances, musicals, artistic artifacts and environmental projects that we observed in the life of the schools. At Broadvale, we sat spellbound as two Cambodian students entertained a middle school assembly with an exhilarating dance routine. The point we want to emphasize here is that young people have so much to contribute to the betterment of society that we ignore their knowledge and insights at our peril. Steering school reform back to the students is essential if we are to revitalize schools and improve the educational opportunities and life chances of the most disadvantaged groups in society. We have argued that the process of transforming schools must begin by creating the kinds of places to which students want to belong. Unless young people feel connected to a school community where their concerns are taken seriously and where they have a genuine voice in decision-making, little meaningful learning is likely to occur.

Fostering a sense of identity and belongingness is clearly important, but it needs to be accompanied by educational experiences that broaden students' horizons and promote active citizenship. Giroux (1986) claims that schools 'need to be reconceived as "democratic counterpublic spheres"—as places where students learn the skills and knowledge needed to live in and fight for a viable democratic society' (p. 66). To bring about such change, school will have to engage with the problems and concerns of students in their everyday lives as well as cultivating a spirit of critique and respect for human dignity.

Reform of the kind we are talking about here has implications for school organization, pedagogy and the ways in which teachers relate to young people. Many teachers in the project schools recognized that their long-term survival depended on the adoption of teaching practices that were more attuned to social learning and relational issues rather than entrenched pedagogies. But this shift is easier said than done. How can teachers break down the institutional barriers that work against educative relationships with students? How do teachers learn to negotiate curriculum with students? In short, how can teachers reinvent themselves for young people? These questions are explored in the next part when we turn our attention to teachers' lives.

PART THREE

Adult Lives

CHAPTER FIVE

Teachers reinventing themselves . . . for kids!

Introduction

In this section, we shift our attention on the issue of adolescent schooling from young lives to adult lives. Bearing in mind the concerns, aspirations and insights voiced by students in the project schools we ask: How are teachers reinventing themselves for young people? Our choice of the term 'reinventing' teaching is quite deliberate; indeed, we had been using the term for several years before we discovered Deborah Meier's (1992) reference to it. We liked the term, particularly in relation to teaching with young adolescents, because of the way it conveyed a sense that those who were most intimately and directly involved had a large measure of control in bringing their experience and creativity to bear on reworking a project that had fallen into some disrepair. What the notion of reinvention captured for us was a sense of reclamation, rediscovery, regeneration or rejuvenation that comes from having a passion about something. It also conveyed a sense of the need to rework ways of doing things in the light of wider changes occurring beyond schools.

Reinvention carried too the connotation of being prepared to go considerably beyond tinkering around the edges, and of having to fundamentally re-examine the construction and design of teaching, and question how well schools as institutions are working, and what needs to be changed in the light of experience. The notion

of 'remaking teaching' also captured this sentiment of looking expansively at ideology, policy and practice (see Smyth & Shacklock, 1998). Words like 'reform,'
'improvement' or 'change' were too narrow, too loaded or too worn-out for us.

Meier (1992) nicely captured the pervasiveness and the depth of what we
believe is involved in reinventing teaching around something as crucial as working
with young adolescents, when she said: 'Teachers need to relearn what it means to
be good in-school practitioners' (p. 594). In other words, it is not sufficient to assume
knowledge or to continue to rely on habit:

> We can change teaching only by changing the environment in which teaching takes
> place. Teaching can only be changed by reinventing the institutions within which
> teaching takes place—schools. Reinvention has to be done by those who will be stuck
> in the reinvented schools. It cannot be force fed—not to teachers, nor to parents and
> children. (Meier, 1992, p. 600)
>
> If teachers are not able to join in leading such changes, the changes will not take place.
> Politicians and policymakers at all levels may institute vast new legislated reforms; but
> without the understanding, support, and input of teachers, they will end up in the same dead
> end as . . . past reforms . . . For all the big brave talk, they will be rhetorical and cosmetic,
> and after a time they will wither away. (Meier, 1992, p. 594)

The changes needed are not changes in the solo acts teachers perform inside
their classrooms . . . We are talking about creating a very different school culture,
a new set of relationships and ideas. (Meier, 1992, p. 599)

What we are talking about here is something as fundamental, as courageous and
as passionate as re-thinking and re-working the institution of schooling if we are
to get it right for young people.

In this chapter, we want to do two things. Firstly, we want to show what it is
that teachers of young adolescents need to reinvent themselves *against*—that is,
working against the grain of the current educational policy direction to make themselves different, while at the same time trying to make a difference in the lives of
young people. And secondly, we want to sketch out the emerging features of what
such a reinvention or 'imaginary' of teaching might look like (and does look like in
some instances). In other words, we want to reveal something of what it is that some
teachers are actively resisting, and why, and provide some insights into what it is they
are striving for, how they are going about it, and with what effects.

Working against the policy discourse

Just what it is that teachers are struggling against is not easy to define precisely or
to delineate. In the broadest sense, what is being resisted by many maverick teachers, and which is of profound importance, is their attempt to try and limit the worst

excesses of the broad project of what is termed 'global governance' (Fonte, 2005). In its simplest forms this means envisaging teaching within a broader project in which significant forces are working to undermine notions of democracy. Fonte (2005) has referred to these as 'transnational bureaucracy' by which he means the political arrangements being engineered beyond nation states. He depicts the global governance regime as being:

> . . . promoted and run by complementary and interlocking networks of transnational (mostly western) elites . . . These transnational elites are for the most part ideologically compatible . . . Nation states . . . continue to exist, but their authority is increasingly circumscribed by the growing strength of global institutions, laws, rules and ideological norms. (p. 19)

So, how does this relate to teachers, and specifically how does it impact at the level of young adolescents?

Teachers' work is something of a perplexing anomaly. At one level, in the wider public, media, political and policy domain, teaching of a kind that requires high levels of autonomous professional judgment is treated dismissively, derisively and perfunctorily, and is deemed to be of little value or importance. In other words, teaching is frequently portrayed as not being especially complex or difficult work, is of a limited technical kind, and is readily able to be scripted and codified in ways that will render it even more compliant and susceptible to outcomes-oriented forms of treatment. Yet on the other hand, over the past three decades enormous ideological effort and expense has been incurred internationally in trying to circumscribe, prescribe, calibrate, measure and ultimately control the work of teaching. The consequence of this has been that as long as teaching is able to be construed as basically technical work, then the attempt to control it by external means is legitimated. This argument is further bolstered by the way in which schools are bolted onto the economy, particularly at the secondary level in ways that say, in effect, schooling is for work.

These are not an especially new or novel set of ideas, but what is giving them added urgency at the moment is the fact that they are not working out quite as planned. Large number of students around the world are disengaging, switching off or making the active choice to 'drop out' of school completely. To take one indicator, albeit one of growing interest and angst to educational policy-makers, it is estimated that in the United States 'the number of disengaged students may exceed two thirds of the high school population' (Cothran & Ennis, 2000, p. 106)—and this may be only the tip of the iceberg.

The tension, therefore, that is becoming increasingly evident is that instrumentalist forms of teaching are not translating into happy, switched-on and productive students. Quite the contrary, and in part this explains the resort to muscular and coercive strategies like high stakes testing, benchmarking, standards and punitive forms of teacher evaluation. There is a mounting and compelling body of evidence that teachers know better, and have for some time understood 'what works' with young adolescents in school—and it is vastly different from the narrow, reductionist, atomistic, impersonal ways in which teachers are being pushed by the policy gurus. They live daily with the damaging effects of these policies.

Class matters[1]

Where the mismatch between the educational policy trajectory and the lived experiences of young adolescents becomes most glaringly apparent is among the increasingly large number of young people who are coming from families and backgrounds that have been ravaged by the effects of economic globalization. Where the 'interactive trouble' (Freebody, Ludwig & Gunn, 1995) occurs is in the yawning chasm between the middle class ideology of schools and their increasing working class student clientele. In other words, when the gap between what the school promises and the means it has on offer to realistically deliver on its promises through an instrumentalist workforce agenda becomes untenable or totally distasteful to young people, particularly those from backgrounds that differ from that of the school and its teachers, then something is bound to give—and in this case, schooling takes a king hit in terms of its perceived (ir)relevance. The irony in all of these is that as front-line professionals, teachers have in many instances long known what kind of conditions have to be sustained and maintained for educative relationships to be possible with young people from increasingly disadvantaged backgrounds, but they are rarely consulted, listened to or involved in such discussions.

It is worth briefly reiterating the context of the schools we were involved with in this book. Using Thomson's (2002) shorthand, they were from a 'rustbelt' state, like many others around the world, going through 'hard times' in terms of the process of global de-industrialization. The consequence is that half of the public schools in the state, which includes all the ones studied here, fall within the increasing gradient and definition of being 'disadvantaged' (Kimber, 2002)—meaning they have communities of low income, are suffering from forms of social dislocation, high un(under)employment, family breakdown, ill-health, and often multiple forms of economic and social distress.

In an analysis of a celebrated US instance of a progressive approach to this kind of institutional mismatch (see Wiggington, 1985), Margonis (2004) argues that what is needed is a focus on 'relational sensibilities' (p. 43). His argument is that the focus of 'attention on pedagogical relationships is long overdue' and that if we are to advance the life chances of the most marginalized students in ways that include them in the benefits of schooling, then we will need to reconsider 'why those relationships between students and teachers are failing' (p. 40). Put another way, we need to 'better understand the relational preconditions for powerful learning and teaching' (p. 40).

According to Margonis (2004), at the core is the middle class tendency to label such students in terms of individual or family 'deficits' and to then focus in on 'resentful,' 'rebellious,' 'angry,' 'lazy' and 'rude' behavior. What is required instead of such victim blaming approaches are ways of understanding these behaviors as systematic forms of resistance. The focus needs to be shifted to possible ways in which the social relationship might be transformed from one of 'student resentment and apathy,' to one of becoming 'motivated, engaged and productive' (p. 41). In other words, a shift from a situation in which young people feel imprisoned by school, to one in which they are (and feel) respected and trusted, and respond as a consequence in 'engaged learning in the classroom' (p. 41). The issue here is really around what Sennett and Cobb (1977) refer to as 'reciprocal respect across class boundaries' (p. 47)—how the middle class institution of schooling listens to the lives, experiences and aspirations of working class students, and how they in turn are incorporated into engaged forms of learning. This is not rocket science, but equally neither is it a perspective that is widely endorsed in the substance, direction, or practices of educational policy-making, nor in the daily leadership practices of many schools. The awesome responsibility for this rests primarily and heavily on the school.

To put it most directly, we need to think about pedagogical relationships sociologically. Margonis (2004) says that in situations of school–student class mismatch:

> . . . it is insufficient to look only at the face-to-face social dynamics played out in the classroom, for those patterns are pre-shaped by the institutional positions of students and teachers. We cannot understand the ontology of social relationships without also considering the institutional influences that frame those relationships. (p. 47)

'The institutional position of students and teachers shapes their relationships, and often the face-to-face exchanges live out those institutional determinations'. (pp. 47–48)

For example, when middle class teachers encounter rural working class students and these 'polarized groups meet in the classroom, both can often feel the tension' (p. 48) because of the way such social relations are lived out in the wider society. 'The tension is experienced by both parties; it is in neither individual but in their relationship; and their face-to-face relationship is inhabited by the historical influences of their respective groups and their groups' relationships' (p. 48). In these situations it is not uncommon for teachers to 'act out their structurally slotted role' (p. 48), and it is no mere coincidence that this often translates into enacting 'the most controlling pedagogies . . . in inner city schools where many of the students are low income and people of color.' (p. 48)

The challenge in these situations where students expect the school to exercise 'stern discipline and distrust' and for school to be 'disconnected from their lives,' is for a pedagogy that gives students significant responsibility and learning that is 'socially and intellectually engaging' (Margonis, 2004, p. 48). Invoking Wiggington, Margonis (2004) says that this amounts to an important case of the teacher 'changing the signals' (p. 48). What occurs here is a pedagogy that works in part because it 'violate[s] the structurally sanctioned terms of middle class teacher/working class student relationships' (p. 49). 'Instead of playing out the game of surveillance and resistance' what the students and teacher create in these situations is 'an institutional position' (p. 49) in which the students use and draw on the resources and the deeper connections to their own historical social location.

This new direction for a pedagogy for working class students can be neatly summarized as one that shows students 'greater degrees of respect while holding them accountable for educational aims' (p. 49). It has fairly minimalist prescriptions:

> . . . a particular pedagogy is not prescribed, but rather a small set of ethical principles. Students want respect from their teacher; they want a classroom pedagogy relevant to their interests; and they want a teacher with enthusiasm and openness. (Margonis, 2004, p. 51).

In other words, 'respectful relationships' built upon a 'process of collective decision making' (p. 51). The title of a recent book says it all—*No Education Without Relation* (Bingham & Sidorkin, 2004). How such a stunningly self-evident revelation has been allowed to elude us, at least officially, is one of the great mysteries of education, and of even greater curiosity is why so little of this percolates through into what passes as educational policy in schools. Willard Waller (1932) puts it with incredible clarity almost a century ago:

> . . . let no one be deceived, the important things that happen in schools result from the interaction of personalities. Children and teachers are not disembodied intelligences, not instructing machines or learning machines, but whole human beings tied together in a complex maze of social interconnections. The school is a social world because human beings live in it. (p. 1)

Middle school pedagogy: a class response

The argument we want to make in the context of the data we have is that the notion of middle schooling, at least in its pedagogical enactment, while certainly a progressive and democratic ideal, in effect amounts to a response by the middle class institution of schooling to accommodate to working class adolescents. In a sense it is a response to Weis and Fine's (2001) claim that the collapse of the wider public sphere and the insertion in its place of notions of individualism, marketization, consumer choice and privatization, when translated into school effectively amount to giving up on school for working class youth.

As the public sphere packs up and walks away from poor and working class youth, it is absolutely essential for the community to reclaim these spaces. (p. 499)

Weis and Fine (2001) do a considerable service by 'offering an alternative voice to the deafening victim mentality' (p. 509) in the way they provide the rhetorical scaffolding and language of 'disruptive and "forceful" pedagogies,' 'counter publics,' and 'pushing the borders' (p. 509) with which to contest the stereotypes and victim mentality constructed by mainstream educational practices for working class children. They provide the beginnings of ways in which the power shifting and stereotypical reversals might begin. As they put it, 'students who never expected to be seen as smart, never expected to get a hearing from teachers or peers, are now opening their mouths, challenging myths and stereotypes and lines of vision [portrayed] as if 'natural,' or even worse, inherently correct' (p. 516). What they are arguing for are the 'social spaces for challenge' (p. 498) that in the end produce 'extraordinary conversations in public schools' (p. 497).

Thrupp (1999) also argues the need for teachers to 'reject the politics of polarization and blame . . . [and instead] building co-operative rather than competitive relationships' (p. 194). He says that teachers need to 'retain a balance between accepting powerful limitations on change and doing the best possible job' (p. 194). This might mean taking a courageous stand:

> They should not be afraid at times to make good use of the gulf between official policy and classroom practice in the service of their students. For instance, when schools are often being asked to impose inappropriate or damaging curriculum or assessment innovations, paying only lip service to what is required may be entirely justified. (p. 194)

The kind of turn around necessary was nicely captured by Erickson (1987):

> The teacher tends to use clinical labels and to attribute internal traits to students (e.g., 'unmotivated') rather than seeing what is happening in terms of invisible cultural differences. Nor does the teacher see student behavior as interactionally generated—a dialectical relation in which the teacher is inadvertently co-producing with students the very behavior that he or she is taking as evidence of an individual characteristic of the student. Given the power difference between teacher and student, what could be seen as an interactional phenomenon to which teacher and student both contribute ends up institutionalized as an official diagnosis of student deficiency. (pp. 337–388)

But just before we move to address in somewhat more detail what a transformative pedagogy for young adolescents around the notion of middle schooling might look like, we first need to sketch out in a little more detail the broader cultural and ped-agogical geography of such a counter-hegemonic tendency—in other words, how middle class teachers might confront the *status quo* and expand their thinking, theorizing and practices in the ways they engage with 'other people's children' (Delpit, 1995) and how schooling might work for all children not just those from backgrounds of privilege.

It is about relationships

Educational researchers and policy-makers are belatedly coming to the realization that generations of teachers and students have known for a long time, that teach-ing is fundamentally about relationships. When schooling does not work for stu-dents, it is invariably because of a corrosion of, or inability to form, healthy and sustainable relationships. Healthy, respectful, trusting and caring relationships between teachers and students, students and other students, and between teachers and the wider community—are all absolutely crucial to successful student learning. Reading the plethora of reports that are appearing internationally on what is need-ed to reform schools you could be forgiven if you came away with the solid impres-sion that teaching was not about relationships at all. According to the policy pundits, it is about: accountability, high stakes testing, standards, benchmarks, league tables, performance indicators, school choice, value for money and interna-tional comparisons of best practice. Not a mention in here of the most crucial ingre-dient of all—a profound need for teachers and students to like and respect one another, or as one commentator delightfully puts it 'making healthy connections with students' (Deiro, 1996).

Obviously to try and canvass a topic as comprehensive and as complex as rela-tionships in teaching is beyond our scope here, and besides not much would be served by tracking over old territory except to say that some people 'still don't get it.' More importantly, we think it is more useful to have some discussion of what relationships mean sociologically in schools. That is to say, when the middle class institution of school meets working class students, what happens relationally speaking?

Willard Waller (1932) in his remarkable seminal work *Sociology of Teaching* probably comes closest to the essence of what schools are about when he described them as a 'despotism in a state of perilous equilibrium' (p. 10) and a 'meeting point of a large number of intertangled social relationships.' (p. 12)

It is a despotism threatened from within and exposed to regulation and inter-ference from without. It is a despotism capable of being overturned in a moment, exposed to the instant loss of its stability and its prestige. It is a despotism demanded by the community of parents, but specially limited by them as to the techniques it may use for the maintenance of a stable social order. It is a despotism resting upon children, at once the most tractable and the most unstable members of the community. (p. 10)

If teaching were as straightforward as a process of developing a set of interpersonal relationships, then the work would be a breeze; it is far from that, and a major impediment and hindrance is the wider context within which teaching has to be enacted. We are referring here in particular to the wider political context within which teaching is encased, and in which large number of teachers are engaged in daily struggles. It would be no exaggeration to say that current so-called 'reforms' to schools and the manipulation of teachers' work that have been engineered from outside of schools are deeply damaging schools, teachers and students.

A range of literature from the youth health areas are beginning to provide strong legitimation for teachers who place a high premium on creating and sustaining productive relationships with students. This literature from quasi-medical quarters refers to relationships and a bundle of other factors as being an indispensable part of teachers and schools providing affirmation to students. Without these strong affirming relationships with students, the likelihood of youth risk behavior increases considerably, including disengagement from school, alienation, disaffection, absenteeism, behavioral problems, eventual 'dropping out,' and a range of other anti-social out-of-school activities. The shorthand way of referring to this is in terms of 'relationships matter' (Klem & Connell, 2004, p. 262).

The pivotal importance of relationships was a recurring theme in our study. Barbara from Broadvale Community School explained how she came to the early realization that unless she could find a way of establishing genuine relationships with her students, any meaningful learning was going to be impossible.

RELATIONSHIPS ARE THE MOST IMPORTANT THING

I had a bunch of kids in my history class who were just ghastly; they were *awful* and I really didn't know what to do and I was at my wits' end with them. Then I said to two of the really tough kids one day: 'Do you do any babysitting?' and they said: 'What! Us!,' and I said 'Yeah.' Anyway, they came around and looked after my kids and after that they'd sort of rock up on the weekend with various boyfriends and take the girls out to a park. But the whole attitude of the class sort of changed toward me because they saw me as someone who gave them a chance to show that they could be responsible. So when I left the school at the end of that year, they gave me a gold bracelet that they'd all saved up for and that was really, really touching, with the name of the class engraved on the back of it. . . . Relationships are the most important thing about middle schooling. You can't teach kids unless you've got some idea of who they are as people.

(Barbara, August 8, 2002)

We have abundant evidence to support Barbara's views in the writings of commentators like Klem and Connell (2004) who argue that positive and constructive relationships between teachers and students are a necessary precursor to learning. Their position is worth quoting at some length:

> An emerging consensus exists in the school reform literature about what conditions contribute to student success. Conditions include high standards for academic learning and conduct, meaningful and engaging pedagogy and curriculum, professional learning communities among staff, and personalized learning environments. Schools providing such supports are more likely to have students who are engaged in and connected to school.
>
> Professionals and parents readily understand the need for high standards and quality curriculum and pedagogy in school. Similarly, the concept of teachers working together as professionals to ensure student success is not an issue. But the urgency to provide a personalized learning environment for students—especially with schools struggling to provide textbooks to all students, hot meals, security, and janitorial services—is not as great in many quarters. While parents would prefer their children experience a caring school environment, does such an environment influence student academic performance? Research suggests it does. For students to take advantage of high expectations and more advanced curricula, they need support from the people with whom they interact in school.
>
> *Experience of support from teachers*
> First, students need to feel teachers are involved with them—that adults in school know and care about them. Students also need to feel they can make important decisions for themselves, and the work they are assigned has relevance to their present or future lives. Some researchers refer to this as autonomy support. Finally, while youth desire respect and the opportunity to make decisions, they also need a clear sense of structure within which to make those decisions. Young people need to know what adults expect regarding conduct, that consistent and predictable consequences result from not meeting those expectations, and that the expectations are fair.
>
> Studies show students with caring and supportive inter-personal relationships in school report more positive academic attitudes and values, and more satisfaction with school. These students also are more engaged academically. (Klem & Connell, 2004, p. 262)

Enabling conditions for learning

Drawing on these insights it is possible to summarize fairly succinctly an enabling set of learning conditions for all young people, but especially for those from disadvantaged or urban backgrounds:

- *High expectations* to students that they can succeed, expressed in terms of the confidence teachers have in the students.
- A *curriculum and pedagogy that are interesting* to students and engaging of their lives, that values what they bring to school, and which students can see as being relevant to their worlds and pathways in life.
- A learning environment that indicates that the school and its *teachers care* about them, and take an individual and personal interest in them.
- Circumstances that are *safe, devoid of fear, respectful, amenable to risk-taking,* and that provide extended opportunities for *joint decision-making by students* about their learning.
- A *consistent and set of structures* that are fair and within which learning can occur with predictable consequences.
- Teachers, administrators, parents and students who work together as a *professional learning community.*

It is not that these are an especially new or controversial set of ideas, at least not for teachers. Nor is it the case that teachers around the world are unaware of the primacy of this constellation of enabling conditions, or that they do not already exist in thousands of classrooms, for clearly they do. It is more the case that while these ideas make good intuitive and practical sense to teachers, they are not ones that are consistently or roundly endorsed in the policy regimes that have been raining in on classrooms around the world for the past three decades. What teachers have been forced to endure and comply with as a consequence of so-called reforms, bear no resemblance at all to even the minimalist conditions for good learning. It would be no exaggeration to say that most of the educational reforms that have been driven into schools in recent memory have been more concerned with controlling teaching, narrowing teaching to reductionist terms, managing (and manipulating) teachers' performance, compelling schools and teachers to artificially compete against one another, and engaging in meaningless and endless charades of measurement and calibration. How these imperatives impact on teachers, how teachers perceive and experience their work, and how this manifests in the way they work with young adolescents, will be addressed shortly in terms of 'confidence, trust and respect' (Willie, 2000, p. 255).

Learning as an engaging activity

For the moment, and from the vantage point of teachers and students, relationships are played out in schools in a multiplicity of ways through a complex web captured by various research literatures and labeled as contributing to the concept of 'student engagement.' Student engagement is something of a slippery term made all the more complex by its adoption as the latest policy fad word in education. Over a decade ago Newmann (1992) attempted to put some clarity around it in these terms:

> We define student engagement in academic work as the student's psychological invest-
> ment in and effort directed towards learning, understanding, or mastering the knowl-
> edge, skills, or crafts that academic work is intended to promote. (p. 12)

Newmann offers a number of caveats that needs to accompany the term student engagement, many of which get lost in translation in more recent usage of this term.

First, it involves an 'investment in learning' and to that extent it requires more than a 'commitment to complete assigned tasks or to acquire symbols of high performance such as grades or social approval' (p. 12). There is pause for reflection here as to what is, therefore, going on in current infatuations with achievement testing in its various forms. Second, students may complete tasks 'without being engaged in the mastery of a topic, skill or craft' (p. 12). In other words, students may (and do) invest much time and energy in 'performing rituals, procedures and routines without developing substantive understandings' (p. 12). Third, the investment and effort required to learn 'are not readily observable' and engagement refers to 'an inner quality of concentration and effort to learn' (p. 13). Fourth, engagement has to be 'estimated or inferred' from indicators like 'participation' (attendance, tasks completed, time spent on academic work), 'intensity of concentration,' the 'enthusiasm and interest expressed,' and the 'degree of care shown in completing work' (p. 13). Fifth, many of the activities students are required to be involved in during the course of a day are 'meaningless, mechanistic reproduction of knowledge, and trivial forms of learning' (p. 13) which do not involve critical capacities, creativity or in-depth understandings. Finally, because 'interest, effort and concentration' are highly dependent on particular circumstances, then the 'social context' (Newmann, 1992, p. 13) of learning is highly relevant.

The behavioral as well as the social, situational and affective nature of student engagement and the agentic role of students in it were well captured by Willms (2003):

> The construct of engagement generally includes an affective or feeling component per-
> taining to students' sense of belonging at school and how much students identify with
> and value schooling outcomes, and a behavioral component pertaining to students' par-
> ticipation in academic and non-academic activities. (p. 18)

This brings us back to our earlier point that students are active decision-makers in the extent to which they are prepared to involve themselves in negotiating and giving their assent to learning. In these circumstances, as San Antonio (2004) puts it, what is occurring is 'much more than a process of pernicious enculturation carried out by active agents (teachers) and imposed on passive recipients (students)' (p. 144). On the contrary, in many instances students are 'active agents of cultural transmission, passing on to their peers values, styles and ways of thinking, [and operating as] active resisters to enculturation that [is] in opposition to their lifestyles and values of their communities and families' (p. 144).

Negotiation and power sharing in learning was well put by Leanne, the principal of Plainsville as she discussed how this came about in her school, how she, her students and staff confronted the issue of how to do it, and what happened as a result. As we can discern from the following portrait, sharing power has to occur at several levels, and it can be a complex and multi-faceted activity.

HAVING POWER OVER THINGS . . .

A couple of years ago, one of the kids said to me, 'How are you going to make sure we're successful, because there's heaps of us here, and at some stage or other we are going to need to talk to each other. How will we know if we're successful?' And that's one of the places we started when we asked our kids, 'What enhances your learning? What detracts from it?' What came up under 'detract' all the time was what I would call lack of congruence and the kids said, 'You never bloody work out what you're supposed to do. You go to this teacher and they tell you that sitting down and putting your hand up is the right thing, but if you go to the next one, then it's "Have a good time," and then you go to the next one, and you just get it sorted out and it's the end of the year, and you've passed onto the next teacher. How do you ever know?' A lack of congruence was one of the big impetuses for thinking about: 'Well how do we create a place where kids don't feel like that?' It doesn't mean everyone is the same but that there are common beliefs, values and attitudes that underpin our behavior.

To begin with nobody felt they had power over anything. I mean, that wasn't what everyone was saying, but if you looked at people's behavior, teachers were hanging on really tight, families were really angry and kids were really angry. And if you looked at why, it was because none of them thought they had any power over anything and so they were all battling with each other to get it. Initially, we made a conscious decision not to look at empowerment within a classroom because we didn't want to push people's power buttons. My theory is you can either do the chipping away routine where you say to people, 'This bit needs to be changed and that bit needs to be changed' and you just keep chipping away; or you can do immersion which is to change the world around and so the world that they've got to live in is different and then they may see the need to make those changes for them-selves. We went with the second one and on reflection that was a good choice.

The second thing we did from the very beginning was to say that we were going to target all three groups so, no matter what change process we were going to enter into, we would always establish a student team, a staff team and a community team. The question we asked ourselves was: How many authentic decisions do children make in our school and in our classroom? That was really our starting point and we talked about the importance of an authentic decision. So we set up a whole range of teams in relation to looking at this question and one of the key ones was a team which looked at out-of-class learning. The end result was that that probably ended up with 25 out-of-class learning programs.

The success of these programs helped us to move onto the next stage. The kids said: 'We're making all these decisions outside of the classroom. How come we're not making any about learning?' So what I said to them was: 'You're being ripped off. The school told you that you could make decisions about bins, toilets and dis-cos. But you haven't made any decisions about what we're really on about;' and my challenge to them was, 'If the core business of our school is about learning, how come you're not making any decisions about that? Is it because you don't want to? Is it because you don't know how to? Is it because you haven't been allowed to?' and 'How are we going to change that?' And what it is, what I said to the kids was: 'Okay, so you keep talking about litter and bins and stuff. Is that the issue or is the issue really that the kids in the school don't value what we have and they don't respect the property?' You know like, let's stop dealing with the end result which is paper around the yard. If you really want to change things, let's look at why the rubbish is there. Let's find out what kids think about the school. Why do they throw stuff around, or why don't they care what it looks like? Is it that they don't care, you know?

And we did the same thing with the governing council; we invested a lot in them in terms of looking at the decisions they'd made. A major task the council under-took was to learn about the key competencies and then work out how to teach our community about it. They produced brochures; they developed workshops, which they ran here. I said, 'It's really good. Have you thought about offering it to other schools?' So they sent out the mail-out to run key competency workshops in other schools and they got business and went all over the state. For two terms we've been running these workshops with kids and parents, and it has had the most amazing impact. These are people who had never spoken in a meeting before, managed to stand up in front of a group of other parents and talk about key competencies. That had an amazing impact on our culture, you know. The next time we went to do something around student-initiated curriculum, fifty hands went up to be on the planning team.

Our kids have been all around Australia and some have even been overseas. All of that have changed families' perceptions of our school. They've seen us in the paper, on television, on the radio and it changed their belief in themselves. Instead of being, 'Oh, we're a crappy school ... it's like Plainsville has won all of these things and so that must mean you're actually a pretty okay community and we've got pretty okay kids.'

(Leanne, February 1, 2002)

What this portrait clearly conveys is the sense that student engagement does indeed have several levels to it, and that pursuing it is a process that requires persistence and a preparedness to learn along the way. But let us pursue this notion in a little more detail through a discussion of the following elements or features of a constellation that makes up student engagement:

- connectedness,
- care and respect,
- belongingness in 'active learning communities.'

Connectedness

In the United States, at the moment the situation of student disengagement from schools is attracting considerable national attention from the medical profession and, in particular, the US Center for Disease Control. Medical authorities are urging national action to 'combat the culture of detachment ... [in which] 40 percent to 60 percent of all students—urban, suburban and rural—are "chronically disengaged from school" ' (Public Education Network, September 17, 2004). The convener of the *Wingspread Declaration*, Robert Blum is reported to have said, 'Essentially, we're telling kids they're on their own, and while many of them succeed, many don't. This is not acceptable' (Public Education Network, September 17, 2004). As the *Wingspread Declaration* (2004) puts it:

Students are more likely to succeed when they feel connected to school. School connection is the belief by students that adults in the school care about their learning as well as about them as individuals. (p. 231)

To put this in some kind of context, what this evidence from the medical and adolescent health research literature is saying is that it is imperative young people make sustainable emotional ties to schools, not simply for future economic reasons as our politicians and business leaders keep reminding us, but making a healthy connection to school is crucial to the avoidance of extremely damaging and risky behavior. In other words, developing a 'positive orientation to school' (Libbey, 2004, p. 274) is seen as a key 'protective factor' in the lives of young people and is essential to their avoidance of 'health compromising behaviors' (Blum & Libbey, 2004, p. 231). In short:

> School connectedness refers to the belief by students that adults in the school care about their learning and about them as individuals . . . [And] when present [it] reduces the likelihood that young people will engage in health-compromising behaviors and concurrently increases the likelihood of academic success. In addition, recent research has shown that students who report high levels of school connectedness also report lower levels of emotional distress, violence, suicide attempts, and drug use. (Blum & Libbey, 2004, p. 231)

Libbey (2004) uses the term 'school bonding' in a similar way:

> Like school attachment, school bonding represents an umbrella term to encompass several aspects of a student's relationship to school. [We define] school bonding as the presence of attachment and commitment. Attachment represents an emotional link to school, while commitment reflects an investment in the group. (p. 274)

According to Catalano, Haggerty, Oesterle, Fleming & Hawkins (2004):

> Bonding to school represents an important area where bonding to positive adults can occur, and has shown to increase positive developmental experiences, decrease negative developmental experiences, and buffer the effects of risk. Thus, school bonding appears to promote healthy development and to prevent problem behaviors. (p. 252)

When students are provided with ways of seeing school as being relevant to their lives they develop the kind of affective relationship in which they are prepared to make an investment that produces engagement and then learning. The following extract from a portrait of Lauren at Gulfview illustrates how a teacher starts from student interests and then finds ways of making connections back to the required curriculum framework. It is not that this is a manipulative process but rather an acknowledgment that learning does have to occur within a public education system. It is about how to both divest responsibility to students while at the same time ensuring that the curriculum is being followed. Clearly this requires a high degree of reflection on the part of the teacher to ensure that they are discharging their dual responsibilities for a relevant as well as a rigorous curriculum.

HOW WE NEGOTIATE LEARNING

How do we negotiate? Well, we go through the process in which we get the kids to reflect on their concerns about themselves before looking at broader issues. I start off by getting the kids to think about it for themselves at home. I tell them, 'you need

to come up with half-a-dozen questions about yourself: things that you're really concerned about, that you think are important,' and then we get together and they work
with a partner that they're prepared to share that information with. We always tell
them that if there's something they've written down they don't want to share,
that's fine—there's no compulsion. They share with a partner and look for common-
ality. Then they get into a larger group of four to six and they do the same process.
Kids come up with great self-questions, like: What are my chances of being
employed in the future and what are my best choices that I could make at school?
What sorts of things can I do to improve myself? Are the things that I value respected in schools? Why do adults get more airtime than students? The whole sub-
school of five classes worked through this process. Beforehand, we did an in-service
with the whole staff and I then did a more intensive in-service with my own sub-
school. We talked about the reasons for negotiating curriculum and how you gath-
er and collate information to get a whole sub-school picture.

When we negotiate with the students we don't overlook the formal curriculum
requirements. What we do is look at the key things the kids want to cover and
match these against our curriculum framework. We ask ourselves, 'Okay, if we've
got eight areas of the curriculum, how can we incorporate their ideas into the content of what we're going to cover? How can we make sure that we address the
essential learnings and key competencies? What explicit skills do we need to teach
the kids?' So we then start looking at the subject areas. And we said, 'Okay, let's take
science. What sorts of things can we do? Well, we've got volcanoes, we've got earth-
quakes, we've got all of the seismographic scientific work.'

(Lauren, March 18, 1997; October 25, 2002)

As we mentioned in Chapter 4, Greg from Plainsville is at pains to make the
point that the curriculum should fit the child. For him, it is clearly a case of students' interests not necessarily being incompatible with a broad required curriculum framework—what it requires is an ability to be flexible on his part as a teacher,
to start from a different point in acknowledging the needs of his students and then
monitoring and mapping how what he and his students are doing fits with the
required curriculum.

There is also another much more sociological sense in which 'connectedness'
is important to young people in schools and it has to do with the way the school
operates to connect them to wider issues of social justice beyond the school. Another
way to put this is how the school works with students to enable them to understand
how things come to be the way they are in terms of power, and the forces operating to keep them that way. The more schools develop this kind of connectedness
(Zyngier, 2003) the further they move toward operating to promote healthy rela-

tions of civic justice, and as a consequence expose students to alternatives to individual consumption and self-centeredness.

Care and respect

There is something of a risk in the use of terms like 'care and respect' when speaking about schools in these tough economic times. These are nurturing-sounding words that are easily dismissed or pilloried by hard-nosed economic rationalists as being warm and fuzzy and therefore of no relevance at all in this cutthroat competitive era of standards, accountability, benchmarks and economic imperatives. As the Australian Federal Minister for Education, Brendan Nelson, is alleged to have said, and this might well be an echo of his political counterparts anywhere in the world at the moment:

> The only benchmarks that will count increasingly are international ones—and they are about standards. We have to drive national consistency on standards. The responsibility of the Government is to drive this agenda. (Grattan, 2005, p. 19)

Such strong words resonate at a certain level with elements of the corporate and business community, and some part of the electorate that understandably want reassurance in these insecure times. Fundamentally, they are an unhelpful and damaging commentary given the diversion they create from the complex and protracted nature of the real issues. The problem with such hairy-chested comments from politicians is that they are not designed to understand the problem at all but rather to convey a false impression of a tough 'can-do' mentality. 'Political spectacles' (Alexander, Anderson & Gallegos, 2005; Edelman, 1988; Smith with Miller-Kahn, Heinecke & Jarvis, 2004) of this kind serve the limited and symbolic purpose of conveying the misleading impression that politicians have a solid handle on the issue, a fallacy we will return to in more detail shortly.

The reality lies in quite a different quarter, one that is much more sophisticated and sociologically informed.

When schools do not work for young people or when schools present as places characterized by fear, intimidation or violence, then it is because of an absence of care and respect. Reviewing school violence in urban schools, where the circumstances are often at their most difficult for teachers, Gladden (2002) puts it like this: ' . . . schools that possess an engaging curriculum and operate as communities characterized by respectful and supportive relationships tend to be safer' (p. 276). What he is arguing for are 'attempts to increase students' attachment to school by modifying a school's curriculum' (p. 276). In other words, ' . . . making schools relevant, valuable, and personable will make them safe' (p. 276). Noguera (1995) agrees:

The urban schools that I know that feel safe to those who spend their time there don't have metal detectors or armed security guards, and their principals don't carry baseball bats. What these schools do have is a strong sense of community and collective responsibility. Such schools are seen by students as sacred territory, too special to be spoiled . . . and too important to risk ones' being excluded. (p. 207)

Hult (1979) speaks to this same issue in terms of 'pedagogical caring'—a deep and interpersonal concern and appreciation for the special uniqueness and circumstances of the person that involves 'overcoming obstacles and difficulties' (pp. 238–239; see also Wentzel, 1997; 1998). But, at the same time, this involves more than a concern for the individual. As Hult (1979) puts it, ' . . . that which is cared for may be an idea as well as a person or a plurality of ideas or persons' (p. 243). In short:

Pedagogical caring refers to the careful . . . manner or style by which a teacher operates. In doing his (sic) professional job with due care, the teacher demonstrates serious attention, concern, and regard for all his (sic) duties . . . even under conditions of adversity. (Hult, 1979, p. 243)

It could be argued that when a school fails to acknowledge or practically address the class, racial or ethnic background of its students, then it is acting in a grossly uncaring and disrespectful way. In other words, when the school as a social institution is oblivious to the unique circumstances of its students, families and communities it is seriously out of sync. In these circumstances there is moral responsibility upon the school to operate in ways that do not marginalize or exclude students because of their background. There is a requirement upon schools and teachers to recognize and attend to mismatches and to do that in ways that are caring, respectful and inclusive of students, families and communities.

Noguera (1995) provides some thoughtful comments from his experience of working in urban schools in which he found that:

. . . the adults don't really know who their students are. The sense of what children's lives are like outside of school is either distorted by images of pathological and dysfunctional families, or simply shrouded in ignorance. (p. 204)

In those circumstances where teachers do understand how to 'cross-borders' and 'negotiate' differences with their students, Noguera (1995) found that students attributed teachers' success in doing this to three things: 'firmness,' 'compassion,' and an 'interesting, engaging and challenging teaching style' (p. 205).

Essentially, what care and respect come down to in the end is adults being able to actively listen—that is to say, silently paying attention to young people when they or their lives speak. Or, put another way, being able to appreciate that there might be another perspective than the singular adult one. Young people have very direct ways of describing what an uncaring and disrespectful attitude by adults looks like. A young person interviewed by Intrator (2003) in his detailed study of a high school expressed the view that: 'Adults treat our generation as if we were infected meat' (p. 105). Another revealed her resentment at the way adults view teenagers as 'lazy, spoiled and materialistic,' and the media's equally simplistic portrayal: 'They think since we care about our clothes, care about music, and care about MTV that we are just bubbleheads, but what they don't do is listen to what we are saying. We care about important stuff. They call our music noise, but it's about important issues like freedom and race. We think about that stuff' (Intrator, 2003, p. 106).

Thoughtful and effective teachers have a profound understanding of the need to know and understand their students and of the uncompromising effect this can have on the quality of learning that is possible. Peter from Investigator puts it as follows.

YOU NEED TO KNOW THE KIDS

Good middle school teachers like the kids. They enjoy being there. They're prepared to be non-judgmental, not to see the stereotype role of the teacher as authority. Half of my students were on negotiated curriculum plans when I came here; three attract individual support and I have a group of girls who are real high fliers. I didn't know how it would all pan out, but it's a sense of wanting to get to know them and to work with them. I know it can sound like a warm fuzzy kind of approach but, as Ted Sizer says, 'I cannot teach a kid that I do not know well.' It's taking that thinking and making it a cornerstone of practice, not just an optional extra, that good teachers have. Middle schooling requires a different sort of practitioner. It's not like the old days of teachers as facilitators. It is much more to do with relationships. I have seen it in my own home group with truants who have suddenly turned that around. Teachers who are able to develop good relationships with their students get much more out of them. When you get a relief teacher, all hell is likely to break loose. Kids are at the stage in their development where their social skills aren't enormously successful. There are some tough kids in our sub-school that I can deal with. Once they know you they will improve dramatically both in terms of learning and socialization. Socialization is the first thing—they've got to want to be here. They have to respect the teacher; otherwise no learning takes place.

(Peter, September 6 and 9, 2000)

There should be no mistaking the absence in what has Peter said of anything even vaguely resembling the uncompromisingly harsh and head-kicking internationally economic competitive imperatives alluded to earlier. Tough punitive tactics of the corporate sector are nowhere to be seen in here. There is a fortunate absence of what Trammell (2005) notes as the folksy but instrumental language of big business, in his case of Exxon Mobil, of 'measuring and fixing, filling and drilling'—reference to what some in the corporate sector claim needs to be done to analyze and fix schools. Rather, what we have instead here is the levelheaded carefully considered judgment of an experienced teacher who knows that unless he carefully cultivates the atmospherics of 'confidence, trust and respect' (Willie, 2000) crucial in any civil society, then real learning is unlikely. Willie (2000) is worth invoking here to provide the contra-distinction to the prevailing impoverished political view:

> Confidence and trust are essential components of civil societies and social organizations. These two concepts are also very important in effective school communities. Confidence is what dominant people of power—teachers and parents—have for subdominant people of power such as children and students. Trust is what subdominant people have in dominant people of power. Effective teachers have confidence their students can learn and trusting students believe that their teachers will not betray them. Teachers cannot educate students in whom they have no confidence and students cannot learn from teachers they do not trust. These reciprocal beliefs when implemented together result in respect manifested in esteem for teachers by students and esteem for students by teachers. (p. 255)

Implicit in these comments by Peter above are some key insights as to how power works in schools and classroom contexts. Noblit (1993) has usefully attempted to move thinking beyond the outdated, simplistic, and unhelpful dualisms of 'teacher-centered' and 'student-centered' by arguing that 'a caring relationship [is not] an equal relationship' (p. 26). That is to say, 'caring in classrooms is not about democracy—it is about the ethical use of power' (p. 24) and student attachment that accompanies 'moral authority.' Viewed in this way, and it is contained in Peter's notion of mutual respect, classrooms become 'collectives' in which 'individuals are connected by responsibilities and obligations to the whole' (Noblit, 1993, p. 32).

Invoking Gilligan, Noblit says 'caring is context dependent and reciprocal' (p. 35). Construed in this way, if we think about what teachers do as exercising 'moral authority,' then what we are dealing with is 'reciprocal negotiation' (Noblit, 1993, p. 37)—the 'willingness [of the teacher] to take responsibility for children to participate in [their learning], and from children themselves who, after all can and often do deny adults the right to control them.' What 'socially constructed and legitimated' construals like this do, Noblit says, is shift us in the direction of an 'emphasis on collectivity,' something that is a helpful and promising correction to current high levels of 'rampant individualism' (p. 37). Peter captures the essence of this in his comment about teachers of young adolescents not being 'judgmental' and not seeing their role stereotypically in terms of 'teacher as authority.'

As mentioned earlier, teaching young adolescents is not simply a matter of being friendly with them or of superficially respecting their rights to a legitimate voice in their learning—it is certainly the latter, but it is also a lot more as well. Having respect, being empathetic, and having a caring attitude brings with it a preparedness to be courageous in experimenting with one's teaching, even 'pushing the boundaries', as Theresa at New Vista can attest. Theresa regarded it as central to her identity as a teacher of young adolescents to give her students the opportunities to experience new ways of learning, even when that brought with it criticism from one's colleagues. Going beyond the conventional ways of doing things and having students learn with and about their communities, could mean tackling what some might regard as controversial, even political topics.

PUSHING THE BOUNDARIES

I taught physics and maths for ten-and-a-half years in an outback town. I had a bit of a talent for working with difficult kids so if a teacher came along who wasn't as good at working with mixed groups of kids I'd tend to pick them up and run courses that were called maths and society and multi-strand science. I could work more flexibly with students than many of my colleagues. I was on all sorts of boards and I was always in trouble for pushing the boundaries. Yeah, I was 'that mad woman from the outback.' Instead of just doing more topics, I actually taught them about enquiry-based learning using the community. It wasn't just that they learnt how to learn from textbooks; they learnt how to frame their own projects, how to use members of the community, how to communicate and how to write reports. I was a bit of a greenie so we did a lot about water pollution, the use of fertilizers and overgrazing.

Two really important things for me are resilience and empathy. Caring for ourselves is a really important resilience tool and that's about being as successful as you can be and taking enough care of yourself to battle life's storms and to take responsibility for your own stuff. Caring for each other and caring for this world is about growing empathy. The kids are going to give the money from their recycling project to Amnesty International because this year is the International Year for the Rights of the Child with Amnesty. That's how they sold their campaign this year and they were talking about that just before the war against terrorism. I wanted the kids to have something powerful that they could do where they felt they were making a difference for children in other countries and standing up and saying, 'Well,

I don't think that children should bear arms and I don't think that children should be exploited for commercial gain.'

(Theresa, August 26, 2003)

Students are able to, and frequently do, speak eloquently to the importance of having a teacher with whom they can develop a relationship and who cares deeply about their educational journey. Indeed, the absence of such a relationship is frequently a harbinger of difficulties for students.

Lucy, a veteran teacher at Seachange spoke of the personal struggle she had in striking a balance between mastery of content material and the importance of getting to know her students. It was as if having a good relationship with students was like having a reserve of goodwill to be drawn upon in difficult times—a point also made by Mark at Plainsville. Behind Lucy's comment, at least in part, seems to be a view that says rapport is so important that to pass students on to another teacher at the end of the year is to run the significant risk of setting these students back markedly—and she says this acknowledging the difficulty she had in getting relationships in a sound footing. According to experienced practitioners like Lucy having good relationships with young adolescents seems to be a crucial precursor to even minimal formal learning, yet it is hard to see where such crucial ingredients feature on the calibrating mechanisms of the benchmarking, standards and accountability-driven ways politicians would have schools organized and enacted. These two worlds appear totally incommensurate, and it would seem that the only way for the Lucy's of the classroom world is learning 'to teach below the radar' (Romano & Glascock, 2002, p. 19). As these commentators put it, when teaching working class children and youth this involves beginning by:

> . . . understanding that ours is both a political and an intellectual project. The work we do in our classrooms is not neutral or value-less. What we do, how we do it, and why we do it is full of values and politics. (p. 18)

While it certainly goes against the political grain of producing compliant students able to fill the metaphorical equivalent of the Exxon Mobil 'skills pipeline' (Trammell, 2005), for teachers like Lucy teaching young adolescents involves:

> . . . [developing an ability] to negotiate difference, to develop a tolerance for ambiguity and complexity, to learn to reflect upon what we [are] learning and mak[e] sense of conflicting positions, and in the process to become critical knowledge producers (p. 19). [Such teachers] . . . help students develop the capacity to question ideas, construct meaning, and think critically about their society . . . [and in the process develop a] robust curriculum instead of anemic lessons of fragmented skills. (Romano & Glascock, 2002, p. 21)

Here is the way Lucy puts it as follows.

I FEEL LIKE I'M JUST A MOTHER TO THESE KIDS

The struggle is probably more of a reflection on me, given that I graduated a million years ago with a Bachelor of Arts and a Diploma of Education with such wonderful topics as Icelandic Sagas and Scott Fitzgerald. The struggle for me has been the whole debate about expertise. I have many days where I feel like I am a millimeter in front of the kids in terms of what I know . . . I just think getting to know kids really, really well and having relationships with them, as well as teaching whatever you have to teach them, is just crucial for this age. I know there are days when I could scream at every single child in my year 8 class, but I can still walk out of there and know that the next time I see them they'll say, 'Hello, how are you?' and we'll actually have some kind of rapport. Sometimes I feel like I am just a mother the whole time with these kids, you know. I'm just a mother that tells them off and the next minute I'm looking at their sore finger or whatever. But I feel that is very important and even though I find them incredibly hard work, I know already I would like to take them through next year because of that rapport I've got with them. I know that if somebody else picks them up they're going to be back to square one just trying to create some rapport before you can even think about getting any work out of them. My boys have gone up to the primary school and run skate board competitions and kept journals and had to write letters and do all those kinds of things. It's worth it even if you have to mop up because so-and-so swore on the microphone and the neighbors over the road heard it and complained to the primary school.

(Lucy, October 14, 2003)

Belongingness in 'active learning communities'[2]

> There is a growing consensus that academic motivation is not a purely individual, intrapsychic state; rather, it grows out of a complex web of social and personal relationships. As Weiner (1990) stated 'school motivation cannot be understood apart from the social fabric in which it is embedded.' (Goodenow & Grady, 1993, p. 60)

Whether students become engaged in and eventually succeed at school is increasingly being shown to relate to the extent to which they develop a sense of affiliation to school. This is particularly so for students from disadvantaged or marginalized backgrounds. In his study of 'withdrawing from school,' Finn (1989) found that early school leavers had low levels of identification; that is to say, they experienced difficulty in developing positive qualities like 'affiliation,' 'involve-ment,' 'attachment' and 'commitment' to schooling, displaying instead negative qualities of 'alienation,' 'powerlessness,' 'social isolation' and 'cultural estrangement.' The more positive notion of identification with school has two components:

> First, students who identify with school have an internalized conception of belonging-ness—that they are discernibly part of the school environment and that the school con-stitutes an important part of their experience. And second, these individuals value success in school-relevant goals. (Finn, 1989, p. 123)

The significance of what is being alluded to here should not be lost or under-estimated. In a study of mostly African American and Hispanic high school stu-dents, Goodenow and Grady (1993) concluded that 'Many urban adolescents have a poor sense of belonging and low school motivation . . . [and] students who do have a high sense of belonging in school are also more likely to be motivated and engaged . . . ' (p. 67).

What is being highlighted is the profoundly important role that schools and teachers can play in the way they embrace, accept, cultivate and work with students particularly those from disadvantaged backgrounds. Creating circumstances with-in schools that break down the individualistic, competitive, adversarial and inhos-pitable way in which some schools relate to students from non-middle class backgrounds, remains one of the most significant challenges confronting contem-porary high schools worldwide. Again Finn (1989) is quite insightful in identify-ing practices and policies that help to minimize negative student attitudes toward school and promote active participation and involvement. At the classroom level he cites 'positive teacher attitudes [towards students] regarding the potential for suc-cess . . . teaching practices that involve students in the learning process . . . a diver-sified curriculum with objectives that are relevant to the need of these students and that are neither too easy nor too difficult to master . . .' (Finn, 1989, p. 137). At the whole-school level he drew attention to the value of 'smaller schools [and group-ings] of students . . . flexible school rules that don't alienate students and discipli-nary procedures that are seen as fair and effective . . . an evaluation and reward structure that is compatible with the abilities of the students . . . positions of responsibility for students, i.e. participation in decision making' (Finn, 1989, p. 137).

From our research in the six Australian case study schools, there was a high level of consistency between what teachers were saying to us and the findings of research by Finn (1989) and others. Respect, trust, relationships and pedagogy were the key themes teachers identified in terms of how they had re-thought and reinvented their practices to foster belongingness toward a school culture that was more inclusive of young adolescents. To elaborate a little on these themes, teachers explained that respect involved:

- conveying the sense that you genuinely like students;
- showing a real interest in students' lives and respect for their families and communities;
- avoiding labeling or categorizing students in universalistic ways;
- being mindful of the obstacles and impediments many students bring with them to school and not be judgmental about these;
- understanding students' desire not to be singled out among peers;
- working with students in ways that are fair and consistent in treatment.

Developing trust meant they had to:

- get to know students as individuals;
- view students as having serious intentions to learn, while 'having fun;'
- regard them as being curious about their histories and communities;
- acknowledge students as having a well-developed sense of fairness and justice.

On the issue of relationships teachers spoke of the need to:

- spend the time allowing students to get to know teachers and one another;
- convey high expectations to students about their capacity to learn;
- construct rules and polices with students, rather impose rules/policies on them;
- pursue positive relationships rather than negative stereotypes;
- avoid interpersonal comparisons between students.

Finally, in terms of the pedagogical aspects of their work, teachers spoke of:

- acknowledging students' need for social affiliation particularly through participative forms of learning;
- teaching in ways that brought students' lives into the curriculum;
- endorsing the multiple ways in which students learn;
- providing ways for students to learn from each other;
- assessing student learning in ways that acknowledge success and growth;
- working with students to provide choices so they understand the consequences of choices they make;
- taking the focus off trivial issues like school uniforms that magnify conflict.

What these teachers were telling us about the traits needed to engage with young adolescents was remarkably congruent with what students also told us about the qualities of a 'good' teacher in the closing phases of Chapter 3.

A way of thinking about how these ideas come together for teachers of young adolescents, as well as for young people themselves, is to think in terms of a cultural analysis of the nature of teaching. In other words, what needs to be made prominent is belongingness within a culture of teaching. It is only when we examine teaching in these terms that we begin to access the underlying issues. This is a long-standing matter that goes back to at least Waller (1932) if not earlier, and it is not our intent to review the voluminous literature around that topic. However, we do wish to invoke Labaree (2000), who argues that there are at least five key elements all of which have to do with social control in schools: client cooperation, compulsory clientele, emotion management, structural isolation and climate of chronic uncertainty about effectiveness.

According to Labaree (2000), the problem of *client cooperation* has important implications for teachers in ensuring students' willingness to learn. Invoking Dewey (1933), he says the reciprocal relationship in teaching is analogous to selling and buying goods in which buyers have to be prepared to buy what is on offer; likewise in teaching, 'you can't be a good teacher unless someone is learning' (p. 228). Cooperation is further complicated through the school's demand for compliance from its *compulsory clientele*, in part a legal requirement, but also through parental pressure on their offspring to 'get an education.' Where this becomes problematic Labaree says is that 'given a choice, students would be doing something other than studying' (p. 229). As Waller (1932) puts it:

> The teacher–pupil relationship is a form of institutionalized dominance and subordination . . . The teacher represents the formal curriculum, and his [sic] interest is in imposing that curriculum upon the children in the form of tasks; pupils are much more interested in their own world than the desiccated bits of adult life teachers have to offer. (pp. 195–196)

Where this leaves us according to Labaree, is in a situation where 'control [is] the central problem facing the teacher' (p. 229). Where it is simply a matter of requiring compliance and cooperation, then teaching would be a relatively straightforward activity, but teachers are required to primarily 'establish and actively manage an emotional relationship with students' (p. 228):

> Teachers need to develop a broad relationship with students for the purpose of understanding their learning problems . . . They also need to establish an emotional link to motivate their students to participate actively in the learning process. (Labaree, 2000, p. 229)

This *emotion management* has to occur in a situation where 'there is no guidebook on how to accomplish [such relationships and in which beginners have to] . . . work things out on their own [and] . . . fumble around for a way in which to establish emotional links with students that is effective and sustainable' (p. 230).

When teachers opt for emotional distancing or detachment, then their problems become exacerbated. Teaching as an activity is predicated on the contradictory requirement of 'emotional closeness,' which in turn has to be used to exercise 'leverage' for other secondary purposes, like—rewarding student performance, ensuring students develop skills of independence, and applying universalistic rules consistently and humanely:

> To be really good at teaching requires a remarkable capacity for preserving a creative tension between these opposites, never losing sight of either teaching's relational means or its curricular goal. (Labaree, 2000, p. 230)

Another of the unique elements of teaching according to Labaree (2000) is its *structural isolation*—'the four walls of the self-contained classroom' with the teacher operating largely alone, trying to figure out how best to manage 30 or more students 'and move them through the required curriculum' (p. 230). There are tangible consequences to teaching being a largely 'private ordeal' (Lortie, 1975) in which the teacher is 'self-made' (Britzman, 1986), the most notable of which is that:

> . . . the teacher must turn the classroom into a personal fiefdom, a little dutchy complete with its own set of rules and its own local customs . . . This leaves little room for the construction of a shared professional culture for teachers . . . (p. 230)

Finally, this happens within a *climate of chronic uncertainty* about the effectiveness of teaching, due in part to unpredictable emotions being at 'the heart of teaching and learning processes' (Labaree, 2000, p. 231). This uncertainty is magnified by several factors: (1) the 'irreducible complexity' of teaching; (2) the multitude of 'intervening variables that mediate between a teacher's actions and a student's response;' (3) our 'inability to measure adequately the effects that teachers have on students;' (4) a lack of clarity as to purposes—'preparing competent citizens,' 'preparing productive workers,' or 'preparing individuals who can compete successfully for social goods;' and (5) confusion over client identity—'the student,' 'the parents,' or 'the community at large' (p. 231).

These are a particularly robust set of professional characteristics of teaching, but they also make teaching extremely resilient to even the most muscular of school reform regimes. Notwithstanding, they are a set of features that teachers are continually mindful of as they struggle to reinvent their identities and practices as they work with young adolescents in difficult times.

Fostering belongingness and a culture of inclusion is, therefore, a fine ideal but it has major political and practical challenge for schools and teachers in a society increasingly marked out by material inequalities, and various forms of social and cultural exclusion. Belongingness seems to come into existence when schools place the notion of being an 'active learning community' at the center of what they do. However, this is becoming harder and harder to sustain in an era in which many schools are struggling with issues of growing inequity and disadvantage. In many respects, disciplinary policies of containment and zero tolerance appear to be positioning many schools in ways that present them as being more like prisons. Delpit and White-Bradley (2003) described this in terms of 'an imprisoning of the spirit' in which 'the scripted nature of many mandated instructional and "management" programs . . . [are having] . . . dehumanizing effect[s] on the ways teachers and students interact, and the resentment [these] instill in the children they are supposed to benefit' (p. 283). They argue that: 'The effect of such reductionism on the work we do in schools is mind-boggling' (p. 283).

To obtain an understanding of what this means, we have to listen to the voices of students, and Intrator (2003, p. 98) provides us with an insight on what this looked like in his research in the US high school:

> At Stanton High maintaining order and discipline is important. Its wide hallways are designed to accommodate the flow of students and enable a quick scan for whoever is out of place. Students need passes to be in the hallway. Stanton prides itself in the decorum of its campus. The year of my research the administration handed down controversial new rules cordoning off the parking lot during school hours. The policy infuriated many students. [One] said, 'They treat us like we are fucking prisoners. I keep my books in my car. What the hell, do they think I'm going to go smoke a bong between Chemistry and English? It's like we have no freedom and no trust.'
>
> People don't listen to us at school. Teachers talk at us or down to us. [From another]: 'School's a jail for the most part, and we just clang our tin cups against the bars and nobody listens, nobody hears, or cares to hear what we have to say. I mean that's why I like work [referring to her job at a Department store]. They ask me questions and they want to hear my answers. Here nobody listens to me, or anybody else. It sucks.' (Intrator, 2003, pp. 90–91)

The notion of the school as an active community of learners struggling with many of these issues is alive and thriving in some quarters (e.g., Plainsville), and to that extent is a useful category within which to pursue belongingness. However, as with many ideals in education there is often a big gap between aspiration and reality. In what follows, we want to provide a window on the notions of inclusion and exclusion through the voices of teachers in one of our case study schools, Broadvale Community School. We think the ironies, the contradictions, the hostilities, the dilemmas and tensions are extremely poignant.

Technologies of inclusion and exclusion: insights from Broadvale Community School

As described in the school portrait in Chapter 2, Broadvale is a culturally diverse, working class community with a high level of poverty and youth unemployment, welfare dependency and social dislocation. A teacher explained that deficit views about the students, their families and the community were a major concern for the school:

[Our] school and the region suffer from a negative image—parents don't own up to a Broadvale address. They want their kids to succeed and to be working but they don't know how to provide the conditions. (Barbara, August 8, 2002)

According to the principal, the school had invested a lot of efforts and resources in trying to change these perceptions and to address concerns about school attendance, literacy, social living and transition to the workforce:

The broad [priorities] are really just around kids being successful at school and about how are we going to increase the engagement and the achievement of these kids so that they can actually make a successful transition from school . . . to work, further training, or whatever. The kids who are not making a successful transition usually have a checkered history of schooling. They have issues around literacy, numeracy and their social development. Often they'll have issues around their family and the relationships within that family. All of those things come to play here at the school. That's what probably makes the work of the school most challenging because teachers are dealing with not only the academic achievement, but also the social development and the welfare of many of the kids that they are working with. (Garfield, April 4, 2003)

At first glance, a commitment to inclusivity and belongingness was quite apparent at Broadvale. The school's motto 'Success for All' stood out boldly on the welcome sign and weekly newsletters gave glowing accounts of individual and group achievement in sporting, cultural and artistic events. It occupied a prominent place in the school's priorities:

Our core purpose is quality learning and teaching R–12 in a supportive, harassment free environment where success and achievement for all is our focus. Our learning and teaching programs are underpinned by collaborative work that: values and builds on student–teacher relationships; ensures equity and social justice in all our actions; has high expectations for student participation and achievement; values and is inclusive of the range and diversity of cultural groups; and, maintains a strong commitment to accountability, innovation and improvement. (School Context Statement, p. 2)

There were tangible signs that this motto was being put into practice. In years 7 and 8, small teams of teachers were responsible for the welfare and instruction of home classes which were restricted to 25 students. Success and achievements were celebrated in student-run middle school assemblies, and an annual 'success trip' funded by the school was the ultimate reward for students who went the extra yard in terms of effort and commitment. A pastoral care program, aimed at developing positive relationships, and social and communication skills, operated across the school in the form of a 40-minute extended home group sessions.

Health and safety issues were taken very seriously. The school had developed and implemented an anti-bullying and harassment policy with clearly defined referral steps for redressing grievances. This policy was complemented by preventative strategies including anger management programs and peer mediation workshops. STudents At Risk (STAR) programs incorporated literacy and numeracy skills workshops, cross-age tutoring and a peer support scheme. Concerned about mental health issues and harassment, the school became involved in Mind Matters, a federally funded project aimed at reducing teenage suicide and promoting mental health (Commonwealth of Australia, 2000). Whole-school closure days and staff meetings were set aside to develop a whole-school approach to enhancing resiliency and building positive relationships through a reinvigorated pastoral care program. There were structures and programs to address the needs of particular groups of students. Indigenous students, for example, had access to an Aboriginal Education Teacher (AET) and an Aboriginal Education Worker (AEW). Special education teachers and English as a Second Language (ESL) support staff operated from R–12. Broadvale's efforts to reduce the incidence of racism and violence involved the appointment of a Khymer-speaking education worker who acted as an advocate, counselor and ESL support person for Cambodian students. Hien was particularly successful in mediating relationships between school and home and helped to significantly reduce the level of school violence.

Technologies of exclusion: 'we've become tougher on kids'

In spite of initiatives, many teachers felt that much more could be done to create a more inclusive school. Speaking about the complexity of the task, the principal exclaimed somewhat ruefully, 'I'm looking for a silver bullet, you know, looking for the magical cure and there isn't any quick-fix solution.' (Garfield, April 4, 2003)

It was also quite apparent that the technologies of exclusion typically associated with high schools were alive and well at Broadvale. Claudia, a special needs coordinator, claimed that the school had lost some its working class connection and was 'moving much more towards a middle class model' with an emphasis on dress code compliance and discipline. 'We've become tougher on kids,' she exclaimed and went on to state:

> [There's] a lot less focus on social justice, which I think, is a problem . . . there's a lot
> more cut-and-dry, 'This is the way. If you don't do that, then we kick you out' . . . I feel
> that I need to advocate for special needs kids—and not, that doesn't mean go soft on
> them, like maintain, these *are* the rules and these are the ways you have to act to be in
> society, but at the same time, to look at the big picture. (Claudia, March 3, 2003)

As an advocate for students on Negotiated Education Plans (NEPs), she was alarmed that mainstream teachers were not always willing to accept responsibility for these students and were inclined to push them into special education classes. She claimed that academic learning had precedence over social learning and that the arts, despite its popularity with students, occupied a low position in faculty hierarchies.

This gap between rhetoric and reality was particularly apparent in the school's assessment and reporting system which incorporated grades, marks and competitive practices which tended to reinforce a sense of failure for many students. Julie-Anne, a middle school teacher, expressed her frustration as follows:

> It's awful. We've gone from portfolios . . . to giving a score out of twenty . . . and a comment which tells you absolutely nothing about the child's learning and has nothing to do with kids. (Julie-Anne, March 3, 2003)

Sorting and streaming practices still prevailed in mathematics where students in some year levels were categorized as advanced, remedial or gifted. Although the school had endeavored to broaden the scope of student and parent participation in decision-making forums, several teachers pointed out that student voice was still in its infancy. In her efforts to encourage student involvement in the Student Representative Council (SRC), Barbara said she encountered both staff indifference and 'a self-destructive culture' in the student body:

> Kids have a really negative view of [participation] so that the kids that are in any kind of student voice things are considered to be nerds. I said to one of the boys who was actively involved in the SRC 'What do you reckon we get little badges that have got SRC on them?'—and he said, 'You're kidding, Miss. I'd get my head kicked in if I wore one of those.' So it's actually about changing an ethos [that says] 'Don't work any harder than you need to; like do enough so that you don't get in strife but don't do so much so you get alienated, and certainly don't get involved—it's not cool.' (Barbara, March 25, 2003)

It is not surprising that young adolescents should feel more comfortable being an unidentifiable part of a group rather than being singled out as individuals with some special status. However, the negative work ethos described by Barbara reinforced educational disadvantage. Like the working class boys in *Learning to Labour* (Willis, 1977), Broadvale students engaged in acts of resistance or passive behaviors that ultimately undermined the potential of schooling to transform their lives.

How do we account for the difficulties and frustrations experienced by these teachers in their considerable efforts to foster belongingness and inclusive practices? What stands in the way of more socially just curriculum? While it may be tempting to locate the blame for these failures within the organizational structures and culture of the school itself, we want to theorize more broadly about technologies of inclusion and exclusion in the contemporary educational policy environment. Our social analysis is informed by Foucault's understandings of the ways in which teacher and student subjectivities are regulated by discourses of power and control that undermine social inclusion agendas in schooling.

Foucault and the regulation of the subject

Policies and practices of inclusion and exclusion are generated within a policy context that has a profound effect on schools. According to Fenwick (2003), education in neo-liberal times is framed within a policy discourse that 'promotes the production of human capital and vocational skills' (p. 336) and accords primacy to individual capacity rather than the public good. Foucault (1977) claims that power is embedded in people's everyday activities and that individual subjects are constructed through 'technologies' that make them an object of knowledge (Fenwick, 2003). Practices like school behavior management can be used to naturalize consent to surveillance and, in the process, reinforce technical conceptions of teachers as implementers of mandated policies.

Foucault's (1977) notion of disciplinary powers is particularly helpful in understanding the ways in which social control operates through the institutional structures and processes of schooling. Lefstein (2002) claims that disciplinary technologies aim to create 'docile bodies' (Foucault, 1977) in four significant ways. Firstly, students in traditional schools are separated from the outside world and partitioned into manageable groups so as to minimize communication among students and maximize surveillance by teachers. Secondly, students' daily life is carefully regulated through routines and procedures that allow for little idle time. Teachers direct the pace and order of student activities. A timetable prescribes when children can eat, when they can play, when they come in and out of classrooms, when they can leave school grounds, and when and what they study. Arbitrary divisions of the school day are reinforced by various message systems, such as school sirens or bells, diaries and calendars. Thirdly, surveillance techniques enable teachers to continually observe students and for principals to observe teachers, the panoptic gaze. In a somewhat unusual but disturbing case, it was reported in Australia recently that a principal has used a 'spy camera' intended to protect the school's computers against theft and vandalism, to 'scrutinize a teacher suspected of underperforming' (Tomazin & Rood, 2005, p. 9), and who was later fired from her job. The action of the principal was officially endorsed. Fourthly, schools set up normative expectations for student behavior and achievement. Teachers engage in testing and examination processes that allow judgments to be made in relation to these norms. Good students are rewarded and bad students punished. Demotion, exclusion, detention and other disciplinary measures help to reinforce these norms and send messages to students that they are a natural consequence of their own actions. More importantly, power is not simply exercised by teachers but is embedded in 'the minute details of spatial, temporal and organizational arrangements' of schools (Lefstein, 2002, p. 1631). Teachers can fall back on institutional sanctions, policies and traditions to back their own judgment: for example, they can use examination grades as the basis for failing students and keeping them back. Reporting practices often involve normative judgments that consign students to good and bad categories, at worst they become payback systems. Although these disciplinary technologies are a legacy of nineteenth century, many still persist in schools today.

Exclusionary structures

Disciplinary technologies reinforce the practices of exclusion that are writ large in the lives of many students. Lacking the social capital of middle class students, many indigenous/working class students experience the 'deepening divide' (Gilbert, 2000) of an education system which favors the rich and powerful through the maintenance of a hegemonic curriculum (Connell, 1993), inflexible pedagogical practices and discriminatory testing regimes. This is most evident in high schools which are notorious for the way hierarchical relations of power operate through a curriculum that is skewed toward university and college.

For their part, teachers occupy a contradictory position when it comes to addressing these inequalities. On the one hand, they serve as a consistent source of emotional and social support for students, but they are also obligated to act as gatekeepers for institutional norms and practices, to distribute rewards and punishments in line with school policies, and to implement competitive assessment and reporting practices that often work against the interests of the most marginalized students. As the teachers are subjected to bureaucratic policies, procedures and normative practices, they are often more preoccupied with issues of administrative efficiency than they are with the development of personal and educative relationships. The problem is exacerbated by organizational structures that restrict the time that supportive teachers spend with students, large class sizes and a lack of professional development opportunities, inadequate counseling services and an absence of pastoral care programs. The upshot is that 'relationships remain superficial, transitory, and interwoven with . . . hierarchical and power and institutionalized inequality' (Stanton-Salazar, 1997, p. 19). These tensions and dilemmas are particularly apparent in the implementation of student behavior management policies.

School behavior management: the politics of crisis management

From the late 1980s education departments in all Australian states and territories introduced comprehensive behavior management codes and guidelines for government schools. Although most guidelines acknowledge the need for inclusive and participatory curriculum, surveillance and control has been extended by 'a range of psychological and management discourses and regulatory practices' (Slee, 1995, p. 164). One of the effects of this behaviorist orientation is to shift attention away from deficiencies in school organization and pedagogy to the 'deviant' behaviors of individual students. In other words, the student rather than the school is the problem.

Although school-based responses to violence, disruptive behaviors and various forms of harassment usually involve a range of preventive strategies (e.g., anger management, conflict resolution, peer support and pastoral care programs), the use of in-school detention, suspension and exclusion measures has become widespread. Moreover, there can be little doubt that schools and teachers are under increasing pressure from politicians, parent groups and the public at large to punish disruptive kids who would not toe the line. Responding to 'the politics of crisis management' (Slee, 1995, p. 117), there has been a growing tendency to criminalize youth misdemeanors and to import, in a largely uncritical manner, criminal justice strategies based on notions of zero tolerance. Perhaps this new approach is best captured in the widespread adoption of an American baseball metaphor, 'three strikes and you're out,' as the cornerstone of discipline policies in schools. Typically, three detentions result in a period of suspension and three suspensions result in exclusion. In spite of evidence that these 'quick-fix' solutions do not work (Cameron & Thorsborne, 2001; Gladden, 2002), many educators believe that punishment is an effective deterrent and a necessary means of ensuring compliance and control.

In a recent study of the experiences of early school leavers we (Smyth & Hattam et al., 2004) found the damaging impact of inflexible and vengeful disciplinary measures on young adolescents' lives. Students suspended and/or excluded from school are often pushed over the brink when it comes to leaving school before successfully completing post-compulsory requirements. There is a sociological dimension to this problem. Research from the United States (Gladden, 2002) and United Kingdom (Blair, 2001) shows that minority students and those with disabilities are disproportionately represented in statistics of school exclusion. In addition, students suspended for relatively minor infractions usually feel less connected to school and are more likely to engage in disrespectful and uncooperative behavior that is counterproductive to their academic success. Slee (1995) maintains that policies that respond to the politics of the marketplace fail to give proper recognition to the political economy, the cultural dimensions of schooling and the individual circumstances of students' lives. In effect, they exacerbate the extent of disadvantage of the most vulnerable students in the school community.

It was apparent from our observations and conversations with teachers that a good deal of this discourse had infected policy and practices at Broadvale. However, as we point out in the following section, several teachers were railing against the most oppressive elements of the student behavior management guidelines.

Student behavior management at Broadvale Community School: 'three strikes and you're out'

We should point out that the discipline code at Broadvale was quite typical of many Australian secondary schools, including some other project schools, insofar as rules, behavior expectations and consequences of infringements, were made quite explicit. Minor infractions, such as non-compliance with the school's dress code and non-attendance in lessons, usually incurred lunchtime community service. Students could be sent to a withdrawal room for disruptive behavior in class, failure to follow instructions, indifference to schoolwork or harassment. Normally, they received three warnings, but if the matter were serious enough they could be sent there immediately or, in the case of acts of violence, face immediate suspension. Students who had been sent to the withdrawal room on three occasions normally faced a mandatory period of suspension from school and were required to go through a re-entry process with their parents or caregivers. Similarly, students who had been suspended on three occasions faced a period of expulsion, during which time the school and the system were required to maintain an educational program at another school or a special behavior management center. The expression 'three strikes and you're out was commonly invoked to describe this system.'

From our observations school discipline involved a huge investment in teachers' time and resources. A teacher explained that the work of the deputy principal, coordinators, assistant principals, counselors and teachers in supervising the withdrawal room, managing suspension, exclusion and re-entry processes, supporting teachers, patrolling corridors and out-of-bounds areas, and enforcing school rules amounted to the equivalent of 10 teachers' salaries. For their part, teachers were required to document instances of inappropriate behavior on a central file and to take action in accordance with the discipline procedures outlined above. The administrative complexity of these processes generated an enormous amount of paper work for the school leadership and home group teachers.

Most teachers recognized the need for a whole-school approach to discipline as a means of supporting colleagues 'so that they can get on with their core business' (Susan, March 4, 2003). Without clear and consistent guidelines, there was a view that effective teaching in a complex environment like Broadvale was impossible. However, there was a good deal of concern about the unfairness of procedures, the enormous amount of teachers' time and energy expended on surveillance and control mechanisms, and the displacement of curriculum. Some teachers went further in questioning the underlying philosophy of student behavior management. This concern was articulated most forcefully by middle school coordinators like Barbara, Sam and Claudia, who found themselves in a difficult position of having to balance the individual care and welfare of students with their institutional responsibilities for enforcing the norms and rules of the school. In what follows, we give some insight into the problematic aspects of the school's student behavior management policy at a time when it became a major agenda item in staff meetings.

We begin with a student counselor's reflections on the philosophy behind the policy:

> I have a frustration with our behavior management policy because I think it doesn't link in with a framework of positive relationships . . . we've got these punitive measures that if you do this, this will happen. Three strikes and you're out . . . I *don't* agree with it philosophically. I don't agree with the system. (Monica, March 19, 2003)

Citing an example of a student whom she had recently counseled, she went on to explain how minor infractions could lead to a period of suspension which could be quite damaging for those students who were already struggling at school:

> Unfortunately, she is the sort of kid who will get detention for being out of uniform, or hiding in the toilets. This will probably move to a suspension and eventually to exclusion and, if you look at originally, where it started, it was probably something related to not wearing the right pants. (Monica, March 19, 2003)

The three strikes policy was criticized by the Cambodian education worker for its harshness, inflexibility and failure to address the cultural dimensions of behavioral issues. Some of Hien's students had become caught in a disciplinary web of detention and suspension that eventually led to a period of school exclusion. He argued that the incidence of violence could be minimized through staff/student dialogs that promoted an understanding of the causes of violence and consideration of conflict resolution strategies.

I KNOW THESE KIDS. I TEACH THEM THE KHMER LANGUAGE

The problem with the young people here is they get into lots of fights and they're forming groups, and they don't know how to solve their own problems so they take their problems in their hands and how they solve their own problems is being angry. They do it with the physical action and things like that . . . And all these problems, the fighting, detention, withdrawal and the suspension, will probably lead to exclusion and things like that. I know all these kids. I used to teach them in the Khmer Ethnic School and I teach the Khmer language . . . I understand them and can communicate with them. I try not to persuade or push them to do things that they don't want to do, but to give them options and lead them, let them make their own decisions.

(Hien, March 3, 2003)

In a similar manner, Claudia drew our attention to the disproportionate number of special needs students punished under the current guidelines:

> When we used to have suspensions written on the board, you'd go up there and you'd have a look and probably half of the names are the kids on negotiated education programs because of course they find it *so* difficult to tap into the curriculum. Their only real way of saving face is either by sort of pulling heads in and doing nothing or, particularly the boys will muck up. (Claudia, March 3, 2003)

Claudia's comments about curriculum relevance and resistant behaviors highlight 'the unproblematic acceptance of indiscipline as a student-centered problem' (Slee, 1995, p. 1), rather than a curriculum issue. This emerged quite strongly in a conversation with Sam:

> The problem with behavior management systems is that first of all they're external; secondly, they work from the teachers' point of view . . . 'You will change your behavior,' just like that. 'When you come back from withdrawal, you're going to be a different person.' Now we know in fact that it takes 27 to 29 times of consecutive operation of the changed behavior, *perfectly*, for it to even hold in that person's system. (Sam, April 2, 2003)

Having undertaken a professional development course in this area, Sam questioned the value of a policy where the locus of change rested squarely with students who were expected to modify their behavior in accordance with school rules and norms.

As an assistant principal, Susan felt that her curriculum role was undermined by her responsibilities for student discipline in a system that was too concerned with compliance and control:

> There's *much* more focus on . . . get your school uniform right, get your behavior management right, get all those other things right and curriculum is not getting much of a look-in. (Susan, March 4, 2003)

Echoing these concerns, Monica spoke of a preoccupation with crisis management to the neglect of student participation and more enduring strategies for addressing student alienation and indifference to learning:

> I think we spend a lot of time running around in circles having to fix a situation or a problem with a kid [and] we don't actually have the time to institute some of these things like student voice. (Monica, March 19, 2003)

Despite the existence of explicit behavior management guidelines, it seems that some teachers were able to circumvent or at least minimize the most damaging consequences of suspension and exclusion practices. Sam's non-compliant stance was quite evident in a middle school meeting when he categorically refused to exclude a student, despite recommendations from the school administration. He claimed that the boy was 'basically a good kid with a shithouse home life' and said that he had spent an hour with him on values, goals and behavior. Supporting Sam's course of action, Monica said the student had no power in his life and needed opportunities to participate in school activities and take on positions of responsibility. We also heard of instances where teachers went out on a limb for their students in giving them more than three chances, overlooking minor infringements—especially in situations where students were dealing with some crisis in their lives and negotiating more appropriate consequences for misdemeanors. Some home group teachers wanted to be more directly involved in counseling students, negotiating re-entry processes and working constructively with students to achieve their goals.

What is being highlighted through these discussions is 'the politics of success' (McGinty, 2004, p. 169) displayed in the apparent paradox of both having structures but at the same time possessing the capacity to allow teachers to 'cut the slack,' especially for students from less conventional backgrounds. As McGinty (2004) puts it:

> Cutting the slack occurs when the teacher bends the rules for a student whom the teacher knows is genuinely disadvantaged by school rules and regulations. This notion relates to and is an extension of idiosyncratic credit. [i.e.] . . . a tacit belief among some staff that a 'little difference is delightful.' (p. 168)

'Cutting the slack' is especially important for disadvantaged students which when looked at from the student's perspective can make the crucial difference between success and failure. Again from McGinty's (2004) study of young women:

> When a student found a teacher who understood the stressors in her life and adapted the program accordingly, this made for success. Success for the young women in this study meant seeking out teachers who cut the slack for them. The teachers allowed these young women a lot of freedom to take control in these situations even if it meant the teachers risked being censured by the administration. Students who did not have the capacity to form trusting relationships that led to the slack being cut found it difficult to succeed at school. (pp. 169–170)

While the prevailing tenor at Broadvale was to maintain a tight ship, it nevertheless says something about Broadvale's commitment to open dialog that a major policy issue could be discussed and debated so freely in staff forums. We also gained an appreciation of the advocacy role of middle school coordinators and teachers and their efforts to create a culture of belongingness and trust in their classroom. Barbara, who had negotiated classroom rules with her students, commented:

We're very good at telling people what they need; we don't actually sit around long enough to find out what *they* think they need. You know, we seem to think that we know it all. (Barbara, March 25, 2003)

Although the instances of resistance and non-compliance described above may suggest that teachers at Broadvale were not held captive to policy, the fact remains that a control-focused approach to student behavior management exercised a powerful regulating influence on teachers' subjectivities. For all their efforts to develop trusting and supportive relationships, teachers and middle school coordinators spent much of their time and energy on behavioral matters at the expense of curriculum renewal and community development. Though some politically engaged teachers managed to subvert the more oppressive elements of the 'three strikes' philosophy, they were swimming against the tide of a powerful accountability discourse.

Responding to the pressures of the marketplace it seems that disadvantaged schools like Broadvale have a tendency to reinvent themselves around middle class values with a major emphasis on dress code, school discipline and functional approaches to literacy and numeracy. The shift toward local school management has placed added pressure on these schools to attract 'better students,' to find a niche in the market and to sell themselves to their communities. In this context, it was quite apparent that the student behavior management code at Broadvale functioned as a disciplinary technology with the capacity to alienate the school's most vulnerable students. At the extreme edge, these technologies can be likened to the border protection measures of neo-liberal countries where 'policing and incarceration emerge as part of a larger pattern of social context' (Giroux, 2002, p. 1150). In the case of schools, surveillance mechanisms coupled with in-school detention and suspension and exclusion policies serve as a means of controlling young people and maintaining institutional authority.

However, we do not want to suggest that the disciplinary technologies of the kind described above are a totalizing phenomenon. As this chapter has shown, hegemony is never complete; there are spaces for teachers to challenge inequitable arrangements and promote more compassionate and inclusive practices. Schools can draw on successful alternatives to control-based approaches to student behavior management through an engaging curriculum that connects schoolwork with the community and the real-life experiences of students, integrates students' culture into lessons, provides academic support for failing students, emphasizes the importance of relationships between staff and students, and ensures that students have an active voice in school decision-making structures. Although significant barriers to the establishment of trust and attachment lie outside the domain of the school (Stanton-Salazar, 1997) educators can form alliances with community groups to challenge the oppressive nature of racism, sexism and class conflict, and work for progressive social change.

Concluding remarks

In this chapter, we have made a case for teachers reinventing themselves for young adolescents. We have suggested that this is a difficult and demanding task that involves both working against the grain of a somewhat hostile policy environment as well as working for a set of worthy ideals and values to guide the directions of teachers' work. For many teachers in the project schools these values were expressed in words and phrases like respect, trust, care, relationships, belongingness, connectedness to kids' lives and engaging pedagogy. How these are translated into practice will be discussed in some detail in the next chapter "Transformative Pedagogy for Students."

Notes

1. Here we wish to acknowledge bell hooks' (2000) use of this phrase in her book *Where We Stand: Class Matters* (New York: Routledge).
2. This is a term we borrow (and elaborate on in some detail) from San Antonio (2004, p. 155).

CHAPTER SIX

Transformative pedagogy for students

Introduction

The framing or guiding question this chapter seeks to address is one that logical-ly follows from the previous chapter: How do teachers reinvent themselves for stu-dents? In other words, what are the practices, school cultures and organizational features that enable teachers to work successfully with young adolescents? We want to take a broad view of this because to envisage what is going on here in a reductionist or prescriptive way would be to miss the point about the broad con-tours of a transformative pedagogy for students. The questions above are interest-ing ones, not least because they lead us into some fairly contentious territory characterized by major tensions. These tensions reside within forces that seek to more closely control, constrain and prescribe the work of teaching and a counter-vailing set of predispositions that regard successful teaching as much more of an improvisational activity, albeit one that has to occur within a framework (Sawyer, 2004). These are by no means a new set of tensions, but they are being given poignancy at the moment for a number of reasons, not least of which has to do with forces that wish to more stringently control all aspects of social life, including schools, teachers and students in the alleged interest of the economy.

Broadly conceived from vantage points beyond classrooms and schools, teach-ers are considered to be 'a problem,' and 'the solution' is argued to lie in better 'managing' them. Where this diagnosis becomes highly problematic, indeed dangerous, is that in most instances the claim that schools are 'failing' is false, unsustainable, or the evidence is simply manufactured or fabricated (Berliner & Biddle, 1995; Bracey, 1997). The consequence for schools, teachers and students is that they are forced to operate within policy regimes that misunderstand the nature of schooling, that falsely and mischievously construe it as technical work in need of tighter control, and in the process devise measures and strategies that fail to support or nurture the conditions necessary for learning.

There are several ways of describing the agenda underlying the move to more closely circumscribe teachers. Moore (2004) refers to this tendency in terms of a 'dominant discourse in teaching' that purports to be about constructing 'the good teacher'—hardly a notion likely to be opposed by any sane person. Where it becomes problematic is in terms of whose interpretation. One of us has caricatured this in terms of a policy orientation of what might be termed a 'preferred teacher;' that is to say, one preferred by current educational policy-makers. This emphasis, incidentally, is one that treats teachers in highly individualized ways that would privatize them and subject them to competitive market forces in order to 'reform' them. It went like this:

> Within the kind of educational reform context described here teaching is increasingly being constructed as work in which there needs to be maximum opportunity for a flexible response to customer needs and where the teacher is hired and dispensed with as demand and fashion dictates. This ethos of schools as marketplaces also means a differentiated mix of teachers, some of whom are fully qualified, others who are cheaper to employ for short periods of time and who can rapidly be moved around within auxiliary and support roles to help satisfy growing niche markets. Coupled with this is a mindset in which the teacher is required to act as a kind of pedagogical entrepreneur continually having regard to selling the best points of the school, promoting image and impression, and generally seeking to maximize the school's market share by ensuring that it ranks high in competitive league tables. A crucial element of this educational commodity approach to teachers' work is the attention to calculable and measurable aspects of the work, especially educational outputs, for without that kind of information the capacity of the school to successfully promote itself will be severely circumscribed. There will be a need for the teacher to be a team member within the corporate culture of the school always mindful that anything she may do will impact in some way on the schools' outside image. However, team membership which will sometimes be glorified with terms like 'collegiality,' 'partnerships' and 'collaboration' will reside very much at the operational and implementation level, for to incorporate strategic decision making, might be to threaten the wider mission of the school. Interactions with students will occur within an overall framework of 'value added' in which students are 'stakeholders,' continually deserving of receiving educational value for money. Teaching will be increasingly managerial in nature, both as teachers are managed and themselves

manage others—there will be clear line management arrangements with each layer providing appropriate performance indicator information to the level above about the performance of individual students against objectives, and the success of the teacher herself in meeting school targets and performance outcomes. The remuneration of both the teacher and the school will be based on attaining these agreed performance targets. This sketch may not be that inaccurate, for as one teacher in the UK puts it:

I think we can predict what schools will look like by the end of the century. A much increased private sector, government specials, . . . and at the bottom, an under-resourced state sector. You won't be able to tell the difference between supermarkets and schools. Middle-class areas will have Marks and Spencers types of schools, and corner-shop types for the inner-city. Marketing, targeting and performance indicators will be the language of education. Heads getting together boasting about the quality of their sponsors. We'll have cigarettes and beer advertised in the school and we'll be told that it improves the pupils' discussion skills, to prepare them to make real choices in the real world. This lies behind all the policy changes now taking place. They're not as benign as they look. It would have seemed like fantasy ten years ago. Now, you are regarded as a liberal reactionary if you oppose the brave new world (Mac an Ghaill, 1991, p. 299).

(Smyth & Shacklock, 1998, pp. 122–123)

It is fairly clear that the preferred teacher is also the compliant or acquiescent teacher. Notably missing from this cameo, which is now largely upon us, are the important ingredients which coalesce around a teacher who is connected to her students, their concerns, lives and aspirations.

In Chapter 5, we saw something of the grounds upon which the case for teachers reinventing themselves for young people might be constructed: around themes of care, respect, trust, belongingness and schools that were humane places, committed to advancing learning. These themes were pervasive in the literature as well as in the voices of the teachers in the project schools. In a sense, we were addressing the question. In this chapter, we want to turn our attention to the question of how teachers with the support of their schools, refashion themselves in pursuit of a transformative pedagogy for students. We intend doing this around three broad themes which we can represent as given in Figure 6.1.

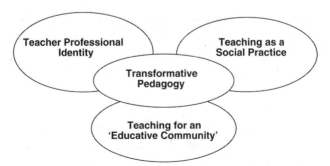

Figure 6.1. Transformative Pedagogy

In what follows, we elaborate a little on the notion of transformative pedagogy, and describe what it involved in practice in the project schools with reference to three themes:

1. Teaching for an identity: professional identity as argument.
2. Teaching as a social practice: taking a broad emotional-relational view.
3. Teaching for an educative community: where everyone is learning.

Transformative pedagogy: rethinking the fundamentals

'Transformative pedagogy' is the kind of word that is increasingly being attached to all kinds of activities and is in danger of becoming, as Brookfield (2000) says, a 'premature ultimate—a term that once invoked forestalls further debate or critical analysis . . . [for example like the phrase] "meeting needs" ' (p. 141). From our vantage point, transformative pedagogy is not so much a well-defined category or a set of strategies or procedures, so much as it is an orientation or way of thinking. Speaking of the way, the word transformative is increasingly being misused and evacuated of meaning, Brookfield (2000) invokes Mezirow's work (1991; 1992; 1994; 1997) as an instance of someone who uses it in a quite specific and helpful way. Mezirow's use of the term refers to 'a transformation in perspective, in a frame of reference, in a personal paradigm, and in a habit of mind . . . a fundamental reordering of assumptions' (Brookfield, 2000, p. 139). How we get to this point is less than straightforward:

> We transform frames of reference through critical reflection on assumptions supporting the content and/or process [of what we do]. We transform our habits of mind by becoming critically reflective of the premises defining the problem. (Brookfield, 2000, p. 142)

When we invoke the notion of transformative pedagogy, what we mean here is an active process of 'speaking out' against educational practices that are unjust or oppressive, as well as 'speaking up' for a different state of affairs. Elsewhere one of us (Smyth, 1993) has argued that teachers are enacting a transformative pedagogy when:

- they speak out against those practices which are more concerned with measurement against standards of performance than ways of enabling them to connect with the lives of their students;
- there is an emphasis on better ways of helping teachers to counteract

mindless bureaucratic incursions into their classrooms that have no educational foundation to them;

- they are able to discern in what ways their voices are being progressively
silenced in the debates about school reform, and how the media hype
about accountability is being used as a way of legitimating managerialism;
- they have an opportunity to expose and transform authoritarian and hierarchical structures that captivate [them] and their students; and
- they are able to engage in the study of the academic culture of teaching,
so as to provide one another with an active, informed commentary on one
another's teaching (Smyth, 1991, p. 75, paraphrased).

What we are referring to above is a set of frames of reference, habits of mind
or orientations that capture positively what it is that we need to be working for or
doing differently as educators and what needs to be confronted and supplanted. As
a starting point, we need to listen more to our voices as teachers and less to the cap-
tains of industry. We need to work in ways that not only acknowledge but also loudly celebrate teachers' theories about what works. Importantly, we need to treat
teachers in ways that acknowledge teaching as a form of intellectual struggle, teachers are not unthinking technicians. We need to be more trusting of teachers and stop
treating them in ways that are implicitly distrustful. We should acknowledge the
complex nature of the work teachers do and put to rest the nonsense that teaching
is something any fool can do. When students do not learn as well as we expect, we
should be less hasty in pointing the finger at teachers and look more closely at the
context within which teachers work and ask ourselves if they are being properly
supported.

Curriculum should be constructed around the live experiences of children and
teachers rather than crafted around national priorities that are allegedly aimed at
making us more internationally competitive or that aim to reduce the trade imbal-
ances. We need to encourage 'deliberate improvisation' in teaching, so that we can
move beyond mindless processes that produce 'compliant' and 'defiant' kids. We need
to provide the kind of circumstances in which teachers feel comfortable with and
compelled to call into question the basic assumptions about teaching and learning
and to radically change those if experience tells them otherwise. Teaching and
schooling ought to be about engaging with the 'big questions' that fire the 'imagination,' the 'spirit,' the 'feelings' and the 'intellect' (Clifford & Friesen, 1993).
Finally, we need to support and foster teachers who are collaborative (not competitive) learners in schools (Smyth, 1993).

This list of predispositions fit with what Biesta and Miedema (2002) claim to
be some of the necessary orientations for a transformative view of education.
According to them, teachers in their research in the Netherlands, and this applies

as well to teachers in other places, are becoming increasingly dissatisfied with such things as:

- an increasing emphasis on measurable (i.e., quantifiable) outcomes and accountability criteria;
- a constantly closer linkage between values of the curriculum and the market economy, resulting in the idea that the curriculum should be determined exclusively in terms of what is economically useful;
- a growing tendency to specify and prescribe in great detail what aims should be reached by individual pupils and schools;
- the formulation of the so-called 'professional profiles' for teachers that emphasize technical–didactical skills and where there is only a minor role for the pedagogical dimensions of teaching; and,
- an overemphasis on the role of cognition (p. 175).

It is important that we emphasize the positive and constructive dimensions to transformative pedagogy, and the teachers in the Biesta and Miedema (2002) study were able to articulate what that looked like. It had much to do with norms and values that are antithetical to the instrumentalist direction currently being pushed by educational policy-makers in most parts of the world. These different priorities identified by Biesta and Miedema (2002) have something quite different to say about what is regarded as important in teaching:

- relationships with students (p. 175);
- assisting students in 'gaining a sense of what is right and wrong' (p. 176);
- a viewpoint informed by the concept of a 'whole sense of student identity' (p. 176);
- teaching that reflects on the 'ways in which people live together' (p. 176);
- a view of learning as being an active process of an 'exchange of meaning' (p. 179) between teacher and students;
- involving the learner 'in the act of interpretation' (p. 179);
- regarding the student as a 'whole person' (p. 180);
- conceiving teaching as a 'shared' and 'collective' activity (p. 180);
- placing 'participation' (p. 180) at the center of teaching and learning;
- acknowledging that 'feelings, beliefs, attitudes, values, emotions, volitions, habits, predispositions, and actions' (p. 180) are crucial to teaching and learning;
- non-separation of 'instructional' from 'pedagogical' work (p. 180);
- facing up to the reality that 'students are the real curriculum makers' (Bloomer, 1997).

This leads us into the obvious question of how teachers live the divided life and how they sustain predispositions like these toward young adolescents.

We want to theorize this a little further now, before returning to what some of the project teachers had to say.

Teaching for an identity: professional identity as argument

It became clear to us that many of the teachers in the project schools were 'continuously engag[ing] in "reinventing old roles" ' and that they had adopted an 'openness and orientation to change' (Carlson, 2005, p. 31). The vast majority of the 64 teachers in the study came from a secondary teaching background and had little experience of team teaching, curriculum integration and planning beyond the confines of traditional subject faculties. Reinventing themselves for young adolescents created numerous challenges, not the least of these being how to teach outside an area of subject specialization, how to teach as part of a team and how to negotiate curriculum with students. Although some teachers had participated in retraining programs and post-graduate education studies, we developed the impression that personal biography played an important part in their transformation. Who they were as people, where they had taught previously, inspiring colleagues they had encountered along the way, life-changing experiences beyond school and their general demeanor and understanding of young people, emerged as crucial factors in the interviews, portraits and the snippets of conversation we had while inhabiting their schools. Typically, secondary-trained teachers explained that they learnt a great deal from colleagues with a primary teaching background and experience. Stewart summed up his learning experience at Gulfview as follows:

> The people who were at the best advantage in terms of coming to grips with middle schooling were the two primary-based people appointed here. The rest of us came from traditional secondary structures so we're very much subject specialist. We learnt a lot from these people about how to teach a range of subjects, how to integrate, how to involve kids in giving them a say into curriculum and responsibilities. Now a lot of that was trial and error like it is in any first year. It was hit and miss. I think what's happened over the years is that we've educated ourselves by taking on those extra subjects. When you look at what you have to cover in some of those subject areas, they're not often content driven, they're more skill driven and if teachers are prepared to look at the skills involved, it's not so hard to actually teach a range of different subjects. (Stewart, November 6, 2002)

Stewart's reorientation involved a change in headset from a focus on subject content to a consideration of student' interests and needs as a starting point for curriculum planning. It was, he says, 'a hit and miss' process that involved a gradual shift in teacher attitudes and dispositions rather than overnight change. But to leave this transformation entirely at the level of the personal would be to risk omitting some crucial things that were occurring systematically and institutionally that was facilitating this identity formation. There is another dimension to it as well, and elsewhere we have put it thus:

> Coldron and Smith (1999) argue that professional identities are constructed through a process of 'active location in social space' (p. 711)—'active' in the sense that knowing what it means to be a teacher is relational, and is continually being modified in light of experience. That is to say, there are 'traditions' or 'repositories of possible or actual practices and structures' (p. 713) that constitute fields of choices that either enhance or diminish the spaces within which teachers see themselves as having to make pedagogic decisions. How teachers regard themselves in their work, therefore, has a lot to do with what kind of spaces they envisage themselves as having, and the kind of relationships possible within them. Coldron and Smith note that 'policies that impose greater degrees of uniformity and conformity threaten to impoverish the notion of active location' (p. 711). (Smyth, 2002a, p. 470)

The significance of social space on teacher identity and development was revealed during the weekly breakfast sessions at Plainsville when staff met to discuss the implications of the 'essential learnings' contained in a recently released state curriculum framework. What follows is an abridged account of our observations:

> By 8.05 A.M. there are 11 teachers and school support officers in the staffroom breakfasting on pancakes prepared by the groundsman. Leanne, the principal, chairs the session on the topic of communication and values. There is some initial discussion about how to develop debating skills. A teacher suggests that talking-circles could be safe places for kids to discuss and debate current issues. Later the discussion turns to the topic of values which was a major learning activity at the school. Leanne argues that teachers can play a critical role in challenging prejudices and stereotypes that children bring to school. One of the challenges is getting kids to talk more openly about values. Posing moral dilemmas is an important aspect of this. Leanne suggests that teachers prepare dilemma cards for use in talking-circles, e.g. is it ever okay to tell a lie? . . . is war ever justified? A teacher expresses a concern that many students cannot read well. Leanne asks, 'How do you set up a learning environment where kids will want to learn to read?' Teachers suggest increasing the range of texts and materials, especially those which connect to youth culture and everyday literacy practices, e.g. comics, magazines, train timetables, advertising broadsheets and junk mail. A teacher talks up the relevance of videos, DVDs, play stations and audio visual resources. Leanne says that kids have to be able to locate these kinds of resources themselves from web sites and other sources. (Field notes, February 5, 2003)

Apart from the socialization value, these breakfast meetings were an important ingredient in an ongoing induction program for new teachers that enabled them to make quite explicit connections between the classroom learning and the local community. As we have described elsewhere, poverty and acute hardship characterized the lives of many students at Plainsville, and there was a strongly held conviction that didactic teaching approaches that simply followed the official script were a recipe for disaster. In this informal setting, teachers were able to share ideas, resources and practices, and talk about strategies that worked for them. The contextualized nature of this professional development meant that they were constantly reflecting on the lives and circumstances of the children in their classes. Invariably their response to mandated curriculum was framed by the question 'what does this mean for our kids at Plainsville?'

What we saw at Plainsville, and other project schools, was an example of the ways in which teacher identity and development undergo change in the light of local knowledge and experience. Significantly, teachers in disadvantaged schools tended to see themselves as serving working class communities and often sought to distinguish themselves (and their practices) from colleagues in the middle class suburbs—the 'leafy greens' as they were often called. In other words, class-based topographies and geographies of difference came to exercise quite a powerful influence on how teachers constructed their professional identities. However, as Maclure (1993) argues, identity is always in a state of decay and reformation. As she points out:

> While identity is a site of permanent struggle for everyone, teachers may be undergoing a particularly acute crisis of identity, as old models and exemplars of teacherhood disintegrate under contemporary social and economic pressures. (p. 311)

Identity is not 'fixed or unitary' (Coldron & Smith, 1999, p. 712) but rather, as Kelchtermans and Vandenberghe (1994) maintain, it is:

> . . . a complex, multidimensional and dynamic system of representations and meanings which develops over time and as the result of interactions between the person and an environment. (p. 47)

From the position we are pursuing here, the most helpful way of thinking about teacher identity is provided by Maclure (1993), when she says it is not so much a quality that teachers 'have' so much as 'something they *use*' (p. 312). To explain what this means, Maclure says:

> . . . something that they *use*, to justify, explain and make sense of themselves in relation to other people, and to the contexts in which they operate. In other words, identity is a form of argument. As such, it is both practical and theoretical. It is also inescapably

moral: identity claims are inevitably bound up with justifications of conduct and belief. (p. 312)

We find this way of thinking about teacher identity to be particularly helpful because when we are dealing with something as perplexing and tension-ridden as teachers' professional lives, focusing on how it is that teachers 'argue for themselves' or how they present their 'biographical attitude' (Maclure, 1993, p. 311), provides us with insights into how they frame and reframe their aspirations in working with young people. Another way of putting it is that teachers' identity is 'an organizing principle in teachers' jobs and lives' (p. 311).

Where this line of thinking takes us is in the direction of regarding the identity teachers construct for themselves as being essentially *for students* and against *nonsensical systems imperatives* and discourses. In other words, a resource for defining what they are not as well as what they are. In our project, we were not specifically asking teachers to tell us about how educational policies were impacting their work, but inevitably in telling us their stories they were implicitly making such statements. While we did not specifically encounter the uniformly depressing and cumulative effects of educational reforms alluded to by Maclure (1993), this may have been an artifact of the more optimistic contexts in which we were working. It certainly felt to us as though in speaking of their work and passion, they felt for the young people they were teaching, these teachers brought to their teaching a *biographical project* (i.e., a network of personal concerns, values and aspirations) against which events could be judged and decisions made (Maclure, 1993, p. 314).

Some sense of this biographical project and the values which teachers bring to their work is captured in the portrait of Macca, an experienced classroom teacher who has spent much of his career in rural communities. Although he is a strong advocate for middle schooling, he describes himself as a traditionalist and rejects some fashionable ideas about ownership and negotiation of curriculum. Yet in other ways, he reveals himself as an inventive teacher who places a lot of emphasis on personal relationships and the value on hands-on learning. His description of himself as a 'fiddler' nicely captures his philosophy about learning.

MAYBE SUCCESSFUL MIDDLE SCHOOL TEACHERS SHOULD BE FIDDLERS

I began teaching in 1967 in area schools. In 1972, I resigned and went and did other things with my life—like, digging coal in Canada, washing dishes in Europe and driving tractors in Israel. I came back to the city and got the academic side of it under control and then spent a lot of time again in an area school where I had to be resourceful, inventive and adventurous. When I got to Seachange High, which was a very structured and very 'high school' I said, 'This isn't right and it doesn't work for kids.' Fortunately we've had progressive principals and we've had research that's helped me to come to grips with the fact that middle schooling is something in its own right and not just something which prepares kids for their year 12 education.

I think I'm a traditionalist. I'm not sure that I'm ready to involve the kids in developing the curriculum. I kind of think the curriculum belongs to me because I'm employed by society to teach the kids, and while I might instinctively know what's going to interest them, I don't believe that I should only teach those things that they want to learn about. Kids of the age group that we're talking about are interested in their bodies, so we'd be silly to ignore that, in science for example, and delay physiology until they were 15. We'd be much better off to teach our science courses related to physiology because that's what they are, they are self-centered little dears and they really want to know about themselves and their bodies and how they work. It's our job to teach it because that's what we're paid to do. I think there are other ways that I can get kids to negotiate and make group decisions rather than messing about with what I see as my business. I think I'm guilty of imposing my learning style on my classes in the first instance. I'm the kind of person who will unpack a new video camera and play with it to see how it works. Then I'll look at the instruction manual. So that's a learning style that I'm stuck with and one that I impose on my classes. So I say to them, 'Here's something. Will you play with it,' which is as frustrating as hell to some of the kids in my year 11 chemistry class who want a step-by-step approach with everything labeled and nicely set out. I'm trying to say to them; we'll work through this intuitively first. I believe in a hands-on approach first because *everybody* can do that, supposedly—and again. Everybody can fiddle with things. People who know things, tell us that that is the way we learn and I think that kind fits in with what I said before about, 'I'm a fiddler.' Perhaps that has got to do with my background as a kid where that's what you did, you fiddled with it and then you had something happen and you said, 'Oh, that's how that works.' Maybe that's what makes me a successful middle school teacher. Maybe successful middle school teachers should be fiddlers.

It's really important to know the kids and families. So for example, that young fellow that walked through here just now, I know his mum and I know his sister and I know that his dad died in May this year. He's having a rough time coming to grips with it, so I've got to make allowances for his circumstances. Knowing the kids, where they come from and how they are enables me to establish what I'm going to accept from one person and not from another. I've another kid in my class who was shipped into here—and I used the word 'shipped in'—because he wasn't getting on with his home group and my response to him was to quietly say, 'Well, you've got a new chance to start here, now take your time. I know I make allowances for his aberrations.' A kid said to me, 'Why do you always let him go early?' I said, 'I let him go early because he needs to go early.' I was able to give a little bit more in answer to that later on. I was able to say, 'Well, he cleans up quickly, he does his work quietly, he has finished, he has packed up and he's ready to go so my response was to let him go.' She accepted that and just said, 'Oh, okay.' I mean they all recognize that they are individuals and they've all got individual differences.

There are some teachers in our school who want the Pollyanna solution to behavior management, like 'I have a problem and I will send it away and it will be fixed.' And they're the sort of people that want us to employ a coordinator in student behavior management. I happen to think that I'm stuck with the kids that I'm given and it's my responsibility to deal with them. If I can't deal with them, then I'll have to devise ways to do it. I resent the fact that there's a detention room, so I try not to send my kids there. I would reckon that I've sent a kid to the detention room once or twice in its existence, which is four or five years. The detention room is a whole school thing and we have all agreed that it is a necessary thing—and I use the term 'we' there, loosely—and so we've all agreed that we would take one lesson a week above our normal load, in supervision of that room. But I don't believe in the Pollyanna solution. I don't believe that if I send a kid to detention, the problem is going to be fixed. I would much sooner remove a kid from my class to let the rest of the class get on with it and have them working in a nearby room. I'd much prefer to say to some of my buddies, 'This bloke is giving me the shits, look can you have him in here for a while?' Sending kids who are angry to a detention room is no good for them either.

And at the heart of being a parent and, I think, being a teacher is just to care about the kids. I talk to kids about an emotional bank balance, about a reputation and how you can build up a bank balance: 'You can build up a bank balance with me, if you're, if you do your work and you're good and you smile at me and you say hello in the yard and you do all these things, then you're allowed to have one or two lapses, you're allowed to have some grumpy days because you've built up an emotional bank balance and it's the people who have run out of capital, emotional capital and actually are in deficit who are the people who get themselves into strife.' That's another approach I use with kids to persuade them they ought to be caring and they ought to think about other people and ought to consider other people's feelings, and at the very heart of it is just selfishness—you're building up emotional capital. You know, kids can understand that, I think.

(Macca, October 21, 2003)

What emerges quite strongly in this account is that middle school teachers like Macca feel a strong sense of ownership of their students and do not fall back on institutional norms and sanctions as a means of maintaining their authority. This comes through most clearly in his rejection of behavior management practices which tend to transfer responsibility for dealing with infractions from home group teachers to administrators. Macca attaches a great deal of weight to building trust and respectful relationships with his students and assisting them to develop a sense of right and wrong, something which is nicely conveyed in the idea of building emotional capital. He has his own views about how students learn and his role in the choice of curriculum themes and content and does not follow fashionable trends for their own sake.

Reading the transcripts and constructing the portraits certainly gave us a sense that many teachers in the project schools, like those in Maclure's (1993) study, were actively providing us with:

> ... personal testimony and life history as oppositional strategies for combating the punitive abstractions and reductions of dominant discourses ... By insisting on the unheroic smallness and interiority of their personal 'voice,' this particular form of the biographical attitude amounts to an insubordinate refusal, by those on the margins, to play the generalizing games of the powerful ... (p. 312)

As Halpin & Moore with Edwards, George & Jones (2000) put it, 'teachers' professional identity is neither given nor static, but is continually being worked on, revised or renewed. . . . ' (p. 140), and this can mean living the tension between what Bernstein (1996) identified as the 'dislocation between the culture of the pedagogic discourse and management culture' (p. 75). In other words, the tension between 'seeking to do what is essentially "right" for one's students' (Halpin & Moore et al., 2000, p. 140), and 'the management structure [which] has become the device for creating an entrepreneurial competitive culture' (Bernstein, 1996, p. 75). To return to the previous portrait, Macca's insistence that students in his class should, and could, be treated differently according to their circumstances, illustrates how teachers can break down the institutional barriers that often inhibit learning for kids facing hard times. His making allowances for individual students, even against institutional norms, is a classic illustration of McGinty's (2004) 'cutting the slack' referred to in Chapter 5. Doing the right thing by his students involved Macca in some critical judgment about the appropriateness of school rules and policies for particular individuals. While he did not openly defy collectively agreed school policies, he did not meekly submit to managerialist discourses nor was he willing to have his work defined in instrumental ways.

To summarize and draw this discussion of teacher identity to a close, we are concurring with Maclure's (1993) view that ' . . . identity claims can be seen as a form of argument—as devices for justifying, explaining and making sense of one's conduct, career, values and circumstances' (p. 316). What is implicitly being argued against are official policy versions of how they should be as teachers—compliant technicians, dutiful servants, instrumental providers, impartial conveyors of information, non-controversial suppliers of 'client' choices and satisfiers of customers' needs. The teachers we talked to were engaged in a 'pedagogy of reinvention' akin to what Mitchell and Weber (1999) referred to as one of:

> Creating new images [in] an active process that transforms the creator. As teachers, we want to . . . recreate ourselves rather than become the objects of someone else's study or reform plans. We use the term 'pedagogy of reinvention' to describe the process of making both the immediate and distant past usable. It is a process of going back over something in different ways, of studying one's own experience with insight of awareness of the present for the purposes of acting on the future. (p. 8)

We now want to turn our attention to more specifically focus on what it is that makes teachers' work unique, especially teachers who work with young adolescents. There are two parts to this complex ensemble that we want to explore: teaching as a social practice and teaching for an 'educative community.' Both constitute the kind of 'active location in social space' that Coldron and Smith (1999, p. 711) refer to as permitting, fostering and promulgating teachers' professional identities.

Teaching as a social practice

Despite what might be said about it outside of schools and classrooms, teaching is very special work—indeed Connell (1996) has described good teaching as ' a gift relation . . . [that] is founded on a public rather than a private interest' (p. 6). The consequences of the relational effects of teaching extend considerably beyond the extractive personal residue that individual students might gain from good teaching. In a nutshell, Connell (1985) puts it that teachers work daily at converting often what amounts to 'an amorphous mess' (p. 73), into what Hewitson (2004) refers to as engaging young people in 'new insights, new enthusiasms and excitement over the experience of connecting with the world, starting with the self' (p. 166). When schools fall within the increasing gradient of poverty as is currently happening in public schools in most western countries, then the work of teaching becomes even more amazing, as teachers ' . . . regularly perform astonishing (and unheralded) feats of human relations, overcoming age, class and ethnic barriers, breaking through resentment, suspicions and fears, to establish workable educational relationships' (p. 63). The reason for this is not hard to discern when it is remembered that ' . . . the core of the problem is social. Education is inherently a social process, acting through social relationships. Education involves the development of the capacities of the person as well as the development of the capacities of society' (Connell, 2002b, p. 30) and ' a social transition occurs between teacher and student, between learner and learner, and an educational relationship is constituted' (Connell, 1996, p. 5).

Educational relationships are social and creative in the sense that they are fundamentally about bringing new capacities into existence among learners at a number of levels:

> ... [over] the full range of types of social action; *productive capacities*, used in economic life; *symbolic capacities*, used in making culture; *capacities for collective decision making* used in politics; and *capacities for emotional response*, used in personal life. (Connell, 1996, p. 5)

Connell (1993) gets to the core when he says of the social and relational nature of teaching:

> Being a teacher is not just a matter of having a body of knowledge and a capacity to control a classroom. That could be done by a computer with a cattle-prod. Just as important, being a teacher means being able to establish human relations with the people being taught. Learning is a full-blooded, human social process, and so is teaching. Teaching involves emotions as much as it involves pure reasoning. (p. 63)

Probably, the least acknowledged but one of the most important aspects of teaching according to Connell (1993) is that it is 'emotion work'—something we have documented in this book through the portraits of Greg, Barbara and Lucy. The point is acknowledged more recently by writers like Blackmore (1996) and Hargreaves (1998; 2001a, b):

> Teachers establish relations with students through their emotions, through sympathy, interest, surprise, boredom, sense of humor, sometimes anger and annoyance. School teaching, indeed, is one of the most emotionally demanding jobs. (Connell, 1993, p. 63)

In these circumstances teachers are extremely vulnerable. It is work that needs to be actively, constructively and productively supported (Smyth, 2002b; 2003a, b; 2004b, c). As Connell (1993) says:

> 'Making it harder' is much easier to do. All you need is to insist on pupil time on-task, tell teachers they are slack and need to get back to basics, demand teacher productivity, throw in a few standardized tests, and presto! The job is done. (p. 64)

On the contrary, fostering and facilitating this special kind of relational work require having the wisdom, vision and courage to stand up to those who have a diminished or impoverished view of the nature of the work of teaching:

> 'Supporting it' means providing resources (especially time), teacher autonomy (because human relationships cannot be planned), advice (especially from networks of other teachers), and recognition (that this is an important part of teaching). (Connell, 1993, p. 64)

In other words, the question of *how* teachers learn to reinvent themselves for young adolescents is intimately bound up with the idea of teaching as a social practice. Teachers may have their own ideas about what works for them, but as Hargreaves (1992) points out:

> Teachers do not develop entirely by themselves . . . They also learn a great deal from contact with many other people who are knowledgeable about and have experience of teaching and learning. They learn from 'experts' by taking courses, studying for higher degrees, or undergoing programmes of staff training in new techniques and approaches. . . . Teachers learn from many groups, both inside and outside their own schools. But they learn most, perhaps, from other teachers, particularly from their colleagues in their own work place, their own school. (p. 216)

Depending on district priorities, teachers in the project schools were able to access professional development programs on middle schooling sponsored by the education system. This was especially true for staff at Seachange and New Vista schools where the district superintendent and school principals had invested heavily in training and development programs conducted by middle school experts, such as Paul Deering (2003) from the United States. But overwhelmingly, it seems that staff knowledge of middle school pedagogies was being advanced through support networks at the school, district and state level. In particular, our informants spoke of the importance of team teaching, mentoring and other collaborative arrangements that enabled them to learn from their colleagues. Hannah, a curriculum coordinator from Seachange, explained what was needed to become a middle school teacher.

A LOT OF PEOPLE HAVE BECOME LITTLE ISLANDS IN THEIR CLASSROOMS

You have to be able to step outside of yourself and know that you're going to make mistakes along the way and that you've got a bit of learning to do—like when we first came out of teachers' college. You've actually got to get back and have a look at the way you do things and critically analyze them to find out what could be without throwing away everything because a lot of knowledge and experience has been gained throughout the years. The second thing is you've got to put yourself on the line if you're going to buddy up with someone, which I did last year with maths and science because I'd never taught them before. You've really got to lay yourself open to accepting somebody else's way of teaching. And thirdly, you've got to be prepared to work with other people even in your own subject area, to expand on what you have already. So being ready to accept other people's ideas and work is probably one of the biggest hurdles. A lot of people have become little islands in their classrooms and they don't want to take that next step and put themselves out for criticism, if that's the way they see it. It's quite threatening. I think that is one of the biggest areas that needs to be broken down. The first step is to be with somebody else and hand over a little bit of responsibility and accept some ideas from other people, instead of just running with your own ideas all the time.

(Hannah, October 21, 2003)

In a similar vein, teachers' knowledge of middle school practices was promoted through sub-schools teaching teams at Investigator High School. What follows is a brief insight into the workings of the team by two senior members. In the first instance, an arts teacher describes the ways in which sub-school meetings support curriculum planning, and in the second instance, an English coordinator talks of the benefits of teaching in a public space:

> At Investigator we talk about ourselves as learning teams and we have lots of dialogue about the curriculum and the kids themselves. Some of this occurs in a weekly sub-school meeting. There's a lot of support amongst staff about how we deal with kids. In particular, a lot of very honest professional debriefing occurs amongst the core group of teachers that deliver the bulk of the curriculum. Other sub-school staff members form part of an extended group who sometimes come to our meetings and discuss how they can contribute to the cross-curriculum themes in their specialist subject areas. Everyone gets to put items on the agenda and people feel like they've had their say. Every semester we have half a day when we go to the pub and have a nice lunch and do some debriefing and planning for the next semester. During these sessions we look for ways of linking ideas from a range of subjects. (Penelope, November 6, 2000)
>
> Being in a middle school setting teachers have an opportunity to learn from team colleagues. There's a sense of seeing yourself as a public self as a teacher. If you go in your classroom and the walls are up it's a very private environment and there's a sense that you're a private self—you've got control over this space if nowhere else in the world. I like the way middle schooling encourages this sense of public self. You see what other teachers are doing. You know that you are being seen, and the feedback that you get is not like performance management. It's just comments—it's just the way we work with people. It's a very nice dynamic that starts to happen. Teaching is not a science—it's more of the art idea of teaching and things that you pick up through practice. We learn from each other. (Peter, September 6, 2000)

Peter's remarks highlight the importance of team teaching practices in breaking down the culture of individualism (Hargreaves, 1992) that is so pervasive in high schools and indeed many primary schools. Rather than relying on tips and second-hand advice, novice teachers were able to witness at first-hand an experienced teacher in action in an open-space environment. More importantly, they were able to work with and alongside their colleagues in planning curriculum, developing resources, teaching specific aspects of the program, supporting students with special needs and evaluating students' learning. Fortnightly, middle school meetings enabled teachers to discuss curriculum matters and issues concerning students in their classes. The following quote from our field observations gives some indication of the importance of social relationships in teaching:

> The 'gossip' session was a regular item on the middle school meeting agenda—a time for teachers to share information (some of it quite disturbing) about their students and their engagement with schooling. We heard about teachers' concerns for a student whose grandfather had recently died and the possible impact this might be having on his learning. We heard of the concerns for the welfare of a girl whose sister was seriously injured in a vehicle accident . . . about a girl subject to domestic violence . . . about a boy harassed by peers. In each of these cases there was discussion about possible support strategies from teachers and inter-agency personnel. Several things captured our attention here including: (a) the importance of relationships to good teaching and learning—these teachers clearly understood that school could not be quarantined from home and the broader society; (b) the ways in which the political economy and cultural issues penetrate schools—unemployment, racism, poverty, sexism, etc. all impact on schooling and (c) the day-to-day survival of teachers in these schools is dependent on the support they give to each other. (Field notes, March 22, 2000)

The point we want to make here is that the key to curriculum reform depends on teachers having a shared understanding of students' lives and the impact this has on their eventual success at school. This is not just a matter of survival for individual teachers—though we were often told that going public was the key to keeping one's sanity—rather, dialog of this kind was crucial to developing a much closer bond with students and their caregivers.

In canvassing teaching as a social process as we have done here, it is not our intent to provide an exhaustive discussion of the many merits of teaching; our purpose is much more circumscribed. We want to provide a brief set of pointers to why it is that some teachers of young adolescents (like some of those we encountered in this project) seem to 'work out how to do it.'

Trying to understand how some schools seem to be able to create the conditions that foster and protect this kind of relational work is not an easy task. At best, we have to surmise. For example, when schools are assailed with policies, regulations and requirements that demand increasingly institutionalization of relationships, then some degree of relational corrosion with students is inevitable. In other words, when there is increasing formalization of relationships between students, teachers, the administration of the school and system policy-makers, there is a deper-sonalization as each layer is pushed to communicate with other layers through the officially sanctioned discourses. Policies, practices and strategies are not of teach-ers' own making, and over which they have only limited discretionary control. While the official intent is to try and make more predictable, rational, calculable, and hence measurable, the haphazard and often whimsical relationship between teachers and students, the effects can be quite devastating. To provide a specific example: by insisting on policies of zero tolerance, 'three strikes and you are out,' hardening suspension/exclusion/expulsion policies, school uniforms, homework, standards, benchmarks, testing regimes, more 'consumer'-oriented forms of report-ing and the like—the relationship is, in a sense, taken out of the hands of teachers and placed in the hands of seemingly well-meaning, distant, objective, value-free and disinterested autocrats.

A distinguishing hallmark of the project schools was an attempt to foster rela-tional learning and group identity through the creation of smaller learning commu-nities in which a small core of teachers took responsibility for the teaching program and pastoral care arrangements. At New Vista School, home groups were organized so that a pair of teachers was responsible for the bulk of teaching across two class-es. In the following dialogic portrait, we provide an illustration of what this looks like in practice from the viewpoints of Kevin and Lesley who are home group teach-ers of cooperating year 7/8 classes.

THE KIDS SEE US AS ONE TEACHER

'Our cooperation begins with planning units of work,' says Kevin. 'Another aspect is looking at the kids we have and trying to work out strategies for doing things that are best for them. I'm not saying we find all the results but we try and support each other and come up with a range of strategies. Lesley is very good at finding other people to bring in to help out. She never stops trying whereas I tend to occa-sionally think, "Well I've done my thousand percent for that one; I'm going to stop because that kid is absorbing too much of my time. I've got to do something for the others." She tends to keep reminding me that still, we've got to go back to that kid and try and think of something. So that's an example of two different personalities working pretty reasonably for everybody.'

'The kids see us as one teacher in there,' says Lesley. 'Kevin only teaches in these rooms, so he is really the key person who holds both of the classes togeth-er. But if we're both in here together we just put LK for the class. So they could be doing whatever topic or theme we're doing, or it could be that they have me down that end because there's some work needing to be done or Kevin at this end, or there's a group of kids needs some extra maths or they're struggling with something, we can separate them out. Sometimes I'll say "Look, I need to do x" and Kevin will have both the groups and I'm in and out and take them away, some of them away. They are able to relate to both of us, in our own way but as "the teacher" and they do think of themselves as, you know, it's M9 & 10, they both access the same door, they both go through here. I have them both for English, drama and the arts and Kevin has them for maths, society and environment and science. We're rarely out of the room for our non-instruction time. Often we're both in here with the one group so we can give them extra support.'

'Relationships are really important,' Lesley explains. 'If you'd come in this morning you'd have seen my blackboard covered in "harassment, power" and what have you, because we'd had an harassment issue and it's been on-going and . . . We do it whenever it comes up so if it's English lesson and we've had, or if—I tend to respond fairly immediately to things. If it comes up then we talk about it and do some activities and all sorts of things happen. So I didn't send the kids to focus straightaway.' Kevin reinforces Lesley's views. 'Because we've both been primary school teachers all these issues are talked about from the time they're little three-and-a-half-year-olds and they know, they all know, if you sat down with any one of them and you talked about harassment or bullying . . . nicotine, alcohol, marijuana, sexual—sex, they could talk to you very, very well and give all the right answers and say "Yeah, it's not good to harass and this is what harassment looks like and this is what a victim looks like . . ." they can do all that stuff and "This is why we have rules." Harassment is dealt with at a couple of levels. Lesley is talking about a personal way of dealing with it. There's also a structured and systematic way of addressing it in the school. We try to draw parents into it through homework, with very limited success, I might add. Most of them are not willing to talk about these sorts of issues.'

(Lesley & Kevin, August 11, 2003)

It is apparent from our conversation that our informants did not always agree on specific issues and priorities. For her part, Lesley was very concerned with the social and emotional development of students, whereas Kevin tended to focus more on academic learning and argued that parents need to take more responsibility for the moral and social development of their children. There were times when they expressed differences of opinion over issues in front of students. But it was also evident that their students could tap into the unique knowledge and expertise which each teacher brought to the classroom.

It is argued that sanitizing and de-humanizing relationships is in the best interests of schools because it makes schools much more relationally tidier places, less susceptible to violence and idiosyncratic and undisciplined behavior of teachers as well as students. Thus conceived, schools also appear on the surface to be easier places to control, and their images easier to market to discerning consumers who have been inculcated into regarding schools as places of consumption.

However, these alien or interloper discourses and practices of the economy have the effect of scripting and producing a stilted set of relationships between the actors in schools. They produce synthetic and emasculated, rather than authentic and robust relationships that end up forcing teachers, students and administrators to live a lie—that is to say, enacting meaningless, empty relationships that constitute a charade and a sham. Rather than a humanizing set of relationships (Bartolome, 1994; Noguera, 1995) in which teachers and students engage in a struggle with varying degrees of success in getting to know something of one another, what we have instead are coercive relationships that are at best of a limited custodial kind. Any notion that the players can genuinely interact with one another, so as to learn from each other, becomes impossible. The essential ingredient of risk taking is expunged by the working of the policy agenda.

To return briefly to our informants, Kevin and Lesley neither acted in a scripted way with their students, nor did they resort to overly authoritarian practices. Both had an understanding of the 'official' curriculum requirements, but they showed a great deal of flexibility in weaving topical issues and concerns into their lessons. Lesley, for example, addressed social concerns like drugs and harassment in the context of the classroom rather than relying solely on school policies and structures—though Kevin recognized the importance of an institutional response.

In essence, what we have been trying to disclose here is what amounts to ' . . . undoing the institutionalization of the teacher–student relationship' (Smyth et al., 2003, p. 189) demanded by adherence to a range of policy imperatives, including the competitive academic curriculum. Our more general argument is that what is needed as an antidote is the pursuit of 'the notion of middle schooling as a progressive school reform category [capable of] problematiz[ing] the institutionalization of relationships in high schools' (Smyth et al., 2003, p. 191), which is what this book is basically about.

Teaching for an 'educative community'[1]

There is an extensive and burgeoning literature on 'schools as professional learning communities' (e.g., see Hord, 2004; Huffman & Hipp, 2003; Huffman & Jacobson, 2003; McLaughlin & Talbert, 2001; Proudford, 2003), most of it ultimately unhelpful because it ends up describing an 'enchanted workplace' of schooling that does not exist, or has no hope of doing so in the current cold climate toward schools. The major shortcoming of this literature is that one is left with the impression of the lives of real people in schools being ridden over. The distinct feeling left is that the real lives of people in schools does not matter, and that what is more important is hearing from organization and management experts on how categories like the 'learning society' or the 'learning organization' might be translated into schools. We believe schools require and deserve better than this, and so our focus here will be on some general principles that are more indigenous to and drawn from actual schools that we believe better exemplify what we would argue real 'professional learning communities' are about. We prefer to use Romano's (2000) term, that is 'educative communities.'

At the outset, we should say that the notion of an educative community, elements of which were present to varying degrees in all of our project schools, is an aspiration or an orientation being worked toward rather than a set of prescriptions to be followed, or processes, practices or structures to be replicated. As Romano (2000) is at pains to point out, forging an educative community 'is very hard work because the teacher must reinvent himself or herself, acting deliberately against school experiences in K–12 and perhaps even experiences in teacher preparation programs at college or university' (p. 4)—and we would add, educational policies and reforms being imposed on schools. It is 'not easy work, nor is it fast [because] critically questioning ourselves forces us to interrogate our pedagogy. [I]t offers us options, not habits; reflection rather than reaction; responsibility instead of rote responses' (p. 4). In other words, working toward an educative community is to pursue ideals that amount to 'an engagement of the imagination' (p. 5) rather than becoming a slave to the dictates, prescriptions or agenda of others. According to Romano (2000), an educative community, whether of the kind she studied intensively in the third-grade classroom of Mr. Greg at 'Wetlands Elementary,' or in the high schools we studied, all aspire to a number of touchstones: 'trust, communal ways of understanding . . . [and] compassionate imagination' (p. 105)—the latter referring to 'opportunities to strengthen . . . personal, social and intellectual capacities to engage in public life' (p. 105). To put it another way, 'the space and deliberative pace in which . . . sense-making is cultivated' (p. 3). We have already touched on some of these ideals in our accounts of the ways in which teachers in the project schools extended students' horizons and engaged them in community development projects. Rather than seeing the school as somehow separate from the local community, teachers saw the school as a significant resource for the community and at the same time drew upon the 'funds of knowledge' (Moll et al., 1992) of the community to enrich the school curriculum and the lives of students.

We think Romano (2000) is worth following a little further because of the centrality of her argument that educative communities are about 'striving to locate some balance out of the competing tensions between individuals and the common good' (p. 107). She is especially helpful in the way she invokes Walzer's (1983) notion of 'distributive justice' as a way of understanding educative communities—whether that be of a classroom or a school as a whole—in the 'recognition of all members' so they may engage in the 'exchange' of four kinds of 'social goods' (p. 111) or touchstones.

Firstly, 'capacity to tolerate conflict' (p. 111)—which is another way of saying, 'can sustain disagreement and difference and hold it in creative tension' (p. 111) rather than allowing it to dominate or destroy difference. Practically speaking, this means cultivating places where 'different voices and ideas are listened to and encouraged, and where the potential for shared understanding will be increased' (p. 111). Secondly, 'tolerance for difference' (p. 112)—where each person is recognized and respected, and where difference is not seen as threatening. Thirdly, 'tolerance for ambiguity' (p. 112)—where 'uncertainty is named and recognized' (p. 112), and there is space for people to think through what difference means for them. Fourthly, 'sense of belonging' (p. 113)—which is an outcome of dialog, authentic relations with others, respect and recognition, and where no one feels 'diminished by diversity' (p. 113).

To underscore and reinforce our point that these touchstones for the exchange of social goods are not only ideals to be strived for, we would add that they are also tangible expressions of practical realities lived out in actual schools. We have already described Plainsville's efforts to foster respectful and trusting relationships as a starting point for intellectual and social engagement that involved a shift from teacher-directed to student-centered curriculum. In terms of the touchstones described above, this transformation was indicative of a commitment to democratic practices, a high regard for individual difference and a pedagogical response to students in poverty. Discussions about values, ethical choices and moral dilemmas were an integral part of the learning that occurred at Plainsville as evident in the following observations from a middle school meeting:

> At the outset of the reflection session, the principal, Leanne, talked to 3 middle school groups (some 64 students) about the main purpose of learning in the first two weeks of term. She emphasized the importance of building effective relationships—more often referred to as 'bonding'—and made a connection between this goal and values. She went on to ask 'What is a value?' A girl responded 'a value is something you treasure.' Leanne then began to summarize responses on the white board. It was apparent that some students only recognized value in the monetary sense. This prompted a discussion about the different meanings of value. Once some clarification had taken place Leanne set the students the following learning activity: 'In your personal history folder, share two or three values that you hold and that you try to act upon.' Further comments and discussion followed during which students began to share some of their own values. 'I value diversity, that's why I joined the peer mediation group,' said one girl. Others identified honesty, loyalty and friendship as important values. Lisa suggested

that two girls valued conservation because of their work on environmental issues. The question of whether it is ever okay to tell a lie was brought up. Leanne suggested that this might become a topic for debate. [Comment: Discussions about personal beliefs and values are often left off the education agenda and it is refreshing to see some open discussion about such matters. The focus on values in this session also highlights the flexibility of the curriculum in this school. This was not planned at the beginning of the day but arose out of issues raised by students and teachers in other activities, especially around the notion of respectful relationships.] (Field notes, February 4, 2003)

Inclusion and cooperation are important cultural norms not only for middle schools but also for all multicultural contexts (Beane & Lipka, 1987; Deering, 1996). Indeed, much of the rationale for reform in the middle years is based on the need to develop an inclusive curriculum which focuses on adolescents' interests and concerns and includes their cultural heritage into the program of studies. We have described some of the tensions involved in this endeavor in Chapter 5, but tolerance for difference and an appreciation of cultural diversity were evident to varying degrees in all the project schools. It was reflected in the choice of curriculum topics and themes which engaged students in learning about Aboriginal culture and heritage, the multicultural origins and nature of Australian society, the contributions of women to the political, economic and cultural development of society, and issues of adolescent identity and development. It was apparent in the policies and programs to address serious concerns about the physical and psychological health of students, and the various forms of harassment and alienation experienced by particular groups of students.

To cite a specific example from the project schools, Seachange High School made student well-being a high priority after a whole-school survey raised serious concerns about issues of health, safety, tolerance and respect within the school community. Among a range of initiatives, a well-being committee comprising student representatives introduced programs in values education, pastoral care, mental health, social skills and positive life style choices. The school trialed a program in sexual health and relationships education and initiated a peer support program known as Yellow Ribbon in which students trained in peer counseling acted as trusted friends to students being harassed in the school grounds.

What we saw in the most disadvantaged of the project schools showed a fair degree of correspondence with the Central Park East Secondary School (CPESS) in New York's Harlem district. As described by Meier (1995), CPESS is a stunning illustration of what is possible in terms of an educative community in a high school located in a poverty-stricken urban area. It is also a high school that has reinvented itself against the obdurate, belligerent and 100-year history of the high school as a social institution. This is no mean feat. Sizer (2004) reminds us that the mainstream high school of today, whether in the United States, Australia or elsewhere, is unchanged since the 1940s:

> Most of it [the 1940s regime] is not only recognizable; it is still fully accepted and honored today as a representation of what we call secondary school: *a class* of twenty or so adolescents gathered into *grades* to learn *together* a *subject* for its *content* and for the *skills* embedded in that content taught by a *single teacher* who is responsible for *delivering* that material, assigning *homework*, and *assessing* each student's performance in a uniform manner, all this proceeding in sequential *blocks of time* of forty to sixty minutes each in a specialized *school building* primarily made up of a succession of identical rooms that are used for six hours for fewer than half the days in a year . . . This is what *school* is. (Emphases in original, pp. xi–xii)

According to Meier (1995), the key to turning a school around from the indifferent and inhumane institution described by Sizer (2004), is 'respect'—interpreted variously to mean, of people, ideas, aspirations, decision-making processes and structures. At the center of it all is 'time for consultation and information exchange' (p. 133), which means placing crucial importance on the notion of 'reflectiveness' (p. 133). A major part is also 'collective knowledge of students' lives' (p. 134) so as to underpin 'structures of supportive learning' (p. 133). The drive for this, Meier (1995) says speaking of her role as principal, comes from adopting and maintaining 'a teachers' mindset'(p. 129) and regarding the 'whole school as my classroom' (p. 129). This impetus is also due in no small measure to having an 'intellectual curiosity' (p. 134), an 'active listening' stance (p. 132), and conveying the importance of listening in ways that acknowledge the substance and legitimacy of others' concerns. This plays out in the way teachers have 'collective ownership of the workplace' and regarding it as legitimate to collaborate with colleagues on 'shared challenges' (p. 129). Under these conditions, 'knowing' becomes a case of 'knowing from the inside' (p. 130) and understandings are jointly owned rather than privately garnered. Collegial feedback thus occurs in a climate of 'openness to constructive criticism' (p. 134), rather than an atmosphere of punishment, fear or retribution. Not surprisingly, this kind of knowing from the inside is the basis for 'continuous experimentation' (p. 134) in which individuals feel a genuine commitment to being 'accountable for the work of the whole school' (p. 133) and to the wider community.

But none of this comes easily or without cost, as Fine (1994) notes when she says:

> Trying to nurture educational communities amidst the crusty, fragmented organizations we have called urban high schools requires that parents and educators who are frontrunners do double duty. They do 'what is,' create 'what could be,' transform 'what has been' in their schools, and they press for systemic transformation. In the process, they offend almost every vested interest, and former friend, at some point. (p. 25)

Several teachers in the project schools recalled their painful experiences of daring to challenge the wisdom of conventional secondary school practices. In their initial efforts to promote integrated studies and more student-centered approaches to learning, they were often accused of undermining curriculum rigor and the very foundations of the academic curriculum by their senior school colleagues. Perhaps the most insidious example of these attacks came from a disaffected teacher who pilloried primary-trained teachers in a series of spiteful cartoons. However, as we shall relate in the following chapters, these schools were committed to reinventing themselves for young people and teachers could draw on institutional structures and processes as well as school leadership to support their endeavors.

Closing remarks

In this chapter, we have explored the notion of a transformative pedagogy for teachers. Specifically, we have focused on the practices, school cultures and organizational features of schools that enable teachers to work successfully with young adolescents. Rethinking the fundamentals of teaching and learning in the middle years of schooling is a complex process that demands considerable energy, imagination and courage on the part of teachers and school administrators, especially in the current political context. Drawing on insights from the project schools and the school reform literature, we have argued that a transformative pedagogy involves both a critique of unjust educational policies and practices as well as a set of referent points doing things differently.

In trying to advance our thinking around this idea, we discussed the significance of teachers' biographies and social locations in the reconstruction of teaching practices. We concur with Buendia, Ares, Juarez & Peercy (2004) that 'local knowledge and material arrangements matter greatly in defining educators' practices and school reforms' (p. 855). Although teachers in the project schools could draw on a shared discourse on middle school pedagogy and adolescence, practices were invariably mediated by the local context and school histories. Just as importantly, a great deal of the explanatory nature of transformative pedagogy arose from our understanding of teaching as a social practice. The vast majority of the teachers and principals we interviewed were caring and committed individuals who wanted to make a difference for their students. In spite of tensions and ambiguities in their roles, the humanizing aspects of their work generally took precedence over the managerialist and instrumental conceptions of teaching. A great deal of their professional learning was focused on the relational nature of teaching and it occurred through the social networks, whether as members of officially constituted sub-schools, teaching teams, committees and district groups or informal gatherings. Finally, many of these teachers were engaged in a bigger project of teaching for an educative community, and they saw their work in terms of the contribution it could make to the creation of a socially just community. Again there were dilemmas associated with this transformative role, but progressive programs and practices in a number of the project schools enabled teachers to learn how to develop inclusive curriculum and a tolerance for difference.

How can schools reinvent themselves as more inclusive and learner-centered organizations for young adolescents? What kind of leadership practices are needed to achieve this ideal? What can we learn from the project schools about the viability of whole-school reform in the middle years? What are the challenges, impediments and issues associated with reforms of this kind? These questions are explored in the next chapter, when we consider the broader question of school reform and the localized responses from the project schools.

Note

1.   We are grateful to Rosalie Romano (2000) for drawing our attention to this term.

PART FOUR

School Lives

CHAPTER SEVEN

Schools reinventing themselves for young adolescents

Introduction

Previously, we described how teachers in the project schools were reinventing their practices to address the needs, aspirations and concerns of young adolescents. For some practitioners, these changes were motivated by personal beliefs about the inadequacy of current ways of doing things, but in the main they grew out of school environments that encouraged curriculum innovation and nurtured a culture of collaboration. By and large, these were schools where school leaders worked cooperatively with teachers, students, parents and community members to promote a systematic, whole-school approach to curriculum development. All six schools had made adolescent schooling a priority and all were committed to changing school structures and practices in response to concerns about early school leaving, alienation and student engagement. What we saw in these sites confirmed Meier's (1992) belief that 'teaching can be changed only by reinventing the institution within which teaching takes place—schools' (p. 600). This of course is no mean feat. Schools are remarkably resilient organizations that are not easily transformed by decree and coercion from above. Tyack and Cuban (1995) argue that the basic grammar of schooling has remained largely intact over many decades to the extent that:

little has changed in the ways schools divide time and space, classify students and allocate them to classrooms, splinter learning into 'subjects,' and award grades and 'cred-
its' as evidence of learning. (p. 85)

We would argue that resistance to change is sometimes well founded, especially when reform agendas are driven by ideological interests that are largely disconnected from student learning and the work of teachers. Moreover, school
improvement ultimately depends on local will and capacity for success (Fullan, 1993;
McLaughlin, 1987); it cannot be accomplished without the knowledge and skills
of teachers, the active involvement of parents and the consent of young people
themselves.

The chapters in this part move the story beyond individual agency to an
account of whole-school reform in the realm of adolescence education. We have
taken the view that enduring and substantive changes to classroom practice are only
possible with institutional support and leadership at the school, district and system
level—teachers cannot go about it alone. Since we have already sketched the structural features of school reform in the project schools in Chapter 2, our intention in
this chapter is to explore some of the achievements, dilemmas and tensions associated with these processes, in particular school contexts. In Chapter 8, we move
beyond the project schools and engage in some re-imagining of schooling as we
explore the idea of the pedagogically engaged school. Our account is one of 'hope
without illusion' (Carlson, 2005) insofar as we acknowledge that reinventing schooling for young people in the current political climate is beset with difficulties, frustrations and ambiguities. Notwithstanding a sense of optimism and hope, the
principals, teachers and community personnel in the study were under no illusions
as to the enormity of the task and the amount of 'unfinished business' involved in
their work. Their narratives reveal something of the tensions and problematic elements of moves to steer reform back to students amidst a push for high stakes testing, outcomes-based education and marketization of schooling.

From the outset, we want to emphasize the importance of localized responses
to adolescent education. As evident from the school portraits, the project schools
had quite unique histories, geographies, socioeconomic circumstances, cultural traditions and organizational features. In terms of reinventing themselves for young
people, they were all neither starting from the same baseline nor did they hold the
same view of what was needed to achieve this goal. Broadly speaking, the circumstances and reform agendas of the project schools could be categorized as follows:

- Reinventing an existing high school (Investigator, Seachange and Broadvale
  schools).
- Reinventing school from the ground up (Gulfview 6–12 School).

- Reinventing schooling as a seamless transition from reception to year 12 (New Vista School).
- Reinventing schooling for working class students (Plainsville R–9 School).

We should explain that although Broadvale was an R–12 school it was, until recently, divided into primary (R–7) and secondary (8–12) divisions that functioned largely as discrete schools. As a consequence, many of the practices and routines commonly associated with high school cultures prevailed.

We commence our analysis with an overview of the reform imperative in the project schools from the perspective of our informants. This is followed by a brief explanation of a model of whole-school improvement and a discussion of the progressive and problematic aspects of whole-school reform in selected project schools. Finally, stepping outside the project schools, we discuss the educational policy context and broader issues associated with reinventing schools for young people.

The reform imperative

The processes of going to school and growing up are profoundly intertwined, so much so that many of the "markers of independence" (Hoffman, 2002, p. 24) are traditionally linked to school events and accomplishments. Rites of passage from adolescence to adulthood are symbolically enacted in graduation ceremonies, school assemblies and other rituals that recognize and reward individual achievement in academic, artistic, cultural and sporting fields. But not all students receive certificates and awards, indeed many leave school with little to show, but report cards that are writ large with failure. It is a sad fact of life that schooling is not working for a significant proportion of young people, especially those from working class backgrounds (Smyth & Hattam et al., 2004). Unfortunately, Australia has a particularly poor record of school completion at the post-compulsory level compared with Organization for Economic Cooperation and Development (OECD) countries. From a high of 90 percent in the early 1990s, the figures have fallen to 71.6 percent in the early 2000s (Australian Bureau of Statistics, 2000a, b). Not only is this a concern for individual school leavers and their families, but also it is a major economic and political concern for the nation.

The state government's response to the issue of falling school completion rates has been to raise the school leaving age from 15 to 16 years—in effect to compel young people to stay longer at school—and to review the senior school curriculum with a view to broadening the vocational studies options for students. Through the agency of a social inclusion department, the government has proposed a series of strategies to address issues of emotional and physical well-being, student participation, school organization and community capacity building. However, at the system level most energy has been directed toward monitoring and improving student attendance as the foundation of success at school. At the same time, the education system is involved in a major drive to assess (and supposedly lift) literacy and numeracy outcomes chiefly through basic skills tests conducted in years 3, 5 and 7.

There is no doubt that schools (including the project schools) have been caught in a cross-current of system-driven priorities, many of which stem from a corporatist reform agenda, and priorities developed from their own reading of what is needed to improve teaching and learning in their own communities. The motivation for change in most of the project schools stemmed from the intersecting concerns of school completion, alienation, engagement and underachievement, especially in the adolescent years. Although the nature and extent of problems varied from school to school, teachers typically spoke of a lack of curriculum relevance and the inadequacy of high school structures and programs to meet the needs of young people today. Many cited the impersonal nature of large secondary schools and the lack of attention to individual differences as particular concerns. They spoke of student indifference, disaffection and disengagement as manifested in high levels of truancy, escalating rates of in-school detention, suspension and exclusion, non-compliance with school rules (especially school uniform guidelines), passive resistance—'acting dumb,' 'off-task' behavior in class, and low levels of participation and achievement in academic learning. In some schools, these problems were exacerbated by substance abuse, aggressive and anti-social behaviors, and various forms of harassment.

The notion of 'students at risk' was frequently invoked to convey concerns about the likelihood of particular groups of students leaving school without achieving basic levels of competency in literacy, numeracy and skills for social living. Typically included in this category were indigenous students, those from working class backgrounds, students from non-English-speaking families and those with special needs. In some instances, the problems were deemed to be more acute among boys but, as Conrad from Seachange School pointed out, behavioral matters often disguised deeper learning problems:

> I *really* think that a number of boys, and some girls, have skillfully used the survival mechanism of 'dickheadism' if we can put it like that. There is a culture of 'dickhead-ism.' To mask and overcome scrutiny of the real problems—lack of academic skills—they use their ability to be idiots in class to take the focus by peers and by teachers off their learning inabilities. As a consequence, the focus has gone off maths and English to behavior and the boys when in doubt, very adeptly resort to behavior as a rescuing structure to get them off the emotional hook that would follow scrutiny. The other thing that these boys do is they impose mediocrity on the other boys in the class. If some of the other boys (and the girls) dare to aspire beyond mediocrity to get good grades they

can influence them to lower their targets so as not to achieve too high to offend the ruf-
fians in the class but not to achieve so low as to fail. So there's that sort of, you know:
'It's okay to get a "B" because I won't stick my head up too much, but I don't want to
get a "C" because I'll be in strife at home. So "B" is okay to keep me out of trouble where
I'm going, right. If I'm a good student, a "B" will keep me sort of okay' and there's that
sort of play that goes on. But you can see the behavior games happening as a result of
problems with learning. (Conrad, October 20, 2003)

In the Australian vernacular, 'dickhead' is a rather vulgar, sexually derived term
that is commonly conferred on an individual (generally a male) who engages in irra-
tional, irresponsible and anti-social behavior. Conrad's colorful description of the
culture of 'dickheadism' and the mediocrity that it engenders resonates quite
strongly with Willis's (1977) account of the oppositional behavior of the working
class boys in his ethnographic study, *Learning to Labour*. By doing just enough to
stay out of trouble at home, yet remain 'cool' with their peers at school, the boys in
Conrad's school learnt to survive at school. But it is not difficult to see how the culture of the high school fostered this kind of behavior. As revealed in James's portrait in Chapter 3, high schools in particular are hierarchical and coercive institutions
that tend to incubate a 'them and us' mentality when it comes to staff–student
relationships.

The issue of curriculum is crucial. According to Meier (2002), schools are
often organized around 'passive learning of curricula designed to cover a massive
amount of material.' Learning of this kind discourages exploration, understanding
and creativity, especially when it is largely insulated from the social and emotional
lives of students. Teachers in the project schools spoke of problems associated with
large-class sizes, inflexible timetables, subject specialization and the pressures of
competitive learning environments. They told us that schooling had not kept up with
the changing nature of adolescence, the influence of information and communication technologies on society and the profound impact of media culture on youth
identities. Most regarded the adolescent years as a crucial phase of schooling
because in their view it laid the foundations for success in the post-compulsory years.
In a state with a shrinking youth labor market, possession of a certificate of senior
schooling was seen as especially important passport to employment. In short, there
were many compelling reasons for the project schools to disturb the 'continuity of
practice' in high schools (Elmore, 1987) and establish structures, cultures and programs that were more responsive to the needs and aspirations of students in the
teenage years.

To this point, we have made some generalizations regarding the underlying
motives for change, but we want to stress the contextualized nature of the curriculum response in the project—an issue we take up in the next section of this chapter.

Whole-school change

There is nothing particularly novel about the idea of grassroots reform (Connell, 1993; Fullan, 1993; Goodman, Baron & Myers, 1999; McInerney, 2004), but the practical and political strategies required to achieve such change often remain elusive. How do schools change entrenched practices, structures and cultures? What resources and ideas are needed to bring about long-lasting reforms? To what extent can schools go about it alone? In pursuing these questions, it is worth recording that the idea of 'whole-school change' as a vehicle for school improvement had its Australian roots in the Disadvantaged Schools Program (DSP) established by the Federal Labor Government in 1974 (Connell, 1993). Originally conceived as a compensatory program to offset educational disadvantage for children in poverty, the DSP became a vehicle for democratizing schools and reforming the mainstream curriculum. Since it regarded the individual school as the fundamental site for educational change, the DSP helped to undermine the top-down approaches to school reform associated with a highly centralized education system and acted as a conduit for new ideas. Curriculum development was now invested more strongly in local communities, and teachers, in concert with parent groups, had a much greater say in school programs.

The National Schools Network (NSN), a school reform organization linking schools, teachers unions and governments, also provided a model of whole-school reform in the 1990s, although it attached a much greater emphasis to action research as a means of improving teaching practices and student learning. The NSN view of successful school reform lies in the intersection among three interrelated factors:

1. *Restructuring*: structural and organizational reforms such as changing the use of time and space, grouping of staff and students, staff roles, curriculum organization and the use of technology.
2. *Reculturing*: changing values, beliefs, assumptions, habits, patterns of behavior and relationships in school organizational culture.
3. *Changing pedagogy*: concentrating on classroom "instructional practice," the teaching and learning process and student learning outcomes (Harradine, 1996, p. 4).

We find this heuristic to be a particularly useful way of mapping the features of school change in the area of adolescent education, and it is one that we shall keep referring to in our case studies.

Although schools are sometimes able to access ideas and resources from external sources, including government-funded projects, a good deal of evidence suggests that measures to improve schooling have to be worked out locally by those whose lives are most intimately connected to the education and welfare of students (Griffiths, 1998). In what follows, we look more closely at the three situations in the project schools. As we have already described the pedagogical response to poverty and exclusion at Plainsville in Chapter 3, we will confine our account to case studies which are illustrative of the complexities involved in (1) reinventing an existing high school, (2) reinventing schooling from the ground up and (3) reinventing schooling as a seamless transition from reception to year 12.

Reinventing an existing high school

The task of reforming high schools from within is especially difficult and complex, not least because many of the so-called 'agents of change' inside the schools (i.e. teachers and administrators) often remain unconvinced of the merits of alternatives. Although some may change their stance in the light of successful curriculum innovations and professional development programs, there is always a danger that opponents will engage in acts of resistance and non-compliance that may well derail the reform agenda. In this account, we want to take a closer look at the issues involved in reinventing existing high schools through narrative accounts from teachers and school leaders at Seachange, Broadvale and Investigator schools.

We begin with the observation that high schools are formidable and seemingly immovable creatures when it comes to changing their ways. In a previous publication (Smyth, McInerney, Hattam & Lawson, 1999), we described them as credentialing organizations that help to legitimize compartmentalized knowledge, reinforce hierarchies of power and exercise a powerful role in sorting students according to perceptions of their vocational and/or academic potential. The process is inherently unjust because:

> High schools and the ways they constitute what is important about schooling play a pivotal role in who gets to have a share in society's rewards, and those opportunities are reflective of existing advantage or disadvantage. Allowing and actively constructing some parts of the curriculum so that they reproduce existing power relationships means access to some students and denial to others. Some students get access because of inherited educational capital, while others through no fault of their own are shunted into parts of the curriculum that effectively represent economic cul-de-sacs for later benefits in life. (p. 9)

In Australia, higher education institutions have historically exerted an immense influence on education systems both in terms of what knowledge is valued in schools and the way in which it is assessed. In many ways, they have acted as filters for universities in sorting out the academically able from the less able through public examinations. Although this influence is most profound in the senior secondary years, it has permeated the lower years of schooling in the form of subject specialization, hierarchies of knowledge and an undue emphasis on academic learning that is often disconnected to the lives of students. Aside from these constraints, the relationships in many high school settings are often characterized by power differentials which deny students a real voice in decision-making and impose unreasonable limits on their freedom. In previous chapters, we have described the technologies of exclusion that operate against the most marginalized students in schools, and we have also highlighted the damaging consequences of individualized forms of instruction which supposedly cater to individual differences but paradoxically foster competitive isolated learning environments (Goodman & Kuzmic, 1997).

All of what we have said so far points to the immense challenges confronting would-be reformers. But when there is compelling evidence that traditional schooling is not working for students, as we explained earlier in this chapter, or when the act of teaching itself is badly degraded, the imperative to change becomes apparent. Simply put, it is a matter of survival. Among other factors, the incentive for reinventing an existing high school at Broadvale, Seachange and Investigator arose out of dissatisfaction with the graded classroom, the competitive academic curriculum, the lack of attention to student voice and the highly individualized nature of instruction. In terms of the heuristic described earlier, they involved the following:

- Structural changes including the construction of architecturally designed middle schools, middle school leadership positions, the appointment of a small cohort of middle school teachers, flexible staffing and timetable arrangements, and regularly scheduled middle school meetings.
- Cultural changes in the form of middle school teaching teams, pastoral care programs, and an emphasis on relational and cooperative learning.
- Pedagogical changes including a shift toward integrated and negotiated curriculum, increased student participation in decision-making and some steps toward more authentic assessment practices, including the use of student portfolios.

Leadership

In all three schools, the role of leadership was a crucial factor in establishing middle schooling as a major priority and in redirecting funds to facilitate organizational and instructional changes, and teacher development. Patrick, the principal of

Seachange, offered the following insights into the cultural and pedagogical work of curriculum leaders.

IT'S ABOUT BUILDING LEARNING COMMUNITIES

I place a lot of emphasis on professional development. When I arrived at the school three years ago, we had a budget of $4000 and the comment I made to staff was 'If you can convince your line manager that you need T&D [training and development] to achieve the goals which the school has set, then I'll pay for it.' We didn't place a limit on it and the result was that in the first year we spent over $50,000.

Leadership in the middle school needs to look at how you develop learning communities. I think they need to understand curriculum coherence; to be able to develop some curriculum clarity that is one of the gray areas in middle schooling. They need to understand value systems and decision-making right across from years 6 to 9, not just at some stages of adolescence. We made a commitment that our curriculum leaders would not become management people. So what we did was to buy enough time to be able to give time to some teachers to become year level managers, and the year level managers have very much dealt with the behavioral type issues and kept the oil on the cogs to keep the organization moving. That's freed up our coordinators to focus on their curriculum or learning areas. We didn't flatten the organization but gave other people leadership opportunities in different directions.

Unfortunately I think we didn't *ever* change enough our expectations of those who are coordinators and I think that some have actually gone to sleep. Some will retire next year but that's been part of our problem. And we've got some who are resisting change and while you take the roles away, they haven't accepted the new roles, either. So I think there are some issues there about changing the school culture, that sometimes—while principals cannot select their staff—then I think we'll always have that hangover. I think there's got to be engagement at the classroom level that becomes important. Often we select leaders because of their management skills rather than because of their educative enthusiasm and skills there.

(Patrick, principal of Seachange School, November 6, 2003)

Patrick's insistence that middle school coordinators must be curriculum leaders and not just managers resonates strongly with Sergiovanni's (1996) concerns about the dangers of importing into schools leadership theories and practices that are more consistent with the purposes and nature of businesses or corporations rather than schools. This has led to a situation where:

We now import our theories of leadership from management disciplines anchored in our business schools, and we import our leadership practices from corporations, baseball teams, armies, transportation systems, and other organizations. (Sergiovanni, 1996, p. xii)

In spite of efforts to limit their roles to curriculum leadership, it was apparent in some instances that the work of middle school coordinators was intensified as a consequence of additional responsibilities written into their roles, especially student behavior management supervision and, in some cases, faculty leadership. Another impediment to pedagogical reform arose from the staffing policies of the education system.

Staffing matters

Although project schools were able to draw on the resources of state and federal projects to support adolescent education programs in such areas as mental health, drug awareness and student participation, system support for middle school reform has waned over the past decade. Many of the structures to support middle schooling were in place at the three project schools, but they had a limited capacity to resource and staff new initiatives. Since they were bound by industrial agreements, schools were unable to freely select teachers with the knowledge of and commitment to middle schooling. Sam's account of the history of middle schooling at Broadvale illustrates the limitations of this situation:

> Well I've been connected with the middle school here since they were being touted as the way to go. We developed 'the unit' which has separate classrooms, an activity room, a special interest room and a huge central common area. It was designed specifically for middle schooling when the school was redone about 10 years ago. Four year 8 classes were run on what I considered a true model of integrated curriculum where the teachers took four core subjects and they ran them as a team across the four classes. They had time off to develop an inclusive curriculum program. The key to it was that we initially had committed teachers, a very proactive middle school leader and great support for middle schooling within an R–12 setting. But the unit no longer operates like it used to, although this year it's operating better than it has been over the last two or three years because we have two primary-trained teachers in there with the year 7/8 classes. Nobody has yet come up with a better model of middle schooling that meets the needs of kids at that level. But the other thing that is really important is that our school has not had a reasonable pastoral program. It depends completely on the teacher. It either works or it doesn't. (Sam, April 2, 2003)

Collaboration

Disrupting the institutional arrangements and organizational habits of high schools demands immense commitment and courage on the part of school leaders and practitioners. To work in teaching teams on integrated curriculum, for example, is to work against the grain of a prevailing culture of privatism, subject boundaries and faculty orientation to teaching (McInerney, Hattam & Smyth, 2001). Given the entrenched nature of these practices, it is difficult to compel teachers to move out of their isolated classrooms and teach collaboratively. The Broadvale principal summed up the dilemma in the following words:

> Collaboration is crucial for middle schooling but with any collaborative work there are enormous tensions, whether they are things like time or personalities involved. Invariably the best efforts are the ones that grow and evolve naturally. My experience tells me that when you manufacture or put collaborative groups together it's a very hit and miss process as to their effectiveness. Different people will collaborate at different levels and in different ways. For some teachers, lesson planning or topic planning is good, for others the actual sharing of practice and of working collaboratively is the way to go and for others it's more just a touching base and being there is what they need and a sense of place through a group of teachers who meet together or whatever. Some of the stuff that I've seen that's done in terms of teaching teams and integrated curriculum at this school has been outstanding. Unfortunately, some of it I have seen has been just puerile, just so manufactured that it's lost all its rigor. It's more about teachers working together than kids actually doing meaningful work that leads to a genuine engagement and authentic learning. Some of it is just so contrived. (Garfield, April 4, 2003)

The dangers of contrived collegiality are spelled out quite forcefully in Garfield's remarks, and they probably go some way to explaining why most teaching teams at Broadvale were organized on a voluntary basis and were usually restricted to years 7 and 8. From our observations, progressive middle school practices, such as negotiated and integrated curriculum, tended to dissipate in years 9 and 10 when student learning was bound more tightly to traditional school subjects, and the emphasis on relational learning and pastoral care was much less apparent.

Acting politically and strategically

Advocates for curriculum change in all three schools had to engage with the dynamics of power that operated at the micro-political level of their sites (Goodman et al., 1999). In particular, they had to battle to seek a greater share of the financial, bureaucratic and pedagogical power fused into faculties through budget arrangements, leadership practices and curriculum decision-making processes. This meant that even simple requests for resources took on a political and personal dimension with middle school coordinators having to rely on the goodwill and cooperation of faculty leaders for resources and materials to support interdisciplinary projects.

More than any other structure, the school timetable has come to symbolize the hegemonic character of high schools. Not surprisingly, the battle for control of the timetable became a defining feature of the struggle to transform teaching practices in all three schools. Sally Anne explained the importance of acting politically and strategically in her capacity as a middle school coordinator at Seachange High School:

> The things that I think were crucial to middle schooling were changing structures. The way I did that was to go on every committee that I could, particularly the timetable committee. I could see that the only way I was going to get *big* school changes—whole-school change—was through timetable and curriculum. Getting a budget line through the finance committee was crucial. Being very involved in timetabling enabled me to make changes like block timetabling. When I first started here, there were seven lessons a day and we moved every lesson. The only doubles [i.e. periods] were over a recess or lunch break so you didn't ever get a block of time with a group of students, so we could never deal with issues in the classroom because they were always moving in and out. (Sally Anne, October 28, 2005)

In practical terms, the shift from 40- to 90-minute lessons increased flexibility and allowed for more sustained student engagement with integrated studies and out-of-class learning while creating the possibility of enhanced teacher–student relationships.

Policy and practice mismatch

Since reform was taking place within existing school structures at Investigator, Seachange and Broadvale, middle schooling practices often sat uncomfortably with whole-school policies. Some sense of the mismatch between the school's assessment and reporting practices and middle school ideals is conveyed in the following remarks from Bernard, a middle school coordinator at Investigator High School:

> My students are involved in peer assessment but I think as a school we are a long way off authentic assessment and reporting. That's one of the areas where senior school impacts on the middle school. We use the same assessment terminology used by senior school teachers who are preparing students for the certificate of education. We have to give students a number out of 20 for every subject area at the end of the semester. We have parent/teacher/student interviews once a year but it's not authentic assessment. The kids' input into the official assessment process is nil. I make it work in my own classroom by doing the sorts of things I think you should do in assessing a broad range of outcomes but our assessment process is definitely top-down. It's addressed to the individual so the parents aren't included. What sort of a partnership is that? The ideal thing for middle school is for students to have a portfolio with work samples. This would give parents far more information about their children's achievements. I have been frustrated as hell about the situation. I have put out papers and I've spoken at meetings. I've done everything I can but I just keep hitting a brick wall. We have to try to carry both

middle school teachers' sensibility regarding assessment and the school's official policy. This leads to confusion and ambiguity. The curriculum committee wants a uniform system but the needs of middle and senior students are different. (Bernard, November 23, 2000)

Bernard's remarks show just how difficult it is for individuals to change existing practices without whole-school commitment and support. Although Bernard had tried hard to promote peer assessment and reflective practices in his own class, his efforts had been undermined by a school policy that insisted on grading student achievement according to senior school criteria. In this case, the demand for uniformity across the school led to confusion and ambiguity about the purposes of assessment and reporting in the adolescent years.

In summary, the three schools had made significant progress in reinventing themselves for young people, but there was a general recognition of the unfinished nature of the task and the tensions and struggles to break free from their high school legacies. Although the merits of integrated and negotiated curriculum in years 6–9 had won broad acceptance within the project schools, there was often a gap between rhetoric and practice with the result that the ideal was being carried by a small band of enthusiasts, rather than the staff as a whole. Claudia, a middle school coordinator at Broadvale, expressed her frustrations about the lack of progress in the following words:

I don't think we have an understanding of good practice for middle schooling. The administration does not support group planning. People don't have time. We have it in structure, but I think that's all. We have extra coordinators put in place, so there's more support for the teachers but our role is mostly just behavior management stuff. We just pick up the pieces, non-stop, all the time. We did have that a bit when I first came here in the nineties; our deputy principal was quite committed to student voice and middle schooling and we had the four year 8 classes in the unit. The four teachers *did* do integrated curriculum and they *were* given time to plan together. There *was* some shared teaching, team teaching, but it all depended on the teacher. (Claudia, March 3, 2003)

Reinventing school from the ground up

Very rarely do communities have the opportunity to design their own school, select the staff, develop the curriculum and decide on the best means of grouping students. Certainly in Australia, most school reform takes place within existing institutions—a situation that invariably leads to the kinds of frustration, tensions and compromises discussed so far in schools in this chapter. We rather like the simile invoked by Thomson (1992) when she talks about the inherent difficulties of this project:

> It's been said that changing schooling is like trying to design a 747 in mid air. You don't know what it's going to turn into and you can't let it fall down while you're trying to find out. (p. 25)

Unlike the other project schools, Gulfview was designed from the outset 'to cater for the needs of young adolescents through integrated and negotiated school programs' (Gulfview School Context Statement, 2004). To pursue the aeronautical image, it was not being redesigned in midair. As the school was literally starting from the ground up, it did not have to contend with a history of entrenched secondary school practices that might have stood in the way of the cultural and pedagogical shifts required to implement an integrated curriculum, vertically grouped classes, and interdisciplinary teaching and learning teams. But community acceptance was another matter. When the school was opened in 1996, many parents remained to be convinced of the merits of alternative models of schooling and several teachers were still struggling to rid themselves of the 'cultural baggage' they had brought from their high school experiences.

A license to be innovative

Acceptance of middle schooling in the early years at Gulfview probably owes much to the foundation principal and a leadership team that was skilled in community relations and able to articulate a coherent middle school philosophy. Teachers were given time and resources to develop curriculum and a license to be innovative. But perhaps, the most significant factor was the role of the sub-schools in promoting the idea of learning communities. As explained in Chapter 2, Gulfview originally consisted of architecturally designed sub-schools which functioned as discrete units for the grouping of students and the delivery of the educational program across years 7–9 and learning teams for teachers. Sub-school teams had considerable autonomy in terms of timetabling and staffing arrangements, curriculum development and teaching methodologies. As teachers shared office spaces and teaching areas, they were able to plan together and engage in team teaching practices. Within the teams, they got to 'play their strengths' not only in teaching in their area of subject specialization but also learnt how to develop teaching competencies in other fields. Sub-school coordinators and experienced teachers acted as mentors for novices, and subject specialists took responsibility for developing and sharing resources and school-based professional development. Team formation and identity was reinforced through fortnightly sub-school meetings, curriculum planning days and social events, all of which promoted a sense of collegiality and common purpose.

Curriculum coherence

When curriculum development operates through sub-school teams, there is always a risk that ideas and resources may be trapped in the enclaves of separate work areas or, worse still, that autonomy of this kind may lead to inconsistency in curriculum practices across the school. Several strategies helped to promote whole-school curriculum dialog at Gulfview. Firstly, time was set aside in general staff meetings for sub-school presentations when teachers could learn from colleagues about curriculum planning and development. Secondly, standing committees in technology, literacy, curriculum coordination and areas of study met on a regular basis to discuss and debate whole-school curriculum matters, such as assessment and reporting, and student behavior management. Thirdly, the school developed curriculum benchmarks, incorporating skills and competencies in each area of study, as a basis for a common approach to assessment and reporting. Drawing on successful primary school practices, the reporting system incorporated the use of portfolios as a means of documenting student achievement in eight areas of curriculum. With the assistance of teachers, students maintained an ongoing record of their learning which was used as the basis for dialog about learning in parent–teacher interviews.

Learning communities and integrated curriculum

The sub-school set-up at Gulfview helped to foster educative student–teacher relationships as the foundation for learning. The notion of a learning community was developed in two main ways. Firstly, students were grouped in sub-schools where they related to a small team of teachers each taking them for two or three subjects. Secondly, within sub-schools they were further organized into small vertically grouped home classes with a teacher taking responsibility for their pastoral care. These arrangements tended to create a family atmosphere in which students got to relate to several staff members rather than just one teacher, as they had in the primary years. Students also developed a strong sense of sub-school identity because they were together for most of their lessons, and many remained within the one sub-school for several years.

The notion of an integrated curriculum was well advanced at Gulfview. Although national and state curriculum guidelines helped to define the broad areas of learning for students, decisions about content and emphasis were made by teachers in conjunction with students. Elsewhere in this book, we have discussed the ways in which teachers, like Lauren, negotiated curriculum with the students in her sub-school—a process that involved considerable teacher expertise in extending student's imagination when it came to the selection of topics and in developing a critical edge to issues identified by students.

Tensions and dilemmas

With its purpose-built sub-schools and team teaching arrangements, Gulfview was seemingly well placed to cater to the needs of young adolescents, but over the past five years some of the key principles have been sorely tested and, in some instances, abandoned, as the senior secondary years of a high school have been added to the school. Formally opened on the same site in 2000, the senior school provides an academic and vocational education for students in years 11 and 12. Although the school attempted to provide a seamless transition between the middle and senior schools, the new structures created some major curriculum and staffing problems. Stewart, a teacher who had been at the school since its foundation, expressed his frustrations as follows:

> We have gone off track. We were meant to be the pilot school for middle schooling in the state. But in the first year that the senior secondary school was established the senior teachers started making a noise about students' preparation for years 11 and 12. 'These kids don't know what a simple quadratic equation is,' they complained. 'What's going on down in the middle school? Blah, blah, blah. You need specialists down there.' We've had some problems maintaining sub-school arrangements because we now have a line timetable across the whole school. We've lost our flexibility. I think it's got to the point now that it's totally impossible for people to team because in our sub-school we've got people who may be teaching the odd line in *another* sub-school. Just like a traditional high school where senior people often dictate what happens in the junior secondary, we went through a phase where the seniors were dictating what happened. In terms of timetable changes, specialists were set up to teach the arts and whatever. They didn't want to be middle school teachers.
>
> Our staffing has grown beyond the initial cohort of pioneers and we're getting a lot of traditional secondary people coming who don't really know what this school has lost. These people come in and suddenly they're told, 'Well, you've got to teach your home group, three or four subjects of your timetable' and they say 'Well, I can't do that and I'm just a home economics teacher' or 'I am just an arts teacher,' and that of course doesn't help multi-skilling your team. So you get the disaffected secondary people who don't want to be here and feel a bit sold out because they thought it was like a traditional high school. Many of us who were here from the beginning are quite 'pissed off.' (Stewart, November 6, 2002)

Stewart's comments show how readily middle school practices can be undermined when the sociology of the high school begins to reassert itself. With the senior school credentialing processes bearing down, teachers in the middle years were under increasing pressure to move away from an integrated curriculum to subject specialization and disciplines of knowledge. Following intense lobbying from senior school maths specialists, sub-school coordinators resorted to streaming maths classes—something which ran counter to the school's foundation principles on heterogeneous grouping. The adoption of a line timetable across the school was particularly regressive because it meant that sub-schools could no longer organize their own timetable arrangements. Teachers who had once taught almost exclusively in one sub-school now found themselves teaching in a number of sub-schools where they had to get to know many more students. A stronger faculty orientation coupled with a weakening of sub-school teams corroded the very structures on which the original middle school philosophy was built. To make matters worse, teachers lost the sub-school planning days and found themselves having to do much more of the curriculum development without the support of middle school teams.

Of real concern to Stewart and other 'pioneers' was the loss of historical memory so far as the school's purpose was concerned and the unwillingness of some newly appointed teachers to change their secondary school headsets. Lauren, a sub-school coordinator, puts it like this:

> Many secondary teachers believe that what they are doing is good. Why fix something that isn't broken? They have no understanding of middle schooling or the fundamentals of developing relationships with the kids. (Lauren, October 25, 2002)

Lauren and an older brigade of teachers were struggling to reclaim a set of adolescent schooling principles based on teaming, relationships, integrated curriculum, authentic assessment and multi-skilling, but were struggling against an increasing emphasis on subject specialization, senior school credentialing and individual work practices.

What is the education system up to?

Factors beyond the control of the school also had a detrimental impact on moves to cater to students in the adolescent years. Initially, Gulfview benefited from departmental staffing policies which enabled them to appoint a number of middle school specialists, but the school was no longer able to fill all staff vacancies through the school choice process (schools being allowed to advertise and fill vacancies rather than have teachers sent to the school)—in spite of promises made under local school management agreements. Instead, it had to comply with departmental policies, including the use of contract teachers and rules on permanency. Monique, the principal, shook her head in despair when she exclaimed:

> There are 16 teachers who have been misplaced; who don't want to be here, teaching stuff they don't want to, having to take on middle schooling they don't understand. (Monique, August 21, 2002)

We will have more to say later about the lack of system support for the adolescent years of schooling, but it is worth noting some of the damaging effects of these staffing policies on the effectiveness of the middle school teams. Again Stewart's reflections are quite insightful:

> We had some good contract teachers who were here for two or three years, just winning contract after contract . . . [they eventually] got permanent jobs elsewhere because they lost faith in the system. . . . They just went elsewhere and therefore we had to backfill a lot of people through the transfer system, who've come, again come from that traditional secondary structure. That hasn't helped your teaming at all. So you've got to re-educate those people and that's extra pressure, too, because it takes a while for people to change and as you know, some people won't change. (Stewart, November 6, 2002).

Lauren claimed that the department's policies meant that the school had been unable to secure a pool of committed middle school teachers and had to deal with the damaging effects of misplaced and disaffected teachers. The intensification of work associated with the constant induction of new staff into the culture of subschools and integrated curriculum led to 'an exit of enthusiasm' (Lauren, August 7, 2002) and to 'teacher burn-out' (Petula, October 25, 2002). Our conversions with newly appointed teachers highlighted some real concerns regarding teacher preparation in the realm of middle schooling. Michael's experience was a particularly unhappy one. He saw himself as a subject specialist and questioned the value of subschools, subject integration and timetabling arrangements. In his own words, he was teaching outside his comfort zone and was very critical of staffing policies.

IF MY DAUGHTER WAS IN MY ENGLISH CLASS I'D BE UP IN ARMS

When I came here they said: 'You'll be expected to teach across curriculum areas. What other subjects would you like to teach?' And so I was given a choice. My areas of expertise are physical education (PE), geography, and society and environment (S&E). But when I was given my timetable for the next year, it included maths, English and science—subjects that I never taught before and I'd never had on my list. The deputy moved some things around so that I lost my science class. He said, 'Would you prefer to lose year 9 science and pick up say, a year 7 and 9 English? Is that easier for you?' I thought, 'It's got to be easier than teaching year 9 science. I mean, I'm not even sure how to light a Bunsen burner.' Fortunately for me, my wife is a maths and science teacher and if it wasn't for her, me going home and saying, 'Um, what's "whole numbers?" Is that a topic?' 'Yes, that's a topic.' 'Oh, what's involved in that?' 'Well, here are some worksheets.' 'Thanks, dear.' 'Here's a textbook, which we use,' and I've got her textbooks and handouts. I don't know if there's a maths coordinator here. At my last school we had a maths faculty and a senior. Everything that you wanted was in the mathematics room. I don't know if there's something like that here but nobody has ever pointed it out to me. There are no textbooks. For your middle school photocopying, you're given 300 sheets for the term and I used them up in two days. Fortunately, somebody gave me a senior school photocopy number because I teach year 10 physical education. . . . Our school is not catering for the needs of kids in middle school. If my daughter was in my English class, I'd be up in arms. If she was in my maths class, I'd be going, 'Oh my god, that's terrible.'

(Michael, October 25, 2002)

Although it may be tempting to blame Michael for a somewhat inflexible approach to teaching, we can also empathize with his situation; after all, 'it is difficult to be pedagogically graceful when you are lost in unfamiliar territory' (Eisner, 1992, p. 611). But more importantly, Michael's dilemma rises serious questions for schools and education systems about the fate of students caught up in staffing problems of this kind. Anecdotally, it seems that many students, especially those in remote regions, are being taught by teachers who lack the necessary qualifications and subject expertise required in the middle and senior years. In these circumstances, it is pertinent to ask: How do teachers learn about curriculum integration without planning opportunities and strong collegial support? and How can they develop more enduring relationships with students if they teach across a number of sub-schools and year levels?

The lack of system support for the education of young adolescents was a frequently occurring theme in our conversations with principals and teachers. Although the education department formulated a middle school action plan in 1994, most of the curriculum support for schools had vanished by the end of the decade. According to Monique, the department's policy was:

focused more on retention [school completion], attendance and keeping kids here till they complete year 12—whether that's the best thing for them or not is another question—and what comes out of the literacy and numeracy tests. (Monique, July 25, 2003)

Hugh, a district education administrator and strong advocate for middle schooling, likened the system's goals to that of journeying down a narrow path of literacy and numeracy rather than focusing on the whole child. He commented:

I worry about any narrow focus. I understand the importance of kids being literate and all those sorts of things but I don't see them as the absolute goal or the end point. (Hugh, August 1, 2003)

The impermanence of reform

The teacher narratives in the Gulfview case study point to the problematic nature of school reform, even in schools whose stated purpose is to provide an alternative to the kind of educational experiences offered in traditional high schools. They tell us something of the impermanence of school reform and the high degree of dependence on local educational leadership. They also remind us of the powerful influence of credentialing bodies and tertiary organizations on schools. At a time when schools are being called to become more accountable to governments and communities through standardized testing regimes and outcomes-based education, it takes considerable courage for educators to challenge the wisdom and fairness of the competitive academic curriculum that has dominated secondary schooling in Australia. To offer an alternative without the resources, policy support and leadership of the education system itself is a very big task. It is a testimony to the will and capacity of a dedicated group of teachers and school leaders that many aspects of the middle school vision, including the negotiated and integrated curriculum in years 7–9, remain alive at Gulfview. Furthermore, the school has embarked on new initiatives to revitalize student voice and youth leadership and now offers a range of community-based programs in drug education, enterprise education and mental health.

Finally, the experience of Gulfview suggests that sustaining an alternative education philosophy and practices within a 7–12 school is especially difficult when staff members are programmed to teach across the school, and the middle and senior sections operate on a common timetable. Of course, it is difficult to avoid these practices in a relatively small school, but in these circumstances there is a real danger that senior school credentialing requirements will drive the middle school curriculum to the point where many students become disaffected with their schooling. As we have suggested above, this problem is further exacerbated when staffing policies fail to take account of the special needs and circumstances of schools like Gulfview.

Reinventing schooling as a seamless transition

The very rationale for middle schooling is often based on the imperative of smoothing the educational transition for students as they move from the self-contained classroom of the primary school to a multitude of classes, teachers and subjects in a secondary school. However, middle schooling has also been conceived as a separate phase of schooling designed to cater for the developmental needs of young adolescents. As we saw at Gulfview, this recognition generated demands for structural, cultural and pedagogical changes to support integrated curriculum, pastoral care programs and team teaching practices as an alternative to the mainstream high school curriculum. But instituting a different set of educational arrangements for young adolescents can create new dilemmas for schools, not the least of these being the issues of curriculum coherence. According to Luke et al. (2003), there is a worrying tendency toward regarding middle schooling as a distinct phase of schooling, instead of viewing it as part of a continuum in the education of young people. In these circumstances, there is a danger that programs and policies designed for students in the middle years may have little connection to curriculum in other years. Thus middle school advocates are confronted with a twofold challenge: how to reinvent schools for adolescents while maintaining curriculum coherence in the various phases of schooling.

As we have described in Chapter 2, New Vista commenced in its restructured form as a reception to year 12 school, consisting of senior, middle and primary school campuses, in the mid-1990s. The circumstances surrounding the origins of the school created a unique opportunity for a seamless approach to schooling. Although each site had its own leadership team and retained a degree of autonomy in terms of local priorities, the school was remarkable for the high level of cooperation across the campuses with regard to governance, administration, curriculum development and school planning. In what follows, we want to explore the idea of New Vista as a networked collaborative community and show how these cooperative arrangements helped to ensure a measure of curriculum coherence across the primary/secondary years.

A networked collaborative community

There is a marked tendency for schools to operate as stand-alone entities. Even when primary and secondary schools are located on the same site, teachers often work in isolation when it comes to curriculum development and professional dialog. Although many high schools have programs to ease the transition of students from the primary to secondary years, few have been able to create the culture and conditions necessary for curriculum coherence from R–12. But at New Vista, the idea of a school as a locally networked community has been enhanced through whole-school decision-making structures, including an R–12 Governing Council, student forums and cross-campus committees, which engage parents, teachers and students in school planning processes and curriculum development. Community consultation in 2003 generated a three-year school development plan incorporating five major priorities: (1) literacy and numeracy; (2) information technology across the curriculum; (3) the development of an R–12 curriculum continuum; (4) school/community links and (5) future education. The latter priority reflected an ongoing interest in a whole-school approach to environmental education, ecological sustainability and applied technologies. Although each campus responded to these priorities in slightly different ways, all had a commitment to incorporating them into existing programs. In the middle years, for example, students were involved in recycling activities, tree planting schemes and the construction of solar- and pedal-powered vehicles. Each of these priorities was maintained as a whole-school focus through standing committees which reported to R–12 staff meetings and organized training development activities and evaluations of their impact at the classroom level. Beyond the local setting, the idea of a networked community was promoted through New Vista's involvement in a regional school cluster and a state-wide middle school association, both of which contributed to teachers' professional development.

Administration and leadership

Leadership practices reinforced an integrated approach to curriculum development and coherence. This is not an easy task in today's educational policy context. There can be little doubt that the move toward local school management in Australia and forms of site-based management elsewhere have resulted in increased work loads for school principals, since many of the administrative responsibilities once handled by the education center have been devolved to schools (McInerney, 2003; Smyth, 2001). As a consequence, school leaders now find that more of their time is devoted to public relations and school administration rather than curriculum leadership. Although the New Vista principal was involved in a good deal of bureaucratic work, other leaders were largely freed from this kind of work because the school maintained a consolidated budget managed by a finance director and an R–12 Resource Management Committee. Janice, the director, spelled out the advantages as follows:

> There is consistency across campuses. We have a global budget for New Vista and by doing all the administration and the finance, which incorporates the facilities and utilities, I actually feel that I've got a broader picture on the needs of the whole school. (Janice, August 26, 2003)

Aside from the administrative efficiencies that could not have been achieved in the small campuses, these structures allowed the campus heads to direct more of their energies to their curriculum responsibilities. The principal explained:

> The heads of campuses are expected to be educational leaders not managers—'they don't do administrative crap.' Their role is to support the work of teacher and to act as curriculum leaders. (Ted, July 23, 2003)

Although the campus heads had local responsibilities, they also worked collaboratively to develop educational programs for the whole district. In a similar vein, the majority of the curriculum coordinators (middle-level leaders) had R–12 roles and were responsible for ensuring a consistent approach to teaching and learning across campuses. Their work entailed a curriculum mapping activity to ensure that topics and themes were not repeated from year to year and key concepts and ideas were developed in a sequential manner. They were chiefly responsible for the school-based training and development of staff and for maintaining and distributing teaching resources to staff. There was also a general expectation that staff appointed to New Vista would work across campuses, especially teachers with curriculum expertise in the areas of technology, music and the arts. Cross-campus sharing of resources and personnel was facilitated by R–12 staff meetings, planning days and curriculum committees.

Curriculum coherence

The emphasis on experiential, relational and vocational learning at New Vista reflected the school's commitment to broaden the scope of the traditional academic curriculum. As a major office bearer for a school leaders' association, the principal, Ted, was an outspoken critic of the current schooling arrangements arguing that secondary education should stand in its own right and not function solely as an entry course for the 30 percent of students with ambitions to attend university in Australia. He offered the following critique and alternatives in a daily newspaper:

> Schools are an 'out-dated concept' and on-the-job training should be equated with traditional classroom subjects. Many students are bored with traditional learning and this is reflected in poor rates [school completion]. Society has changed a lot in the past few years and there's a real question whether school is an appropriate institution any more for kids. We need to adopt a state-wide practice of applied learning where kids are out in the community and really just come to school for social aspects and teacher support. Kids want to learn things which are practical, not to be stuck in the classroom. (Abridged report from daily newspaper, October 19, 2003)

New Vista students could include a broad range of work-related and community-based studies in their formal senior school curriculum requirements and were able to negotiate off-campus time with staff to undertake special interest projects. Not surprisingly, student drop-out rates had declined significantly with 64 percent of students completing year 12 in 2002 compared with a rate of 39 percent in the past. Although students in the adolescent years had much less flexibility in terms of subject choice and access to out-of-school learning providers, they did have opportunities to become involved in an extensive co-curricula program and undertake assignments based on an integrated and negotiated approach to learning.

Thinking curriculum

One of the notable features of New Vista School was an attempt to maintain consistency and continuity in the primary and secondary years through the notion of a thinking curriculum and a common approach to literacy development. This priority was supported by the appointment of a teaching and learning coordinator with a brief to promote a culture of reflective and independent learning. Although each campus had an educational program incorporating learning objectives in the arts, technology, mathematics, science, English and other curriculum areas, a lot of importance was attached to the acquisition of cross-curricula higher-order communication, thinking and problem-solving skills. Beginning in the early years, students were encouraged to think creatively, work cooperatively, evaluate their own learning and become more independent learners. Strategies to promote reflective learning and critical thinking, such as Bloom's taxonomy of cognitive objectives and de Bono's thinking hats, were built into classroom learning activities and assessment tasks and were reinforced in colorful posters and charts displayed in most classrooms. We observed how this operated in Lesley's classroom during a reading activity:

> Lesley talked to her class group about Bloom's taxonomy and asked them to respond to the day's reading activity by framing three levels of questions on their selected text to a prospective or imaginary reader. Referring to instructions on the whiteboard, she asked them to choose questions that went beyond simple recall to analysis and application. She gave examples of questions that could be classified as higher-order thinking skills: (a) remembering questions: asking the reader where and how the action took place; (b) creating questions: asking the reader to do something based on the story, e.g. plan an excursion to where the story took place or design a cover for the book; (c) deconstructing questions, e.g. look at the attributes of the character. (Field notes, August 11, 2003)

In part, the shift toward an R–12 'thinking curriculum' was stimulated by the school's participation in a state government-funded project *Learning to Learn*, which focused on constructivist approaches to learning as a means of transforming teaching practices. One of the cornerstones of this approach was the idea of individual differences, embodied in the notion of preferred learning styles. At New Vista, year 7/8 students were explicitly taught about an integral learning model which assisted them to identify their own preferred learning style according to auditory, visual and kinesthetic domains. In the following extract from a dialogic portrait, two year 8 students give their impressions of what this model entailed:

> 'We get to learn about the different parts of our brain. We do this test at the start of the year to find out which bits we are good at and we have to try and prove which bits

that we're not good at using. I'm good at blue, that's fact based, and green is organized. I have to work on creating and emotions,' says Rachel. Brendan chips in: 'I was a blue quadrant, which was the logical and fact-based learning, and yellow quadrant, which is creative. I'm not that strong in the organizational and emotional-based learning.' Rachel says with some pride 'Oh, I'm good at the yellow, the organized, creative, but I have to work on my red and blue—emotion and feeling based.' (Students, September 3, 2003)

Not all teachers were convinced of the merits of this psychologized model of learning nor of the logic of brain theory—indeed, one teacher described it as a form of quackery—but as Josie, the middle school head, pointed out the intention was to encourage teachers to think about the ways in which individual students learned and the strategies needed to support their learning. She explained:

There's been a lot of personal growth amongst our teachers about catering for the needs of all students and understanding that not everybody works and learns in the same way. It's not necessarily just a middle school thing; it applies from R–12. It doesn't matter whether we're using multiple intelligences or thinking hats, it's all about being aware that we need to be able to work in different ways at different times. There's an expectation that all the middle [level] classes will be using reflection books as an important learning tool and it's an important means of communication with our parents as well. (Josie, August 19, 2003)

An important component in the thinking curriculum was the attention given to reflective learning. Students kept a journal for recording their thoughts on learning activities, and teachers like Josephine were strong supporters of this practice:

What we're doing is reflection techniques: 'What it is I have learnt, how I've learnt it, what I've enjoyed doing, why I've learnt this and not something else,' and that engagement and that energy and that enthusiasm, just spins off in the class, so you haven't got behavior situations occurring because they are engaged. Students are learning social skills as well as acknowledging the need to manage their own time and to use diaries and formatting and feedback and that sort of thing, which helps. (Josephine, August 12, 2003)

Students were aware that their learning involved much more than recall of subject content, and most were able to speak quite knowledgeably about Bloom's taxonomy and other aspects of the 'thinking curriculum.' An emphasis on class reflection and individual diaries ensured that students were used to talking and writing about what and how they learn as a regular part of their schooling. However, as the following comments suggest, these analytical tools evoked some mixed feelings among some students:

'Our teacher loves Bloom's taxonomy,' says Annabelle. 'And de Bono's six hats or whatever they are,' adds Johnny. In a satirical tone he continues, 'For this activity you can use your evaluating Bloom's.' 'So what do you think of all this stuff?' I ask. 'I don't find it helps me,' says Johnny. 'I'd rather just, if we had to do a project, I just—like to use [pause] um, what's the word—I've had a brain freeze.' 'You want to be able to do your own thing,' I prompt. 'Yeah,' they both respond. 'So what do you reckon they're getting at with all the thinking skills?' I inquire. 'Trying to get you to think out of the square you live in,' says Amy. (Johnny and Annabelle, September 30, 2003)

Encouraging students to 'think outside of the square' may be an apt way of expressing the school's philosophy of learning, especially in the adolescent years. Evidence of its success came through most vividly during the annual presentation of learning given by year 7/8 students. As an integral part of the schools' formal assessment and reporting system, these presentations involved students in a 15-minute demonstration of their learning to a panel comprising a community representative, the home class teacher, a parent/guardian and, in some instances, a senior school teacher. (Incidentally, year 9 students also participated in a round-table reporting activity, but the focus was on an independent study rather than broad areas of learning.) We want to elaborate on the presentations to show how schools can break the high school mold in developing reporting practices that promote dialog and reflective learning. What follows is an abridged account from field observations of the year 7/8 formal presentations in which one of the authors was a community member of the panel:

Before the reporting session students selected samples of learning activities, wrote a letter of introduction about themselves for panel members, practiced oral presentations to class members and learnt how to prepare and use cue cards. Students spoke for approximately 10 minutes about three areas of learning that had made a significant impact on them during the year. Sometimes these were subject specific but generally they were about co-curricula activities (e.g. sport, student forum, recycling project). They were required to talk about (a) what they have learnt, (b) how they learnt and (c) the relevance or importance of this learning. At the conclusion of their talks, panel members are invited to ask clarifying questions of the student to make any comments on the presentation. Panel members are given assessment guidelines and are encouraged to provide written comments about (a) presentation skills and (b) content of the presentation.

When it came to the oral presentation, most kids focused on enjoyable and/or challenging aspects of their learning. There was a strong tendency to highlight achievements in home economics, technical studies, arts and PE. Many said they were 'hands-on learners' and liked making things. Two students gave cooking demonstrations and we [the panel] were inundated with products from cooking lessons. Many handed around works of art (sculptures, paintings, designs) and technology studies projects (windmills, pencil cases). Two students explained how to calculate angles in maths using protractors and rules. One student gave a stunning example of a software package that he had designed. Several girls and a boy read poems they had composed. A student demonstrated inertia by slipping a tablecloth from a table leaving all crockery, etc. in place. Students who had participated in a mock local government activity spoke with enthusiasm about the learning involved in decision-making. (Field notes, November 21, 2003)

Having a teacher from the senior school on the panel was an astute move because it helped to address a prevailing criticism about lack of curriculum rigor in the middle years. These teachers were very impressed with the students' knowledge and their ability to talk confidently about their learning. From our observations, students like to talk about success and achievement. While for some students this is sometimes translated into grades, for many others it is about putting in the effort, persisting with difficult subjects, like maths, participating in team sports and having fun in classes. Being liked and accepted by teachers and peers is a high priority for young adolescents. Many talked of the value of friendship and the enjoyment of schooling particularly when they were engaged in group tasks and it was apparent that they could see the value of schooling when they had opportunities to make connections to the bigger picture—not just the minutiae of subject content and skills. With so much of the Australian federal government's agenda geared to grades, benchmarks and narrow indicators of student achievement, it was truly enlightening to observe a group of students talk about the breadth of their learning experiences in such a robust, creative and articulate manner.

In summary, reinventing schooling for young adolescents at New Vista involved a bold endeavor to develop specially tailored programs and practices for students in the middle years while trying to sustain coherent pedagogical linkages across the R–12 years. But this was still a project in the making. Teachers explained that several colleagues remained to be convinced of the merits of integrated curriculum and team teaching practices. As we saw in the other project schools, curriculum innovation tended to taper off beyond year 9 as subject specialization became a reality. Even the progressive elements of the performance model of reporting described above co-existed with an assessment policy that required teachers to assign marks and grades to the products of student learning. Kevin, a year 7/8 teacher, lamented:

We do peer assessment, we do self-assessment and we do reflection but when it comes down to the crunch we've got to write down a report with a mark on it. The school likes that; the kids like it and the parents demand it. (Kevin, August 15, 2003)

Concluding comments

Tyack and Cuban (1995) claim that most junior high schools in the United States did not turn out to be much different to the high schools that they were supposed to reform. 'Instead of providing a new model for the rest of the system, junior high schools appear to have been patterned on high schools' (p. 73). They suggest that it is easier to 'copy another institution than to invent one from the ground up' (p. 73) that in the end 'would-be innovative schools often come to resemble traditional ones' (p. 73). In the case of America, and we would claim Australia too, the high school has provided a model of legitimacy for the educational community that is hard to break. As we have suggested in the project case studies, middle schools which shared grounds, facilities, timetables and staff with senior secondary schools had some difficulties in sustaining distinctive instructional practices and programs that challenged the competitive academic curriculum. Even the purpose-built middle school at Gulfview struggled to maintain a progressive middle school curriculum in the wake of rising senior secondary enrollments. Ultimately, the high school culture with its rigid academic emphasis and faculty-oriented approach to teaching and learning permeated the lower secondary years of schooling and helped to unstitch some of the fabric of reform in the middle years.

These experiences suggest that attempts to reinvent schooling for young adolescents cannot ignore the broader educational context and the differentials of power that operate in conventional secondary schools. Changes to the structures and practices in the middle years will not bring about any long-lasting pedagogical changes without commensurate changes in the primary and post-compulsory phases of schooling. As the New Vista case study revealed, continuity and coherence across the R–12 years can only be achieved with broad agreement about the purposes of schooling and the strategies needed to achieve a holistic approach to the education of young people. This cannot be accomplished without the whole-hearted support of local communities, governments and education systems.

But as our next chapter will hopefully demonstrate, having a vision and being clear about the pieces of the constellation is half the battle when it comes to reinventing schools for young adolescents. To some extent, all of the project schools had a number of the pieces of the puzzle of how to operate educationally with young adolescents, and it is that bigger picture of the 'pedagogically engaged school' that we want to end this book with.

CHAPTER EIGHT

Toward the pedagogically engaged school

Man proceeds in a fog. But when he looks back to judge people of the past, he sees no fog on their path. From his present, which was their far-away future, their path looks perfectly clear to him, good visibility all the way. Looking back he sees the path, he sees the people proceeding, he sees their mistakes, but not the fog.

MILAN KUNDERA

Introduction

At the time of writing this book one of us, Smyth, was reading a fascinating revisiting of the European settlement of Australia, entitled *Dancing with Strangers*. What was captivating about Clendinnen's (2003) reading of the story of 'the imperial adventure in Australia' (p. 3) was her ability to access and bring alive the voices of the very small cast of British observers who made initial contact with the native peoples, the *first* Australians who inhabited our country when the British arrived 200 years ago. In doing this, the author had to go beyond her training as a historian and draw upon other means of representing human experiences—ones that were both profoundly sensitive to the importance of history but that also acknowledged its shortcomings especially around issues of culture. As she puts it:

> Doing history teaches us to tolerate complexity, and to be alert to the shifting contexts of action and experience; anthropology reminds those historians who still need to be

198 | SCHOOL LIVES

reminded that high male politics isn't everything, and that other cultures manage to get along using accounts of the world we find bizarre, even perverse. Historians' main occupational hazard is being culture-insensitive, anthropologists' is insensitivity to temporal change. Both can be insensitive to the reciprocity dynamic between action and context. Together, however, they are formidable, and . . . offer the best chance of explaining what we humans do in any particular circumstance, and why we do it. (Clendinnen, 2003, p. 3)

The reason that this brief excursion into the intersection of history and anthropology is so relevant to the closing chapter is that what we have been trying to do throughout this book is to construct an account of schooling that runs counter to conventional insensitivities on the nature of schools. In this sense we have indeed been 'dancing with strangers'—in our case, by using teachers and students as key informants in helping us render an account of what works in schools for young adolescents. What is missing from most current neo-liberal policy-driven perspectives of schooling and exhortations of the ways schools 'ought to be' is any sense that the informants we accessed have any right to be heard or represented. To put it bluntly, teachers and students are not regarded as reliable 'witnesses.' The consequence is that the version of schooling portrayed and eulogized as mainstream and natural is an entirely false or synthetic one, informed only by the powerful and hegemonic voices of the policy process. The official stereotypes of schools that get to be constructed are ones that uniformly portray schools as places that should be concerned with standards, benchmarks, achievement scores, testing regimes, accountability measures, consumer choice, and reporting schemes that convey to parents and taxpayers the notion that schools are providing 'value for money.'

Like Clendinnen (2003) in revisiting Australian history and trying to move beyond stereotypical interpretations of contact with the *first* Australians, the kind of rendition of schooling for young adolescents we have been trying to give an airing to here is one that is qualitatively different from the cynical portrayals of schools as economic units caught up in the discourses, languages and practices of some horrendous game of international competitiveness. For our part, we have been trying to construct an account of schooling that is more nuanced, tolerant, just, humane, hopeful and optimistic, that goes beyond the simplistically stereotypical conventional one.

Metaphorically speaking, we want to puncture the fog that has been placed upon schools by politicians and policy types but do it in a somewhat different way to that being suggested by Kundera in his historical allusion in our opening quote. We want to move beyond unhelpful stereotypical myths about schools and young people and hear from them instead as valued and important informants of schooling, especially what is happening when schools are exciting, vibrant and above all relational places. Accordingly, we want to present our culminating ideas in the form of an archetype that we are calling the pedagogically engaged school (Smyth, 2003a, b, in press; **see Figure 8.1**). But, just before we give some details on what this might look like, it is worthwhile recapping and reminding ourselves of some of the key ideas that kept reappearing in our research. In various ways the case study schools were involved in a major task of reclaiming the wasteland of the adolescent years of schooling by reinventing themselves as humane places where young people want to learn (McQuillan, 1997). From our vantage point, pedagogically engaged schools are vibrant learning communities where:

- teachers see it as their role (and are encouraged) to provide strong pedagogical leadership;
- students can be confident that their schooling will equip them with a range of skills and dispositions to pursue a worthwhile life;
- students can understand that a 'relevant schooling' means one that acknowledges their needs but that also necessarily occurs within an agreed set of frameworks and structures;
- the aspirations, interests and needs of the majority of students are satisfied, not just those who conform to some narrow norms of society;
- power games are not played out as a way of keeping students in subservient positions;
- there is genuine dialog both within and across the school and its community about where the school is going, who it is working for, how well it is doing, and where and when it needs to refocus and restructure its priorities;
- the school has worked out how it is going to deal with external reforms and the tensions these might produce with the school's own vision and what it steadfastly believes to be important;
- students feel comfortable in speaking out and are not fearful of being castigated or silenced;
- cooperation is considered more important than competition or possessive individualism;
- there is not a culture of complacency that says, 'we have always done things this way in the past, and they seemed to work;'
- there is some attempt to confront the hermetically sealed silos of knowledge called 'subject specializations' that still hold such powerful sway in high schools, in favor of some movement in the direction of thinking about knowledge in integrated, thematic and holistic ways.

It is possible to bring these features together as a heuristic comprising a number of interrelated elements that we have represented diagrammatically in Figure 8.1.

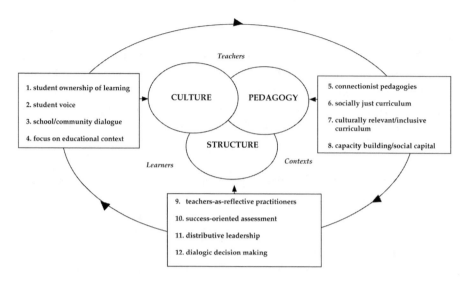

Figure 8.1 The Pedagogically Engaged School

Against this background, it is possible to summarize the key features of the pedagogically engaged school as comprising three interconnected arenas for action, namely: school culture, school structure, and pedagogy, teaching and learning.

Broadly speaking, school culture includes the values, beliefs, norms, assumptions, patterns of behavior and relationships that characterize the daily routines and instructional practices of a school. Although we recognize the limits to the notion of a single school culture embodying shared meanings and collective aspirations of the community, we want to suggest that a pedagogically engaged school has a culture which authorizes student voice, actively promotes school/community dialog and nurtures student-initiated learning. By school structures we refer to the organizational arrangements, including the use of time, space and resources, to facilitate teaching and learning. A feature of the pedagogically engaged school is that these structures promote collaborative relationships, a success-oriented approach to learning, dialogic decision-making and educative forms of leadership. The arena for action encompassed by pedagogy, teaching and learning includes instructional practices, learning theories, educational programs, and assessment and reporting practices that promote an inclusive, connectionist and socially just curriculum.

In what follows we want to elaborate on this heuristic and the elements that make up the pedagogically engaged school.

School culture

1. *Students have high levels of ownership of their learning*
   The school acknowledges the lives, experiences and aspirations of students and incorporates their diverse cultures, interests and concerns into the curriculum. Students are encouraged and supported to become resourceful, independent and creative learners as they explore a broad range of productive and fulfilling pathways from school to adult life.

2. *Student voice is actively promoted as part of learning*
   Schools are configured in ways that encourage students to be activist critical thinkers of how and what they learn in respect to the communities and societies in which they live. Democratic relationships operate within and outside the classroom (Gale & Densmore, 2000), and students are routinely engaged in negotiating curriculum with their peers and adult members of the school. The idea of the school as an 'actual existing democracy' (Fraser, 1994, p. 74) is given added credence through structures and processes that engage students in political dialog and action for change within the school and the broader community.

3. *Active dialog with community about the school and its agenda*
   The school recognizes that the community comprises many groups, organizations and individuals with a legitimate interest in education and a capacity to advance its educational agenda. Utilizing the 'funds of knowledge' within communities (Moll et al., 1992), the school engages in educative dialog with parent, students and community groups in developing a shared educational vision and education programs for young people.

4. *The focus is on educational context within which learning occurs*
   There is a continual focusing on whether everyone understands the wider economic, political and ideological context in which the school is working and the forces that enhance or inhibit the school's agenda. Teachers are aware of the socioeconomic and cultural features of the school community and of the impact of poverty and the various forms of social exclusion on students' lives. The school is actively engaged in counteracting deficit views of its students and their families and in developing an inclusive curriculum in concert with the community.

Pedagogy, teaching and learning

5. *Teachers employ connectionist pedagogies*
   Teachers engage with the diverse lives, backgrounds and aspirations of their

students through pedagogies which connect classroom learning to students' lives and experiences. Generative themes and issues pertaining to youth identity, popular culture, new technologies and the media are incorporated into the curriculum so that learning is meaningful and relevant for young people. Teachers also recognize that they have a responsibility to provide a challenging and rigorous curriculum that broadens students' horizons and encourages them to think outside the square.

6. *A socially just curriculum is being actively pursued*

   The school is able to articulate a socially just and democratic alternative to market-driven and utilitarian approaches to public education. Social justice is included as a guiding principle in school planning and curriculum development and is supported by resources, policies and instructional programs. The questions routinely asked are: 'How are the interests of the least advantaged being advanced in this school?' and 'How is learning being made accessible to all students (not just a few)?' A discourse emphasizing critical literacies enables students to explore the possibilities of creating a more just world through a curriculum which promotes an understanding of inequality and human rights and encourages local and global action in support of the oppressed.

7. *Culturally relevant forms of learning are negotiated with students*

   The school views itself as site for transforming the lives of students not just preserving the *status quo*. Failure (or disengagement) is regarded as a failure on the part of the school system (rather than the student), and as an inability of the school to offer a curriculum and pedagogy captivating of all students regardless of their background. In broad terms, this means offering an alternative to the socially dominant or hegemonic curriculum (Connell, 1993) and contesting the regressive class-based, racist and sexist beliefs and practices that have historically hindered the educational achievement of minorities.

8. *A focus on capacity building and social capital*

   The school regards itself as a significant source of the physical, interpersonal, psychic, cultural and symbolic resources, networks and relationships necessary for all students to enjoy a rewarding life beyond school. Rather than isolating itself from the broader community, the school constitutes itself as part of a 'public sphere' (Fraser, 1994) that contributes to debates about public goods and the future directions of society. The curriculum provides a model of ecologically sustainable and socially just practices for the community at large.

School structure

9. *Constructing teachers as critical and reflective practitioners*
   The school sustains a culture of debate about teaching and learning (Hattam, Brown & Smyth, 1995). Research precedes school planning, and invariably new initiatives are greeted with the question, 'How will this benefit our students' learning?' The school sees that it has a responsibility to provide the time, space and resources for all teachers to engage in dialog with colleagues about their teaching during the course of a school day.

10. *Success-oriented assessment*
    The school has a success-oriented culture with an emphasis on 'achievement for all' in the widest possible fields of academic, social, vocational and cultural learning. Assessment and reporting exist to provide authentic and informative feedback to students on their success and to highlight areas for growth and improvement. The school has multiple ways of assessing student achievement, and students have opportunities to negotiate assessment tasks and to present the products of their learning to their peers, caregivers and members of the community.

11. *Distributive leadership*
    Leadership exists (and is accessed) according to the location of expertise within the school and is not necessarily conceived of exclusively in terms of office or formal status. In the interests of student learning, teachers with valued curriculum knowledge and expertise may be accorded 'provisional authority' over and above the 'assigned authority' roles within a school (May, 1994, p. 98). Distributive leadership of this kind helps to break down the hierarchies of power that can be very destructive of educative agendas (Smyth et al., 1998) while affirming the importance of collective agency as the basis of curriculum leadership.

12. *Dialogic decision-making*
    Decisions are made on the basis of dialog, debate, research and informed discussion within the school community—not knee-jerk reactions to external authority or some manufactured crisis. Dialogic decision-making that promotes dialog around problems and issues posed by students and teachers (Shor, 1996) provides a living example to young people of what it means to live in a democratic community.

An obvious question emerging out of such a constellation is the use of the nomenclature of such an archetype of schools as being 'pedagogical' and describing it as existing in a state of 'engagement.' The reason for our choice of this language is well founded in the reality of what such schools are attempting to do—traces of which we have shown existed to varying degrees in the case study research schools and the lives and experiences of the informants described in this book.

As to the *pedagogical*: Firstly, schools with the kind of orientation we are speaking about have a clear agenda around the imperative of ensuring that what they do has a strong pedagogical focus around teaching and learning. In other words, these schools are not swayed or seduced by whatever fad or fancy happens to be around. They do not see themselves as primarily having a managerial, custodial, marketization or social control agenda, no matter what populist diversions or distractions get hoisted up the government political flagpole. Secondly, schools with a pedagogical persuasion place the learning of young people *as well as adults* in the setting, at core of what it is they do. Thirdly, it almost seems too trite to say it, but these schools think of themselves (and ask to be judged) by how well they perform in terms of turning out students who are passionate about thinking for themselves and the communities and societies in which they live. Such schools do not have to rely on misleading and false league tables that emerge out of government-driven forms of standardized testing. These schools are sufficiently mature and confident in outlook about what they are doing to have developed locally sensitive ways of communicating with their communities that are well tuned into what the school is already doing in terms of promoting educational growth. These schools have no need to convert this important aspect of their work into the kind of three-ringed circus that is currently coming to pass as educational assessment.

As to the notion of *engagement*: This is a signifier or affirmation of how young people respond to having their lives, aspirations and experiences treated respectfully in mature ways, and where they are actively incorporated as important decision-makers in their own learning. In other words, student engagement in learning is regarded as a resounding endorsement (or otherwise) of how well schools are doing in meeting the needs of young people. In short, young people want 'to learn and have fun.' By the former, we mean 'learning in the company of adults' (Meier, 2002, pp. 11–24) and the latter, learning in active and participatory ways that acknowledge that they learn in different ways, often from each other, collectively, respectfully, and in ways that contain variety and that challenges and extends them. They become disengaged, alienated and tune out of school when they are not treated respectfully, where they are not trusted, where the learning environment is not safe enough for them to take risks, or where the methods used are condescending or treat them as immature or unknowledgeable. Engagement then, as Newmann (1992) argues, is an indication of students' preparedness to make the kind of emotional and psychological investment necessary for learning to occur.

So, what is going on here?

What we have been describing in this book through students', teachers' and school lives in six Australian schools amounts to an agenda for *making kids powerful*, and this is highly consistent with an emerging international literature around a number of key themes comprising: student engagement, student voice, middle schooling and the importance of relationships in schooling.

The broader intellectual category we owe allegiance to, or the glue holding all of this together, is what Bryk and Schneider (2002) refer to as 'relational trust.' They define relational trust as 'the distinctive qualities of interpersonal social exchanges in school communities' (p. 12) that comprise core elements of 'respect,' 'personal regard for others,' 'competence' and 'integrity' (p. 124). In other words, when schools work in the interests of young people then 'embedded within all social exchanges in school communities is an interrelated set of mutual dependencies' (p. 124). As Booher-Jennings (2005) puts it, when we refer to relational trust we mean 'the quality of social relationships in a school which strongly influences how well schools operate especially in periods of reform and change' (p. 235).

We concur with Bryk and Schneider's (2002) analysis that over the past two decades, policy arguments and agenda for school reform have tended to focus very much around two broad non-mutually exclusive tendencies. The first of these is a focus on 'structural change' that has included 'governance reform' and matters to do with the 'restructuring of work' involving incentives as well as methods of social control of teachers. The second is an emphasis on 'instruction' in which the claim is made that we must transform the practice of teaching itself through 'enhancing the human resources of schooling' (p. 5), including the improvement of knowledge, skills, training and continuing professional development of teachers. According to Bryk and Schneider (2002) 'both perspectives have merit . . . [but] both analyses remain incomplete' (p. 5) with each failing to adequately grasp the imperative that:

> The personal dynamics among teachers, students and their parents . . . influence whether students regularly attend school and sustain efforts on the difficult tasks of learning. (p. 5)

That there has been so little official policy recognition of the centrality of relationships to all aspects of schooling is one of the major policy mysteries of recent times. As Bryk and Schneider (2002) put it, ' . . . there is relatively little acknowledgment of these relational concerns in either education policy or the more general education research literature' (p. 7).

It is not that there is lack of understanding of the crucial importance of relationships as we have amply demonstrated in this book and as is self-evident in some parts of the literature (Comer, 1993; 2004; Meier, 1995; Newmann, 1992; Newmann & Associates, 1996; Newmann & Wehlage, 1995). Rather, it is a classic case of a deficit of political will and imagination to want to put 'relational ties around the interests of students' (Bryk & Schneider, 2002, p. 6) in the center of the educational frame. Comer (2004) argues that such an emphasis need not deny the importance of high standards, high expectations and accountability, but rather it involves as shift in emphasis of the means for getting there. It would not be too fine a point to say that at the moment, muscular and punitive approaches are undisputedly holding sway through dominant high stakes accountability approaches based on test scores. It is a case Comer (2004) says, of 'right church, but wrong pew' (p. 2) and he puts the message simply, elegantly and stunningly in these terms:

> The direction to the right pew in education—like the real estate mantra of location, location, location—is relationships, relationships, relationships. Good relationships among and between the people in the institutions that influence the quality of child life, largely home and school, make good child and adolescent rearing and development possible. (p. 2)

It all comes down to a case of needing to create 'a relationship context in all schools' (Comer, 2004, p. 2)—not just for a few privileged students. Whether schools are able to work this out or not, has much to do with the degree to which young people are prepared to trust the institution of schooling by acknowledging and affirming 'the institutional legitimacy of the school' (Erickson, 1987, p. 213)—and surely that is the highest stakes test of all.

Appendices

Appendix 1 Summary of interviews in schools and other sites

	Plainsville	New Vista	Gulfview	Broadvale	Seachange	Investigator	Other Sites	Total
Principal	1	1	1	1	1	1		6
Head of School		2						2
Deputy Principal			1	1	1			3
Assistant Principal	1		1	2	2	1		7
Coordinator		1	1	3	1	4		10
Student Counselor		1		1	1	1		4
ESL Support Counselor				1				1
Teacher	4	6	8	2	4	7		31
School Support Officer	1					1		2
Student	5	5	2	3	4	12		31
Former Student	2							2
Parent		1						1
Superintendent							1	1
Teacher Educator							1	1
Social Planner							1	1
Professional Development Provider							1	1
Total	14	17	14	14	14	27	4	104

ESL: English as a Second Language.

Appendix 2 Summary of narrative and dialogic portraits

	Plainsville	New Vista	Gulfview	Broadvale	Seachange	Investigator	Other Sites	Total
Principal	1		1	1	1			4
Head of School		2						2
Assistant Principal	1		1	1	1			4
Coordinator		1	1	3	1	4		10
Student Counselor		1		1	1	1		4
ESL Support Counselor				1				1
Teacher	3	4	3	2	3			15
Student		1	1					2
Former Student	1							1
Parent		1						1
Superintendent							1	1
Total	6	10	7	9	7	5	1	45

ESL: English as a Second Language.

References

Alexander, B., Anderson, G., & Gallegos, B. (Eds.) (2005). *Performance Theories in Education: Power, Pedagogy and the Politics of Identity*. Mahwah, NJ: Lawrence Erlbaum.

Angus, L., Snyder, I., & Sutherland-Smith, W. (2003). Families, cultural resources and the digital divide: ICTs and educational (dis)advantage. *Australian Journal of Education, 47*(1), 18–39.

Apple, M. (1996). *Cultural Politics and Education*. Buckingham, UK: Open University Press.

Australian Bureau of Statistics (2000a). *Schools Australia, Catalogue Number 4221.0*. Canberra: Australian Government Publishing Service.

Australian Bureau of Statistics (2000b). *Schools Australia, Catalogue Number 4202.0*. Canberra: Australian Government Printing Service.

Barratt, R. (1998). *Shaping Middle Schooling in Australia: A Report of the National Middle School Project*. Deakin West, Australian Capital Territory: Australian Curriculum Studies Association.

Bartolome, L. (1994). Beyond the methods fetish: toward a humanizing pedagogy. *Harvard Educational Review, 64*(2), 173–194.

Beane, J. (1991). The middle school: the natural home of the integrated curriculum. *Educational Leadership, 49*(2), 9–13.

Beane, J. (1999). Middle schools under siege: responding to the attack. *Middle School Journal, 30*(5), 3–6.

Beane, J., & Lipka, R. (1987). *When Kids Come First: Enhancing Self-Esteem*. Columbus, OH: National Middle Schools Association.

Beck, U. (1992). *Risk Society: Towards a New Modernity*. Thousand Oaks, CA: Sage.

Bell, N., & Bell, R. (1993). *Adolescent Risk Taking*. Newbury Park, CA: Sage.

Berliner, D., & Biddle, B. (1995). *The Manufactured Crisis: Myths, Fraud, and the Attack on America's Public Schools*. Reading, MA: Addison-Wesley Publishing.

Bernstein, B. (1996). *Pedagogy, Symbolic Control and Identity: Theory, Research, Critique*. Bristol, PA: Taylor & Francis.

Bessant, J. (2004). Up periscope: the future for youth work in Australia. *Youth Studies Australia, 23*(3), 17–25.

Biesta, G., & Miedema, S. (2002). Instruction or pedagogy? The need for a transformative conception of education. *Teaching and Teacher Education, 18*(2), 173–181.

Bingham, C., & Sidorkin, M. (Eds.) (2004). *No Education without Relation*. New York: Peter Lang Publishing.

Blackmore, J. (1996). Doing 'emotional labour' in the education market place: stories from the field of women in management. *Discourse: Studies in the Cultural Politics of Education, 17*(3), 337–350.

Blair, M. (2001). Race and ethnicity in school exclusions: the role of the headteacher. *Curriculum Journal, 12*(3), 331–345.

Bloomer, M. (1997). *Curriculum Making in Post-16 Education: The Social Conditions of Studentship*. London and New York: Routledge.

Blum, W., & Libbey, H. (2004). Executive summary (themed issue on 'school connectedness'). *Journal of School Health, 74*(7), 231–232.

Booher-Jennings, J. (2005). Below the bubble: 'educational triage' and the Texas accountability system. *American Educational Research Journal, 42*(2), 231–268.

Boomer, G. (Ed.) (1982). *Negotiating the Curriculum: A Teacher–Student Partnership*. Sydney: Ashton Scholastic.

Boomer, G., Lester, N., Onore, C., & Cook, J. (Eds.) (1992). *Negotiating the Curriculum: Educating for the 21st Century*. London: Falmer Press.

Bottery, M., & Wright, N. (2000). *Teachers and the State: Towards a Directed Profession*. London and New York: Routledge.

Bracey, G. (1997). *Setting the Record Straight: Responses to Misconceptions about Public Education*. Alexandria, VA: Association for Supervision and Curriculum Development.

Brennan, M., Sachs, J., & Meritt, L. (Eds.) (1998). *Integrated Curriculum: Classroom Materials for the Middle Years*. Deakin West, Australian Capital Territory: Australian Curriculum Studies Association.

Britzman, D. (1986). Cultural myths in the making of a teacher: biography and social structure in teacher education. *Harvard Educational Review, 56*(4), 442–456.

Brookfield, S. (2000). Transformative learning as ideology critique. In J. Mezirow & Associates (Eds.), *Learning as Transformation: Critical Perspectives on a Theory in Progress* (pp. 125–148). San Francisco, CA: Jossey-Bass.

Brotherhood of St. Laurence (2003). *Submission to the Senate Community Affairs References Committee Inquiry into Poverty and Financial Hardship in Australia*. Melbourne: Brotherhood of St. Laurence.

Brown, E., & Saltman, K. (Eds.) (2005). *The Critical Middle School Reader*. London and New York: Routledge.

Bryk, A., & Schneider, B. (2002). *Trust in Schools: A Core Resource for Improvement.* New York: Russell Sage Foundation.

Buendia, E., Ares, N., Juarez, B., & Peercy, M. (2004). The geographies of difference: the production of east-side, west-side and central city school. *American Educational Research Journal, 41*(4), 833–863.

Burgess, R. (1988). Conversations with a purpose: the ethnographic interview in educational research. In R. Burgess (Ed.), *Studies in Qualitative Methodology: Conducting Qualitative Research* (pp. 137–155). Greenwich, CT: JAI Press.

Cameron, L., & Thorsborne, M. (2001). Restorative justice and school discipline: mutually exclusive? In H. Strang, & J. Braithwaite (Eds.), *Restorative Justice and Civil Society* (pp. 180–194). Cambridge: Cambridge University Press.

Carlson, D. (2005). Hope without illusion: telling the story of democratic educational renewal. *International Journal of Qualitative Studies in Education, 18*(1), 21–45.

Carnegie Council on Adolescent Development (1989). *Turning Points: Preparing American Youth for the 21st Century.* New York: Carnegie Corporation.

Catalano, R., Haggerty, K., Oesterle, S., Fleming, C., & Hawkins, J. (2004). The importance of bonding to school for healthy development: findings from the Social Development Research Group. *Journal of School Health, 74*(7), 252–261.

Catholic Social Services Victoria (2003). *Submission to the Senate Inquiry into Poverty.* Melbourne: Catholic Social Services.

Chadbourne, R. (2001). *Middle Schooling for the Middle Years: What Might the Jury Be Considering.* Southbank, Victoria: Australian Education Union.

Clendinnen, I. (2003). *Dancing with Strangers.* Melbourne: Text Publishing.

Clifford, P., & Friesen, S. (1993). A curious plan: managing on the twelfth. *Harvard Educational Review, 63*(3), 339–354.

Coldron, J., & Smith, R. (1999). Active location in teachers' construction of their professional identities. *Journal of Curriculum Studies, 31*(6), 711–726.

Colman, R., & Colman, A. (2004). Youth monitor: a national roundup of recent press reports on youth issues. *Youth Studies Australia, 23*(2), 3–10.

Comer, J. (1993). *School Power: Implications for an Intervention Project.* New York: Free Press.

Comer, J. (2004). *Leave No Child Behind: Preparing Today's Youth for Tomorrow's World.* New Haven, CT: Yale University Press.

Commonwealth of Australia (1997). *Bringing Them Home: National Inquiry into the Separation of Aboriginal and Torres Strait Islander Children from Their Families.* Sydney: Human Rights and Equal Opportunity Commission.

Commonwealth of Australia (2000). *School Matters: Mapping and Managing Mental Health in Schools.* Carlton South, Victoria: Curriculum Corporation.

Connell, R. (1985). *Teachers' Work.* Sydney: Allen & Unwin.

Connell, R. (1993). *Schools and Social Justice.* Leichardt: Pluto Press.

Connell, R. (1996). *Prepare for interesting times: education in a fractured world.* Inaugural Professorial Address. University of Sydney, Sydney

Connell, R. (2002a). Making the difference, then and now. *Discourse, 23*(3), 319–327.

Connell, R. (2002b, 23 October). Rage against the dying of the light. *The Australian,* 30–31.

Cormack, P. (1991). *The Nature of Adolescence*. Adelaide: Education Department of South Australia.

Cormack, P. (1996). Constructions of the adolescent in newspapers and policy documents: implications for middle schooling. *South Australian Educational Leader, 7*(6), 1–11.

Cothran, D., & Ennis, C. (2000). Building bridges to student engagement: communicating respect and care for students in urban schools. *Journal of Research and Development in Education, 33*(2), 106–117.

Cribb, A., & Gewirtz, S. (2003). Towards a sociology of just practices: an analysis of plural conceptions of justice. In C. Vincent (Ed.), *Social Justice, Education and Identity* (pp. 15–29). London: RoutledgeFalmer.

Croninger, R., & Lee, V. (2001). Social capital and dropping out of high school: benefits to at-risk students of teachers' support and guidance. *Teachers College Record, 103*(4), 548–581.

Davis, N. (1999). *Youth Crisis: Growing Up in the High-Risk Society*. Westport, CT: Praeger.

Deering, P. (1996). An ethnographic study of norms of inclusion and cooperation in a multiethnic middle school. *Urban Review, 28*(1), 21–39.

Deering, P. (2003). What's driving you crazy? A question to drive collaborative, inquiry-based middle school reform. *Middle School Journal, 34*(5), 31–49.

Dei, G. (2003). Schooling and the dilemma of youth engagement. *McGill Journal of Education, 38*(2), 241–256.

Deiro, J. (1996). *Teaching with Heart: Making Healthy Connections with Students*. Thousand Oaks, CA: Corwin Press.

Delpit, L. (1995). *Other People's Children: Cultural Conflict in the Classroom*. New York: New Press.

Delpit, L., & White-Bradley, P. (2003). Educating or imprisoning the spirit: lessons from Ancient Egypt. *Theory into Practice, 42*(4), 283–288.

Denzin, N. (1997). *Interpretive Ethnography: Ethnographic Practices for the 21st Century*. Thousand Oaks, CA: Sage.

Dewey, J. (1933). *How We Think*. Lexington, MA: D.C. Heath.

Dewey, J. (1963). *Democracy and Education*. New York: The Macmillan Company.

Donnelly, K. (2004). *Why Our Schools Are Failing: What Parents Need to Know about Australian Education*. Sydney: Duffy & Snellgrove.

Dwyer, P. (1996). *Opting Out: Early School Leavers and the Degeneration of Youth Policy*. Hobart: National Clearinghouse for Youth Studies and Youth Research Centre.

Edelman, M. (1988). *Constructing the Political Spectacle*. Chicago, IL: University of Chicago Press.

Eisner, E. (1992). Educational reform and the ecology of schooling. *Teachers College Record, 93*(4), 611–627.

Eisner, E. (2002). The kind of schools we need. *Phi Delta Kappan, 83*(8), 576–583.

Elmore, R. (1987). Reforming and the culture of authority in schools. *Educational Administration Quarterly, 23*(4), 60–78.

Epstein, D., Hewitt, R., Leonard, D., Mauthner, M., & Watkins, C. (2003). Avoiding the issue: homophobia, school policies and identities in secondary schools. In C. Vincent (Ed.), *Social Justice, Education and Identity* (pp. 120–136). London and New York: RoutledgeFalmer.

Erickson, F. (1987). Transformation and school success: the politics and culture of school achievement. *Anthropology and Education Quarterly, 18*(4), 335–356.

Eyers, V., Cormack, P., & Barratt, R. (1992). *The Report of the Junior Secondary Review: The Education of Young Adolescents 11–14*. Adelaide: Education Department of South Australia.

Farrell, E. (1990). *Hanging In and Dropping Out: Voices of At-Risk High School Students*. New York: Teachers College Press.

Fenwick, T. (2003). The 'good' teacher in a neo-liberal risk society: a Foucauldian analysis of professional growth plans. *Journal of Curriculum Studies, 35*(3), 335–354.

Fincher, R., & Saunders, P. (Eds.) (2001). *Creating Unequal Futures: Rethinking Poverty, Inequality and Disadvantage*. Sydney: Allen & Unwin.

Fine, M. (1991). *Framing Dropouts: Notes on the Politics of an Urban High School*. Albany, NY: State University of New York Press.

Fine, M. (Ed.) (1994). *Chartering Urban School Reform: Reflections on Public High Schools in the Midst of Change*. New York: Teachers College Press.

Finn, J. (1989). Withdrawing from school. *Review of Educational Research, 59*(2), 117–142.

Fisher, N. (1993). Developing a national training market: Is it a sensible strategy? *Unicorn, 19*(4), 27–33.

Fonte, J. (2005, 15–16 January). A world of difference. *Weekend Australian*, 19.

Forte, I., & Schurr, S. (1991). *Middle Grades Advisee/Advisor Program*. Nashville, TN: Incentive Publications.

Foucault, M. (1977). *Discipline and Punish: The Birth of the Prison* (A. Sheridan, Trans.). Harmondsworth: Penguin.

Fraser, N. (1994). Rethinking the public sphere: a contribution to the critique of actually existing democracy. In H. Giroux, & P. McLaren (Eds.), *Between Borders: Pedagogy and the Politics of Cultural Studies* (pp. 74–98). New York and London: Routledge.

Freebody, P., Ludwig, C., & Gunn, S. (1995). *Everyday Literacy Practices In and Out of Schools in Low Socio-economic Urban Communities* (Vol. 1). Melbourne: Curriculum Corporation.

Freire, P. (1993). *Pedagogy of the Oppressed*. London: Penguin Books.

Freire, P. (1998). *Teachers as Cultural Workers*. Boulder, CO: Westview Press.

Fullan, M. (1993). *Successful School Reform: Probing the Depths of Educational Reform*. London: Falmer Press.

Furlong, A., & Cartmel, F. (1997). *Young People and Social Change: Individualization and Risk in Late Modernity*. Buckingham and Philadelphia: Open University Press.

Gale, T., & Densmore, K. (2000). *Just Schooling: Explorations in the Cultural Politics of Teaching*. Buckingham and Philadelphia: Open University Press.

Geertz, C. (1973). *The Interpretations of Cultures*. New York: Basic Books.

Gibson, M. (2005). Promoting academic engagement among minority youth: implications from John Ogbu's Shaker Heights ethnography. *International Journal of Qualitative Studies in Education, 18*(5), 581–603.

Giddens, A. (1991). *Modernity and Self Identity: Self and Society in the Later Modern Age*. Oxford: Polity Press.

Gilbert, P. (2000). 'The deepening divide'? Choices for Australian education. *Australian Educational Researcher, 27*(1), 31–46.

Giroux, H. (1985). Theories of reproduction and resistance in the new sociology of education: a critical analysis. *Harvard Educational Review, 53*(5), 257–293.

Giroux, H. (1986). Radical pedagogy and the politics of student voice. *Interchange, 17*(1), 48–69.

Giroux, H. (1996). *Fugitive Cultures: Race, Violence and Youth*. New York and London: Routledge.

Giroux, H. (2002). Democracy, freedom and justice after September 11th: rethinking the role of educators and the politics of schooling. *Teachers College Record, 104*(6), 1138–1162.

Giroux, H. (2005). The conservative assault on America: cultural politics, education and the new authoritarianism. *Cultural Politics, 1*(2), 139–164.

Gladden, M. (2002). Reducing school violence: strengthening student programs and addressing the role of school organization. *Review of Research in Education, 26*, 263–299.

Goodenow, C., & Grady, K. (1993). The relationship of school belonging and friends' values to academic motivation and achievement among urban adolescent students. *Journal of Experimental Education, 62*(1), 60–71.

Goodman, J., & Kuzmic, J. (1997). Bringing a progressive pedagogy to conventional schools: theoretical and practical implications from harmony. *Theory into Practice, 36*(2), 79–86.

Goodman, J., Baron, D., & Myers, C. (1999). The local politics of educational reform: issues of school autonomy. *Research for Educational Reform, 4*(2), 22–49.

Goodson, I. (1991). Sponsoring the teacher's voice: teachers' lives and teacher development. *Cambridge Journal of Education, 21*(1), 35–45.

Goodson, I. (1994). Studying the teacher's life and work. *Teaching and Teacher Education, 10*(1), 29–37.

Grattan, M. (2005, 20 February). Nelson reins in states. *Sunday Age*, 19.

Grieg, A., Lewins, F., & White, K. (2003). *Inequality in Australia*. Cambridge and New York: Cambridge University Press.

Griffiths, M. (1998). Towards a theoretical framework for understanding social justice in educational practice. *Educational Philosophy, 30*(2), 175–190.

Haberman, M. (1991). The pedagogy of poverty versus good teaching. *Phi Delta Kappan, 73*(4), 290–294.

Halpin, D., Moore, A., with Edwards, G., George, R., & Jones, C. (2000). Maintaining, reconstructing and creating tradition in education. *Oxford Review of Education, 26*(2), 133–144.

Hamburg, D. (1992). *Today's Children: Creating a Future for a Generation in Crisis*. New York: Times Books.

Harding, A., & Greenwell, H. (2001). *Trends in income and expenditure inequality in the 1980s and 1990s*. Discussion Paper No. 57. Canberra: National Centre for Social and Economic Modelling.

Hargreaves, A. (1992). Cultures of teaching: a focus for change. In A. Hargreaves, & M. Fullan (Eds.), *Understanding Teacher Development* (pp. 216–240). New York: Teachers College Press.

Hargreaves, A. (1998). The emotional practice of teaching. *Teaching and Teacher Education, 14*(8), 835–854.

Hargreaves, A. (2001a). Emotional geographies of teaching. *Teachers College Record, 103*(6), 1056–1080.

Hargreaves, A. (2001b). The emotional geographies of teachers' relations with colleagues. *International Journal of Educational Research, 35*(5), 503–527.

Hargreaves, A., & Earle, L. (1990). *Rights of Passage: A Review of Selected Research about Schooling in the Transition Years*. Toronto, Ontario: Ontario Ministry of Education.

Harradine, J. (1996). What research tells us about school reform. *National Schools Network Newsletter, 2*(2), 4–5.

Hattam, R., & Smyth, J. (2003). 'Not everyone has a perfect life': becoming somebody without school. *Pedagogy, Culture and Society, 11*(3), 379–398.

Hattam, R., Brown, K., & Smyth, J. (1995). *Sustaining a Culture of Debate about Teaching and Learning*. Adelaide: Flinders Institute for the Study of Teaching.

Hewitson, R. (2004). *A critical ethnographic account of teacher professional development*. Unpublished Doctor of Philosophy, Flinders University of South Australia, Adelaide.

Hoffman, L. (2002). Why high schools don't change: what students and their yearbooks tell us. *The High School Journal, 82*(2), 22–37.

Holt, J. (1970). *The Underachieving School*. London: Pitman Publishing.

hooks, b. (2000). *Where We Stand: Class Matters*. New York: Routledge.

Hord, S. (Ed.) (2004). *Learning Together, Leading Together*. New York: Teachers College Press and National Staff Development Council.

Huffman, J., & Hipp, K. (2003). *Reculturing Schools as Professional Learning Communities*. Lanham, MD: Scarecrow Press.

Huffman, J., & Jacobson, A. (2003). Perceptions of professional learning communities. *International Journal of Leadership in Education, 6*(3), 239–250.

Hult, R. (1979). On pedagogical caring. *Educational Theory, 29*(3), 237–243.

Intrator, S. (2003). *Tuned In and Fired Up*. New Haven, CT: Yale University Press.

Kaplan, A. (2000). Teacher and student: designing a democratic relationship. *Journal of Curriculum Studies, 32*(3), 377–402.

Kelchtermans, G., & Vandenberghe, R. (1994). Teachers' professional development: a biographical perspective. *Journal of Curriculum Studies, 26*(1), 45–62.

Kimber, P. (2002). The index of educational disadvantage. *Primary Focus, 16*(3), 29–30.

Kincheloe, J., & McLaren, P. (1994). Rethinking critical theory and qualitative research. In N. Denzin, & Y. Lincoln (Eds.), *Handbook of Qualitative Research* (pp. 138–157). Thousand Oaks, CA: Sage.

Klein, M. (2000). *Teaching Mathematics against the Grain: Investigations for Primary Teachers*. Katoomba, New South Wales: Social Science Press.

Klem, A., & Connell, J. (2004). Relationships matter: linking teacher support to student engagement and achievement. *Journal of School Health, 74*(7), 262–273.

Kohl, H. (1994). *I Won't Learn from You*. New York: The New Press.

Kozol, J. (1992). *Savage Inequalities: Children in America's Schools*. New York: Harper Perennial.

Kozol, J. (2005). *The Shame of the Nation: The Restoration of Apartheid Schooling in America*. New York: Crown Publishers.

Labaree, D. (2000). On the nature of teaching and teacher education: difficult practices that look easy. *Journal of Teacher Education, 51*(3), 228–233.

Lefstein, A. (2002). Thinking power and pedagogy apart—coping with discipline in progressivist school reform. *Teachers College Record, 104*(8), 1627–1655.

Libbey, H. (2004). Measuring student relationships to school: attachment, bonding, connectedness and engagement. *Journal of School Health, 74*(7), 274–283.

Lortie, D. (1975). *School Teacher: A Sociological Study*. Chicago, IL: University of Chicago Press.

Lounsbury, J., & Vars, G. (2003). The future of middle level education: optimistic and pessimistic views. *Middle School Journal, 35*(2), 6–14.

Luke, A. (1993). Critical literacy. *The Reading Teacher, 44* (77), 518–519.

Luke, A., et al. (2003). *Beyond the Middle. A Report about Literacy and Numeracy Development of Target Group Students in Middle Years of Schooling* (Vols. 1 and 2). Canberra: Department of Education, Science and Training.

Luxembourg Income Study (2002). *Relative poverty rates for the total population, children and the elderly*. Available at http://www.lisproject.org./kerfigures/povertytable.htm [2005, 2 July].

Lynch, K., & Lodge, A. (2002). *Equality and Power in Schools: Redistribution, Recognition and Representation*. London and New York: RoutledgeFalmer.

Mac an Ghaill, M. (1991). State-school policy: contradictions, confusions and contestation. *Journal of Education Policy, 6*(3), 299–313.

Macedo, D. (1994). *Literacies of Power: What Americans Are Not Allowed to Know*. Boulder, CO: Westview Press.

MacKenzie, D., & Chamberlain, C. (2002). The second national census of homeless school students. *Youth Studies Australia, 21*(4), 24–31.

MacKenzie, L. (1998). A pedagogy of respect: teaching as an ally of working class college students. In A. Shephard, J. McMillan, & G. Tate (Eds.), *Coming to Class: Pedadogy and the Social Class of Teachers* (pp. 94–117). Portsmouth, NH: Boynton Cook.

Maclure, M. (1993). Arguing for yourself: identity as an organising principle in teachers' jobs and lives. *British Educational Research Journal, 19*(4), 311–322.

Maran, M. (2001). *Class Dismissed: A Year in the Life of an American High School, a Glimpse into the Heart of a Nation*. New York: St. Martin's Griffin.

Marcus, G. (1998). *Ethnography Through Thick and Thin*. Princeton, NJ: Princeton University Press.

Margonis, F. (2004). From student resistance to educative engagement: a case study in building powerful student–teacher relationships. In C. Bingham, & A. Sidorkin (Eds.), *No Education without Relation* (pp. 39–53). New York: Peter Lang Publishing.

May, S. (1994). *Making Multicultural Education Work*. Adelaide: Multilingual Matters.

McGinty, S. (2004). The student–teacher axis: idiosyncratic credit and cutting the slack. In H. Waxman, Y. Padron, & J. Gray (Eds.), *Educational Resiliency: Student, Teacher, and School Perspectives* (pp. 157–173). Greenwich, CT: Information Age Publishing.

McInerney, P. (2003). Moving into dangerous territory? Educational leadership in a devolving education system. *International Journal of Leadership in Education, 6*(1), 57–72.

McInerney, P. (2004). *Making Hope Practical: School Reform for Social Justice*. Flaxton, Queensland: Post Pressed.

McInerney, P., Hattam, R., Lawson, M., & Smyth, J. (1999). *Middle Schooling from the Ground Up*. Adelaide: Flinders Institute for the Study of Teaching.

McInerney, P., Hattam, R., & Smyth, J. (2001). *'We're in for the Long Haul': Middle Schooling for Year 8s at Christies Beach High School*. Adelaide: Flinders Institute for the Study of Teaching.

McLaughlin, M. (1987). Learning from experience: lessons from policy implementation. *Educational Evaluation and Policy Analysis, 9*(2), 171–178.

McLaughlin, M., & Talbert, J. (2001). *Professional Communities and the Work of High School Teaching*. Chicago, IL: University of Chicago Press.

McQuillan, P. (1997). Humanizing the comprehensive high school: a proposal for reform. *Educational Administration Quarterly, 33*(Suppl., December), 644–682.

Meier, D. (1992). Reinventing teaching. *Teachers College Record, 93*(4), 594–609.

Meier, D. (1995). *The Power of Their Ideas: Lessons for America from a Small School in Harlem*. Boston: Beacon Press.

Meier, D. (2002). *In Schools We Trust: Creating Communities of Learning in an Era of Testing and Standardization*. Boston: Beacon Press.

Mezirow, J. (1991). *Transformative Dimensions of Adult Learning*. San Francisco, CA: Jossey-Bass.

Mezirow, J. (1992). Transformation theory: critique and confusion. *Adult Education Quarterly, 42*(4), 250–252.

Mezirow, J. (1994). Understanding transformation theory. *Adult Education Quarterly, 44*(4), 222–232.

Mezirow, J. (1997). Transformation theory out of context. *Adult Education Quarterly, 48*(1), 60–62.

Mitchell, C., & Weber, S. (1999). *Reinventing Ourselves as Teachers: Beyond Nostalgia*. London and Philadelphia: Falmer Press.

Moll, L., Amanti, C., Neff, D., & Gonzalez, N. (1992). Funds of knowledge for teaching: using a qualitative approach to connect homes and classrooms. *Theory into Practice, 31*(2), 132–141.

Moore, A. (2004). *The Good Teacher: Dominant Discourses in Teaching and Teacher Education*. London and New York: RoutledgeFalmer.

Newmann, F. (Ed.) (1992). *Student Engagement and Achievement in American Secondary Schools*. New York: Teachers College Press.

Newmann, F. & Associates (Eds.) (1996). *Authentic Achievement: Restructuring Schools for Intellectual Quality*. San Francisco, CA: Jossey-Bass.

Newmann, F., & Wehlage, G. (1995). *Successful School Restructuring: A Report to the Public by the Center on Organization and Restructuring of Schools*. Madison, WI: Center on Organization and Restructuring of Schools, University of Wisconsin-Madison.

Noblit, G. (1993). Power and caring. *American Educational Research Journal, 30*(1), 23–38.

Noguera, P. (1995). Preventing and producing violence: a critical analysis of responses to school violence. *Harvard Educational Review, 65*(2), 189–213.

Panelli, R., Nairn, K., Atwool, N., & McCormack, J. (2002). 'Hanging out': print media constructions of young people in 'public space'. *Youth Studies Australia, 21*(4), 38–48.

Peel, M. (2003). *The Lowest Rung: Voice of Australian Poverty*. Melbourne: Cambridge University Press.

Poplin, M., & Weeres, J. (1992). *Voices from the Inside: A Report on Schooling from Inside the Classroom. Part One: Naming the Problem*. Claremont, CA: The Institute for Education in Transformation, Claremont Graduate School.

Postman, N., & Weingartner, C. (1969). *Teaching as a Subversive Activity*. New York: Delacorte Press.

Proudford, C. (2003). Building professional learning communities for curriculum change. *Curriculum Perspectives, 23*(3), 1–10.

Public Education Network (2004, 17 September). *Emotional ties to school vital to success.* Available at http://seattletimes.nwsource.com/html/opinion/2002034444_raspberry14.htm [2004, 20 September].

Quartz, K. (1995). Sustaining new educational communities: towards a culture of school reform. In J. Oakes, & N. Quartz (Eds.), *Creating New Educational Communities* (Vol. 1, pp. 240–252). Chicago, IL: University of Chicago Press.

Roman, L. (1996). Spectacle in the dark: youth as transgression, display, and repression. *Educational Theory, 46*(1), 1–22.

Romano, R. (2000). *Forging an Educative Community: The Wisdom of Love, the Power of Understanding, and the Terror of It All.* New York: Peter Lang Publishing.

Romano, R., & Glascock, G. (2002). *Hungry Minds in Hard Times: Educating for Complexity for Students of Poverty.* New York: Peter Lang Publishing.

San Antonio, D. (2004). *Adolescent Lives in Transition: How Social Class Influences the Adjustment to Middle School.* Albany, NY: State University of New York Press.

Sawyer, K. (2004). Creative teaching: collaborative discussion as disciplined improvisation. *Educational Researcher, 33*(2), 12–20.

Scott, J. (1999). Geographies of trust, geographies of hierarchy. In M. Warren (Ed.), *Democracy and Trust* (pp. 273–289). Cambridge: Cambridge University Press.

Sennett, R., & Cobb, J. (1977). *The Hidden Injuries of Class.* Cambridge: Cambridge University Press.

Sergiovanni, T. (1996). *Leadership for the School House.* San Francisco, CA: Jossey-Bass.

Shor, I. (1992). *Empowering Education.* Chicago, IL: University of Chicago Press.

Shor, I. (1996). Education is politics: Paulo Freire's critical pedagogy. In P. McLaren, & P. Leonard (Eds.), *Paulo Freire: A Critical Encounter* (pp. 25–34). London: Routledge.

Silberman, C. (1970). *Crisis in the Classroom: The Remaking of American Education.* New York: Random House.

Sizer, T. (2004). *The Red Pencil: Convictions from Experience in Education.* New Haven, CT: Yale University Press.

Slee, R. (1995). *Changing Theories and Practices of Discipline.* London and Washington: Falmer Press.

Smith, M., with, Miller-Kahn, L., Heinecke, W., & Jarvis, P. (2004). *Political Spectacle and the Fate of American Schools.* London and New York: RoutledgeFalmer.

Smyth, J. (1991). *Teachers as Collaborative Learners: Challenging Dominant Forms of Supervision.* London: Open University Press.

Smyth, J. (1993). *Education and economic rationalism: have we lost our way?* Inaugural Professorial Lecture, 8 October, Flinders University of South Australia, Adelaide.

Smyth, J. (1999). Researching the cultural politics of teachers' learning. In J. Loughran (Ed.), *Researching Teaching: Methodologies and Practices for Understanding Pedagogy* (pp. 67–82). London and Philadelphia: Falmer Press.

Smyth, J. (2001). *Critical Politics of Teachers' Work: An Australian Perspective*. New York: Peter Lang Publishing.

Smyth, J. (2002a). Unmasking teachers' subjectivities in local school management. *Journal of Education Policy, 17*(4), 463–482.

Smyth, J. (2002b). But, are we damaging teachers and students? *EQ Australia*, Winter, 11–12.

Smyth, J. (2003a). Engaging the education sector: a policy orientation to stop damaging our schools. *Learning Communities: International Journal of Learning in Social Contexts, 1*(1), 22–40.

Smyth, J. (2003b). Undamaging 'damaged' teachers: an antidote to the 'self-managing school'. *Delta: Policy and Practice in Education, 55*(1 and 2), 15–42.

Smyth, J. (2004a). Social capital and the socially just school. *British Journal of Sociology of Education, 25*(1), 19–33.

Smyth, J. (2004b). Modernising the Australian education workplace: a case of failure to deliver for teachers of young disadvantaged adolescents. *Educational Review, 57*(2).

Smyth, J. (2004c). Policy research and 'damaged teachers': towards an epistemologically respectful paradigm. *Waikato Journal of Education, 10*, 263–281.

Smyth, J. (2005). An argument for new understandings and explanations of early school leaving that go beyond the conventional. *London Review of Education, 3*(2), 117–130.

Smyth, J. (in press). Toward the pedagogically engaged school: listening to student voice as a positive response to disengagement and 'dropping out'. In A. Cook-Sather, & D. Thiessen (Eds.), *International Handbook of Student Experience in Elementary and Secondary Schools*. Dordrecht, The Netherlands: Springer Science Publishers

Smyth, J., & Down, B. (2004). Enhancing school retention: building 'geographies of trust' and 'socially just' schools. Paper presented at the *Annual Meeting of the Australian Association for Research in Education*, Melbourne.

Smyth, J., & McInerney, P. (in press). 'Living on the edge': a case study of school reform working for disadvantaged young adolescents. *Teachers College Record*.

Smyth, J., & Shacklock, G. (1998). *Remaking Teaching: Ideology, Policy and Practice*. London and New York: Routledge.

Smyth, J., Hattam, R., & Lawson, M. (Eds.) (1998). *Schooling for a Fair Go*. Sydney: Federation Press.

Smyth, J., McInerney, P., Hattam, R., & Lawson, M. (1999). *Placing Girls at the Centre of Curriculum: Gepps Cross Girls High School*. Case Study Series: Teachers' Learning Project. Adelaide: Flinders Institute for the Study of Teaching.

Smyth, J., Hattam, R., Cannon, J., Edwards, J., Wilson, N., & Wurst, S. (2000). *Listen to Me, I'm Leaving: Early School Leaving in South Australian Secondary Schools*. Adelaide: Flinders Institute for the Study of Teaching; Department of Employment, Education and Training; and Senior Secondary Assessment Board of South Australia.

Smyth, J., McInerney, P., & Hattam, R. (2003). Tackling school leaving at its source: a case of reform in the middle years of schooling. *British Journal of Sociology of Education, 24*(4), 177–193.

Smyth, J., & Hattam, R., with Cannon, J., Edwards, J., Wilson, N., & Wurst, S. (2004). *'Dropping Out', Drifting Off, Being Excluded: Becoming Somebody without School*. New York: Peter Lang Publishing.

Social Inclusion Board (2004). *Making the Connections: The South Australian Government's Action Strategy to Keep Young People Connected to Learning and Opportunities.* Adelaide: Government of South Australia and Social Inclusion Initiative.

Social Inclusion Unit and the South Australian Department of Human Services (2003). *Youth Views—Stay Involved? Young People's Feedback on School Retention.* Adelaide: Government of South Australia.

South Australian Council of Social Service (2002). *Submission to the Social Development Committee of the South Australian Parliament.* Adelaide: South Australian Council of Social Service.

Spoehr, J. (2004, 29 October). Tale of two cities. *The Adelaide Review, 7.*

Stanton-Salazar, R. (1997). A social capital framework for understanding the socialization of racial minority children and youths. *Harvard Educational Review, 67*(1), 1–40.

Stilwell, F. (1994). Economic rationalism: sound foundations for policy? In S. Rees, G. Rodley, & F. Stilwell (Eds.), *Beyond the Market: Alternatives to Economic Rationalism.* Leichardt, New South Wales: Pluto Press.

Tanner, L. (2003). *Crowded Lives.* North Melbourne: Pluto Press.

Teese, R. (1998). Curriculum hierarchy, private schooling and the segmentation of Australian secondary schooling. *British Journal of Sociology of Education, 19*(3), 401–417.

Thomson, P. (1992). Risking school change. *Education Links, 43,* 25–29.

Thomson, P. (2002). *Schooling the Rustbelt Kids: Making the Difference in Changing Times.* Crowsnest, New South Wales: Allen & Unwin.

Thomson, P., & Comber, B. (2003). Deficient 'disadvantaged students' or media savvy meaning makers? Engaging new metaphors for redesigning classrooms and pedagogies. *McGill Journal of Education, 38*(2), 305–328.

Thrupp, M. (1999). *Schools Making a Difference: Let's Be Realistic!* Buckingham: Open University Press.

Tomazin, F., & Rood, D. (2005, 9 February). Bracks backs school's classroom spy camera. *The Age, 9.*

Trammell, L. (2005). Measuring and fixing, filling and drilling: the Exxon Mobil agenda for education. In D. Boyles (Ed.), *Schools or Markets? Commercialism, Privatization and School–Business Partnerships* (pp. 31–46). Mahwah, NJ: Lawrence Erlbaum.

Tyack, D., & Cuban, L. (1995). *Tinkering toward Utopia: A Century of Public School Reform.* Cambridge, MA: Harvard University Press.

Valencia, R. (Ed.) (1997). *The Evolution of Deficit Thinking: Educational Thought and Practice.* London: Falmer Press.

Waller, W. (1932). *The Sociology of Teaching.* New York: Wiley.

Walzer, M. (1983). *Spheres of Justice: A defense of Pluralism and Equality.* New York: Basic Books.

Weiner, B. (1990). History of motivation research in education. *Journal of Educational Psychology, 82*(4), 616–622.

Weis, L., & Fine, M. (2001). Extraordinary conversations in public schools. *International Journal of Qualitative Studies in Education, 14*(4), 497–523.

Wentzel, K. (1997). Student motivation in middle school: the role of perceived pedagogical caring. *Journal of Educational Psychology, 89*(3), 411–419.

Wentzel, K. (1998). Social relationships and motivation in middle school: the role of parents, teachers and peers. *Journal of Educational Psychology, 90*(2), 202–209.

Wexler, P. (1992). *Becoming Somebody: Towards a Social Psychology of the School.* London: Falmer Press.

Wiggington, E. (1985). *Sometimes a Shining Moment: The Foxfire Experience.* New York: Anchor Press.

Williams, R. (1989). Hegemony and the selective tradition. In S. de Castell, A. Luke, & C. Luke (Eds.), *Language, Authority and Criticism: Readings on the School Textbook* (pp. 56–60). London: Falmer Press.

Willie, C. (2000). Confidence, trust and respect: the pre-eminent goals of educational reform. *Journal of Negro Education, 69*(4), 255–263.

Willis, P. (1977). *Learning to Labour: How Working Class Kids Get Working Class Jobs.* Farnborough, England: Saxon House.

Willms, J. (2003). *Student Engagement at School: A Sense of Belonging and Participation. Results from PISA 2000.* Paris: Organization for Economic Cooperation and Development.

Wingspread Conference Participants (2004). Wingspread declaration. *Journal of School Health, 74*(7), 231–234.

Wood, G. (1992). *Schools That Work: America's Most Innovative Public Education Programs.* New York: Dutton.

Wyn, J., & White, R. (1997). *Rethinking Youth.* Sydney: Allen & Unwin.

Yecke, C. (2005). *Mayhem in the Middle: How Middle Schools Have Failed America—and How to Make Them Work.* Washington, DC: Thomas B. Fordham Institute.

Zevenbergen, R. (2004). Reconceptualising numeracy for new times. *Curriculum Perspectives, 24*(3), 1–7.

Zyngier, D. (2003). Connectedness—isn't it time that education came out from behind the classroom door and rediscovered social justice? *Social Alternatives, 22*(3), 41–49.

Subject Index

Author Index

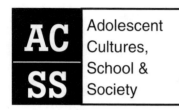

Adolescent
Cultures,
School &
Society

Joseph L. DeVitis & Linda Irwin-DeVitis
GENERAL EDITORS

As schools struggle to redefine and restructure themselves, they need to be cognizant of the new realities of adolescents. Thus, this series of monographs and textbooks is committed to depicting the variety of adolescent cultures that exist in today's post-industrial societies. It is intended to be a primarily qualitative research, practice, and policy series devoted to contextual interpretation and analysis that encompasses a broad range of interdisciplinary critique. In addition, this series will seek to provide a pragmatic, pro-active response to the current backlash of conservatism that continues to dominate political discourse, practice, and policy. This series seeks to address issues of curriculum theory and practice; multicultural education; aggression and violence; the media and arts; school dropouts; homeless and runaway youth; alienated youth; at-risk adolescent populations; family structures and parental involvement; and race, ethnicity, class, and gender studies.

Send proposals and manuscripts to the general editors at:

Joseph L. DeVitis & Linda Irwin-DeVitis
The John H. Lounsbury School of Education
Georgia College & State University
Campus Box 70
Milledgeville, GA 31061-0490

To order other books in this series, please contact our Customer Service Department at:

(800) 770-LANG (within the U.S.)
(212) 647-7706 (outside the U.S.)
(212) 647-7707 FAX

or browse online by series at:

WWW.PETERLANG.COM